Property, Labour and Legal Regulation

Property, Labour and Legal Regulation

Dignity or Dependence?

Mark Findlay

Professor of Law, Singapore Management University, Singapore
Professor of Criminal Justice, University of Sydney, Australia

Edward Elgar
PUBLISHING

Cheltenham, UK • Northampton, MA, USA

Published by
Edward Elgar Publishing Limited
The Lypiatts
15 Lansdown Road
Cheltenham
Glos GL50 2JA
UK

Edward Elgar Publishing, Inc.
William Pratt House
9 Dewey Court
Northampton
Massachusetts 01060
USA

A catalogue record for this book
is available from the British Library

Library of Congress Control Number: 2015940695

This book is available electronically in the **Elgar**online
Law subject collection
DOI 10.4337/9781784711641

MIX
Paper from
responsible sources
FSC® C013056

ISBN 978 1 78471 163 4 (cased)
ISBN 978 1 78471 164 1 (eBook)

Typeset by Columns Design XML Ltd, Reading
Printed and bound in Great Britain by TJ International Ltd, Padstow

Contents

Preface

> Withhold not good from them to whom it is due, when it is in the power of thine hand to do it.[1]

As part of our wider enquiry into socio-economic sustainability and regulatory principle, this book continues our anthropology of embeddedness,[2] with particular attention to law and private property relations. Specifically, the legal regulation of private property rights (see Chapter 3) is analysed as supporting or subverting market embeddedness and consequent social sustainability. The policy reach of this exercise enables testing which regulatory interests external and internal to market economies, work favouring or against sustainable market conditions in the context of positive social bonding. The special relevance for market economies not currently prioritising sustainability as essential regulatory principle is revealed through laying bare law's discriminatory role in crucial private property arrangements (see chapters 4 and 5).

As with our earlier thinking[3] about the social dislocation of market economies, Polanyi's theorising of embeddedness remains the backdrop for our investigation of legal regulation and sustainability. Regina Kreide rehearses Polanyi's explanation of how the market sphere ceased to be embedded in the life of society, and market economies no longer function to serve the people, but instead social processes and institutions have been shaped to meet market requirements. Central among these is law. We join her in questioning what are the mechanics and instruments that allow for the social reembedding of global markets. Beyond economic musing, the answer to this concern has important ramifications for global governance, which is another significant regulatory arena beyond

---

[1] Bible (KJV), 'Proverbs', 3; 27.

[2] For a helpful discussion of embeddedness in many contemporary regulatory contexts see Joerges and Falke (2011).

[3] Findlay and Lim (2014a).

individual wealth creation and nation state economic growth that we challenge as the book evolves.[4]

> The underlying assumption is that legitimate global governance focuses on the inclusion of citizens into law-making processes on a national, as well as a transnational level, while at the same time it tries to place the expanding markets under the control of popular sovereignty … Law alone does not possess the substance to determine [such systematic social integration] and because of this it has to rely on external normative factors. Law's very own normative character, however, lies in its self-dedication to the processes of law-making and justification, which expresses justice within law. It is precisely this law-immanent normativity which allows it to spell out what legitimate law-making should look like … [for more democratic global governance] minority positions must obtain actual access to the negotiations [of market benefit] and must have the possibility of influencing the decision-making process there.[5]

In a market sense, law has become a major instrument of disembedding, in action and in absence. By seeking out law's negative influence over social sustainability, through orchestrating exclusionist private property arrangements, our argument attempts to close the gaps between the forces of rule setting, and those who are genuinely affected by them (not just those for whose benefit rules are directed). In terms of market governance at least, law must be repositioned in the wider regulatory mission, acting towards rather than against social bonding for the *general good*[6] if market sustainability is to complement broader social sustainability. It is not enough to accuse law of failing to protect the marginalised in either institutional or process settings. The following analysis demands more original and equitable logic of the law in its predetermination of private property arrangements that at present destructively separate economic from social relations, and the disadvantaged in its wake.

The *global/social* is the preferred context for our discussion of legal regulation and private property arrangements, despite our empirical focus on nation states and regional alliances. As we have indicated previously,[7]

---

4 Throughout the book our interest in globalised migrant labour flows and the markets they facilitate represent important regulatory contexts beyond the limits of international human rights and humanitarian laws.

5 Kreide (2011), pp. 43, 55, 59.

6 Without unduly constraining the conceptualisation of general goods, throughout the book we focus on correcting the disenfranchising of labour force and value in migrant labour markets, and the social positives above and beyond fairer labour pricing, that such correction would ensure.

7 Findlay and Lim (2014b).

too much energy in regulatory scholarship has been directed towards refining the potency of the regulatory state, and the public law that is said to empower its regulatory objectives. Private law is easily uncoupled from the *dysfunctionalities* of market economies and its regulatory responsibilities are left unscathed beyond even the more critical investigations of how private law might be implicated in market failing.[8]

A more incisive range of speculation about legal regulation looks at private law as making and remaking excluded, marginalised minorities that cannot be rehabilitated into some form of market presence when law's *ring-fencing* of private property arrangements itself resists regulatory efforts at greater integration and accountability through public law. We disagree that *hard law* can call a halt to this process of law as a social problem. The answer to law's unbalanced market discrimination through property enunciation and enforcement, lies more effectively in the reconstructing (or perhaps in a normative or expressive sense, resurrecting) law's regulatory role from exclusion to a more communitarian and pluralist recognition of the social obligations of the market. We endeavour to deconstruct and rebuild particular legal instrumentalities and arrangements as offering practical pathways to market sustainability, beyond critique and hope.

In his discussion of the market's failure to protect public interest, under the larger rubric of responsible enterprise, Philip Selznick observes that despite the many rules designed to off-set the dangers of short-term gain motivation:

> An especially insidious market failure occurs when a product or service that directly affects the quality of public life is degraded, killed or unborn … As pressure rises for wider markets and higher profits, precarious values are displaced or eroded.[9]

In part this corrosive process can be put down to the manner in which the 'idols of the market', such as private property and investment, are justified by the wealth that they have offered even greater populations than just the wealthy.

> This legacy is troubling, however, insofar as it encourages misplaced enthusiasm for applying free market principles to all spheres of life while ignoring the social and political frameworks on which economic life depends … The

---

8 Bridge and Braithwaite (2013).
9 Selznick (2002), p. 104.

> temptation is to transfer an idea made reasonable by a tacit understanding of its limits into an idea corrupted by a lost sense of connectedness and restraint.[10]

Selznick identifies one of the inappropriately worshipped market idols being *property*, individualised and market-centred as it has become in the ages of unfettered exchange since the seventeenth century in Europe. Part of this idolatry is the law's function in protecting property rights and their transference to the heirs of capitalist exchange. Along with this process have emerged such socially problematic trends as the under-valued commodification of wage labour to feed the fetishism of commodities. Despite the selective attempts of private law to rein in the excesses of capitalist market flow, the 'sibling idols of private property and free exchange exert a powerful influence on public policy, and frustrate the protection of important values from market forces'.[11]

As a plus for market certainty, a market-centred notion of property and the legally endorsed rights pertaining to it has done much to encourage investment and the free flow of capital. However, it is this impersonal and non-situated conception of property which has alleviated enterprise responsibility. The shareholder is distanced from that which gives her shares value. The relationship between ownership and control, such a feature of Fordist capitalism, and the essence of person-centred private property, has retained its purchase on the legal imagination despite the corporate personality, and the fluidity of the market in corporate equities.

At the heart of our challenge for a new relationship between law and private property arrangements is the responsibilisation of property as a market entity. This endeavour at fundamental regulatory transition is not advantaged by the burgeoning of law that limits obligations and de-personalises choice. Selznick argues, along with a more sustainably redistributive invocation of property as a responsible market force, regulation needs reinventing so that it becomes the people's business. The analysis to follow takes the understanding of social equity beyond artificial redistribution regimes, preferring to focus on dignity rather than property as the currency produced from markets in which law's normative principles translate into more inclusive social orders.

Much of the empirical content of this book concentrates on markets for migrant labour. It is no accident that we have selected a disembedded market context which so starkly exhibits relationships of vulnerability created by externalised dependencies which reek of unsustainability. If

---

10 Selznick (2002), p. 95.
11 Selznick (2002), p. 96.

we are to imagine the process of disembedding as a continuum, migrant labour markets are the remotest from the social bonds of *general good* even recognising the short-term (but deeply problematic) benefits of wage repatriation. The analysis to follow invites an understanding of law as now profligate but potentially proactive in re-embedding the value of labour, both within its home and host societies. Law becomes a candidate to assist in repositioning labour markets (and other market settings which they benefit) to more socially embedded locations. The sustainability of labour power and pricing then acts as a fillip to the greater project of returning market economies to the service of the social.

In his introduction to the economic work of the decade Thomas Piketty reflects on the Declaration of the Rights of Man and the Citizen (1789) article 1:

> Social distinctions can be based only on common utility.[12]

Our book draws the inevitable conclusion that law's constituency is to the dignity of the individual and not to their degradation within disembedded market economies. The migrant labourer is not an opportunity for capital exploitation but is gravely in need of the legal re-regulation of her labour pricing. Fair value of labour is not some vague right. Re-enfranchising the worker to the value of their labour in a social as well as a market setting takes law's regulatory potential outside processes of commodification, and on to the recognition that occupation is a vitally valuable social bond in which all workers should choose participation rather than suffer exploitation. This incarnation of labour as more than property ensures the priority of individual dignity through actual and informed choice facilitated by law. And this is law's project in a more sustainable and social market world.

> Indeed the distribution of wealth is too important an issue to be left to economists, sociologists, historians and philosophers. It is of interest to everyone, and that is a good thing. The concrete physical reality of inequality is visible to the naked eye and naturally inspires sharp but contradictory political judgements. Peasant and noble, worker and factory owner, waiter and banker: each has his or her unique vantage point and sees important aspects of how other people live and what relations of power and domination exist between social groups, and these observations shape each person's judgement of what is and is not just.[13]

---

12 Piketty (2014), p. 1.
13 Piketty (2014), p. 2.

The arguments to follow explore the subjective and psychological dimensions to inequality, not with the end-game alone of a fairer sharing of the fruits of labour. On top of the recognition that we are, in the North World recurrently, experiencing a rate of return on capital that exceeds the rate of growth of output and income, the consequent generation of arbitrary and unsustainable inequalities Piketty reveals are radically undermining the meritocratic values from which liberal democracies claim economic and social legitimacy. The challenge therefore is for the normative and functional foundations of democratic governance (not to mention of sustainable economic models) to regain control over the market, ensuring general goods take precedence over socially destructive private property arrangements. Law, we argue, is at the centre of this regulatory repositioning. In the grand sense, law is now faced with fundamentally assisting, not fragmenting, the viability of the planet and ensuring its relevance in that project.

Acknowledgements

This book is about millions on the move. Many are robbed of the true value for their labour, and their dignity is denuded. Others – men, women and innocent children – are deported, detained indefinitely or drowned as a consequence of little more than seeking a better, fairer life.

If I were to offer a dedication without condescension it would be to each one of them.

My understanding of the realities of migrant labour and the relationships of obligation and dependency on which the market feeds came from many sources, very different locations and across time. That said, the common story was of state hubris, law's complicity, and the careless view of civil society that we are doing these people a favour.

The research done by my students in the 'Law and Regulation' course, coming from the personal experience of these workers and the knowledge of committed NGOs, has provided crucial and often confronting first hand insights into the world of exploitation and uncertainty which is the migration/labour nexus.

In Sydney and Singapore my research assistants, and my research scholar Jacqueline Krynda, Lee Hsin and Lim Si Wei helped with substantive information on migrant domestic labour in Singapore, the EU and ASEAN comparative perspective, details on the transition in the European regulatory environment, and human rights concerns in the Middle East. Editorial assistance and bibliographic compilation was also their valued contribution. For originally introducing me to the windows of knowledge in Polanyian thinking, Lee Jia En deserves abiding thanks.

Various parts of the text have been exposed to conference critique in Europe and Asia. The thinking on legal regulation and private property arrangements in labour markets benefitted especially from these discussions.

Research support from the Singapore Management University, and from the University of Sydney is, as always, gratefully acknowledged.

The book could not have been written without the people who are its central concern. Asylum migration and migrant labour marketing is a stain on globalisation. How national interest and world economic priorities trump humanitarian obligations on us all is perhaps the shame of this generation. My concluding emphasis on restoring human dignity is a place to start if the challenges developed here are to be seen by readers as personal as well as perpetual.

1. Property rights and the regulation of immigrant labour

> In fact, 'property' is always a bundle of rights, responsibilities and prohibitions each of which is contested and historically determined … perhaps today all would agree that humans themselves should not be private property … [1]

INTRODUCTION

Through the examination of fundamental and fraught intersections between law and private property arrangements this book challenges law's regulatory utility. From the critical understanding of exclusionist and oppressive private property relationships, endorsed, enabled and empowered by law, which shore up the cavernous and catastrophic wealth gaps threatening to irretrievably divide emergent and transitional economies, we critique law in failing the global sustainability project. We argue it need not be so.

This analytical endeavour would chart an easy path if it remains examining normative and practical contradictions.[2] However, our more proactive enterprise is advancing a strategy whereby legal regulation, particularly in its contract mode can be transformed in order to assist in making private property arrangements more inclusive, accessible and generally beneficial. If this can be achieved, rather than undermining such aspirations, law and legal regulation will contribute to the essential social bonds that establish and ensure sustainable market economies now and into the future as economic frames change.

The governing theme in this text is the emergence of sustainability as a new global regulatory principle, advanced or retarded through law's role

---

[1] Schutz (2011), p. 155.

[2] For a discussion of contradiction in legal analysis see Norrie (2001). This is not to suggest that Norrie's conceptualisation and theorising of contradiction is simple or direct, which it is not. Rather, if we remained in that space we might not have to tackle the 'what next' questions which are an important motivation for what follows.

in private property relations. What gives it particularity is the assertion that law's regulatory function in protecting and perpetuating private property rights can either preclude or promote crucial economic and social relationships essential for sustainability.

In the analysis to follow (see chapters 2 and 7), and in our previous work,[3] sustainability is viewed as social bonding, and compatible regulation therefore becomes a force for bonding which is socially embedded.[4] Social solidarity and resultant sustainability are arguably a *general good*.[5] We have proposed in a broad vision that by looking at South World and transitional societies and economies the regulatory importance of social bonding is more apparent than what often features in North World regulatory states.[6] For our purposes in this book, the focus of our regulatory attention is the manner in which private property relationships act as forces for and against social bonding. Through the later comparative case studies of migrant labour (see Chapter 6) South/North market transitions (as with migrant labour transaction) can be critiqued in a sharper market analysis specifically employing legally-endorsed private property relations to explain the exploitation of labour power.[7]

This introduction sets out law's essential role in regulating private property relationships as a precursor to arguing for a repositioning of law's regulatory purpose and in turn practically reshaping law's regulatory role (see chapters 3, 4 and 5).[8] More than an invocation for principled regulation at large,[9] the argument engages a unique perspective as far as contemporary private law theorising is concerned; social sustainability.[10] The overarching analytical context of this chapter is that contemporary crises in global regulation and governance priorities[11]

---

[3] Findlay and Lim (2014a).

[4] For a discussion of our approach to embeddedness see Findlay and Lim (2014a), chapter 3.

[5] Cotterrell (1996).

[6] Findlay and Lim (2014a); Krippner et al (2004).

[7] We use the notion of 'power' to represent labour as a dynamic and should not be confused with any assumption of the empowerment of labour relations. Such empowerment, we argue, is only possible through a repositioning of private property relations enunciated in contracts of employment.

[8] Also Findlay and Lim (2014a), chapter 7.

[9] For this see Findlay and Lim (2014a), chapter 2.

[10] What work there is in this area has a heavy focus on the construction industry and sustainability through building contract formats. See NBS (2014). The International Institute for Environmental Development has done work on sustainability and investment contracts. See Cotula (2010).

[11] Findlay (2013), preface and chapter 1.

reveal shifts away from individualised wealth creation and exponential economic growth at any price, as the driving motivation for regulatory determinations.[12] This transition, as the recent international financial meltdown and its aftermath reveal,[13] will not be painless. To date legal regulation has not assumed much more than a reactive or curative role in this journey.[14] This arguably being so, the chapter proposes that by reshaping the regulatory principles motivating law's influence over private property rights and protections (and activating law's regulatory involvement through such motivations), social and economic sustainability can be fostered in market settings,[15] which would thereby ensure more enduring social location for labour force and for law.[16]

This text builds on our earlier arguments (Findlay and Lim, 2014) that through considering mechanisms of social bonding in transitional and developing economies, and contrasting these with the regulatory features which dislocate North World market economies,[17] it is possible to speculate on how regulation can advance sustainability in a new economic model. For the purposes of this chapter any such new model, when it comes to the use of legal regulation over private property relations, will value conditions of social bonding and responsibility in a similar way that wealth creation and growth have been the regulatory values of the global economic system now under strain.[18]

What does all this have to say about a more specific appreciation of law and its regulatory utility in emerging and transitional economies,

---

[12] This is not to be confused with the movement for sustainable wealth creation even though we agree with its emphasis on 'recapitalising' social capital. See Singapore Institute of Directors (2008). Rather it involves a fundamental redirection in regulatory principle. See UNESCO (1997).

[13] See Findlay and Lim (2014), chapters 3 and 4.

[14] Buckley and Arner (2011).

[15] Again in this brief discussion we cannot pause to develop our conceptualisation of markets and market settings. Our thinking is shaped by the caution that in perceiving markets in terms of their social embeddedness, we should not take the market itself for granted (Krippner et al (2004), p. 110). The market is a theoretical entity in its own right. Markets are social objects and for the purposes of this project markets provide a framework for the exchange of value through identified social bonds.

[16] See the discussion of market economies and social embeddedness in Findlay (2013), chapter 3.

[17] Courts enforce legal values such as justice as an 'expression of requirements for stable social interactions and for predictable expectations in social relations' (Cotterrell (2010)). See also Cotterrell (1996), p. 17.

[18] Laffont (1994).

such as many of those in South East Asia? The present chapter commences with a brief consideration of the wealth gaps which feature prominently (and some say disturbingly) in market economies where sustainability is in question. From here the argument asserts that an important dimension of unsustainable market economies is exclusionist and oppressive private property relationships, endorsed by law. Building on this position the chapter briefly introduces (to be developed as the analysis evolves) ways in which legal regulation can be transformed to assist in making private property arrangements more inclusive, accessible and generally beneficial, thereby contributing to the essential social bonds which establish and ensure sustainable market economies. These imperatives will drive the development of the book's analysis ongoing.

The case study selected to later demonstrate the unsustainability of market economies, where legal regulation (and its absence) currently contributes to disaggregated private property arrangements, is the migrant labour workforce in transitional and developed markets in the EU[19] and ASEAN.[20] In Chapter 5 we particularly focus that investigation on migrant domestic workers as a unique population made vulnerable and dependent as law (migration and employment directed) perpetuates the discriminatory values of disembedded market economies through labour commodification as a depressed market value. The current chapter will explain the comparative enterprise utilising markets in these regions, and foreshadows the selection of essential characteristics which the law offers private property arrangements that currently challenge sustainability (such as contract and agency – chapters 4 and 5). In the chapter to follow we outline the fragile situation of workforce regulation (or under-regulation) against the migration/employment law nexus. Before that, we return to a critical theoretical matrix for appreciating market sustainability utilising the concepts of markets, morality and mutuality. So as to fully appreciate the utility of this frame we commence by examining income inequality as both a product of neo-liberal economic adventurism and a reason behind the challenge that this model poses to market sustainability. If we locate law's role in propping up the private property arrangements which feed and are fed by income inequality then the importance of this phenomenon is clear.

---

19 Bauer, Dietz, Zimmermann and Zwintz (2005).

20 Hall (2011).

SUSTAINABILITY AND INCOME INEQUALITY

In 2011 the International Monetary Fund produced a Staff Note dealing with interpretations of the income inequality/sustainable growth nexus.[21] The report explores the connection between income gap and unsustainable growth:

> The relationship between income inequality and economic growth is complex. Some inequality is integral to the effective functioning of a market economy and the incentives needed for investment and growth. But inequality can also be destructive to growth, for example, by amplifying the risk of crisis or making it difficult for the poor to invest in education. The evidence has also been mixed: some find that average growth over long periods of time is higher with more initial equality; others find that an increase in equality today tends to lower growth in the near term.[22]

Despite the division of empirical opinion one important finding of their research was that in developing economies growth is not persistent. Therefore, in looking at the projection of a nation state's economic growth where its sustainability is most perilous, it is important to explore how income distribution relates to these sharp growth breaks. The authors speculate that longer growth spells are robustly connected with more equality in income distribution. So the issue for growth in economies, particularly those that have sparked growth through fractured income distribution and structural inequality, is the clear medium-to-long-term damage these policies present for growth if not addressed.

Income inequality is fuelled by distorted labour value. Some commentators put this down to fundamental discrimination in the labour market.[23] In the chapter to follow we will identify how labour pricing inequities create profound conditions of dependency and vulnerability relationships that risk the sustainability of all key stakeholders in the labour market.

Much research on labour market sustainability relates to impoverished workforces.[24] Our analysis chooses to look at how income inequality in host countries, fuelled by labour pricing dysfunction in home and host

---

21 Berg and Ostry (2011).

22 Berg and Ostry (2011), p. 3.

23 Much of the writings on gender income inequality in labour markets identify discrimination as the structural cause. See Arrow (1971); Humphries and Rubery (1984).

24 Kitson M., Martin R. & Wilkinson F. (2000) 'Labour Markets, Social Justice and Economic Efficiency', *Cambridge Journal of Economics* 24(6): 631–41.

countries, has a critical impact on the sustainability of markets in both settings (see Chapter 6). In the case of much of labour migration it is rural poverty which triggers the journey to new markets of exploitation. The chapters to follow will show that labour migration is far from a passage of rags to riches. Even the argument that through remittances, the migrant worker is able to supplement failing markets in their home setting is in fact unsustainable. When NGOs in particular assert that even undervalued migrant labour benefits the worker and those reliant on this income in the home country,[25] they do so by taking the conditions of domestic poverty and economic underdevelopment as a given. While an issue too broad for adequate treatment in this text, the economic/political environments of many if not most of these home nation states are riddled with corruption and economic mismanagement. These essential structural failings are the drivers for rural impoverishment more than any inherent deprivation of organic work opportunity. Sustainable wage and subsistence labour levels would grow in the home economy if these core market characteristics were attacked. Migrant labour remittance relief provides respite for these market vulnerabilities and could be seen indirectly as buffering the inevitable social unrest that their perpetuation must produce. Justifying migrant labour and remittance dependency while not at the same time exposing the agents of domestic impoverishment (and the income gaps which expose their social destructiveness) is in policy terms to maintain unsustainable labour market flows driven from home to host by poverty. Indeed without this poverty trap the depressed labour price feeding migrant worker migration may indeed see some natural correction from home to host economies.[26]

> The full impact of migration on a village's income distribution is multifaceted and complex, and many components of this impact may not be quantifiable. For example, estimates of migrants' net contributions to household income need to take account of the full opportunity cost of migration, including income migrants would have contributed to their households had they not migrated. Migrants' net contributions to household income are a subset of the overall impact of migration on the household's resources and opportunities. For example, migration affects the household's income risk, the household's

---

[25] Jean, Causa, Jimenez and Wanner (2007); Hanson (2008).

[26] The other end of this momentum is evidenced in the employment preferences of migrant workers possessing basic wage labour information on which they can exert some job choice. For instance, many migrant domestic workers accept low paid employment opportunities in Singapore and Malaysia, in the eventual hope of using agency contacts to migrate on to the better paid and somewhat more secure labour markets of Hong Kong and Canada.

> production and investment decisions, the household's rank, and so on. And remittances may favorably affect the distribution of income also via a filtering down effect, e.g., if they result in an increased demand for the products and services of the poorest households within the village.

This World Bank research into the income distribution realities of migrant labour goes on to suggest the development of unsustainable dependencies in home economies which are remittance dependent, especially in workforce markets which often are the least socially unsustainable:

> Diverging views concerning the effect of out-migration on the distribution of income by size in rural sending areas and on rural welfare reflect assumptions about both short-term and long-term externalities associated with migrants' departure from their villages, the size of migrant remittances, and the position of migrant-sending households in the rural income distribution. They also reflect value judgements, in particular the weight attached to distributional versus mean income objectives and the weight attached to incomes of households at different points in the income distribution when calculating indices of inequality.[27]

So it is not just wealth gaps in home or host countries that benefit from the critical lens of sustainability. The dependencies that develop economy-to-economy and market-to-market suggest dynamic forces at work which may assist the understanding of how migrant labour-sustained wealth gaps challenge market sustainability internal within and external beyond the migrant labour market.

Often the inequitable labour pricing of migrants is justified either by the assertion that even meagre wages are much superior to survival subsistence at home, and that the migrant is the rich-man on his/her return. Whether the latter is real or apocryphal, the research suggests that any such introduced wealth gaps do little to enhance social bonding in the home setting.[28] The issue of why the poor stay poor is not only a consequence of urban bias.[29] Studies that examine the wealth gaps between native and migrant workers indicate:

> As pointed out by Gibson et al.[30] wealth differences between immigrants and natives contribute to an intergenerational transmission of disadvantage and to a slowing of immigrant assimilation … policies seeking to reduce income

---

27 Stark, Taylor and Yitzhaki (2013).
28 Barajas, Chami, Fullenkamp, Gapen and Montiel (2009).
29 Lipton (1977).
30 Gibson, Le and Stillman (2007).

> inequalities may remain ineffective in reducing wealth inequalities, as wealth and income are likely to be distributed differently and be driven by different determinants, with bequests and intergenerational transfers being two such examples … Our results show that native-born households are wealthier than immigrant households, even after controlling for household characteristics, the country of origin and migration cohort. This result is robust across the entire net wealth distribution, and is not affected by different economic structures and migration situations of the countries considered although the estimated effects vary. We also find that a higher age at migration carries different penalties across countries.[31]

Associated with this concern, and its ramifications for social cohesion, is the ancillary justification for migrant labour into developed economies: that in the short-to-medium-term at least this population flow can ease the cost of an aging population. Into the longer-term this economic benefit will be negatively offset if migrant workers are not assimilated into the domestic labour market and thereby contributing to social welfare and income taxation (discussed in Chapter 6).[32] Wealth gaps, native to migrant workers, whatever direction in which they are perceived to flow, are a potent impediment to productive assimilation.

To extrapolate further on the consequences for sustainability of wealth gaps and inequitable income distribution, if law facilitates such inequality through private property relations, it should be instructive to examine migrant labour markets in a nation state where this correlation is clear. Singapore provides just such a market example. However, before we examine this example, we engage economic externalities that are challenging the form of domestic labour markets in ways similar to the devalued commodification of migrant labour, to seek out similarities in the way regulation or its absence can negatively impact the longer-term sustainability of labour markets.

LABOUR VALUE AND THE FAST-APPROACHING DEMAND LABOUR AGE

Rousseau in his *Discourse on Inequality* argues on from the dominion of greater physical strength, that in modern societies the creation of laws and property has corrupted natural men and created new forms of inequality, neither being in accordance with natural law or natural selection. As unjustifiable, unacceptable forms of *morality* through legal

31 Mathä, Porpiglia and Sierminska (2011), pp. 8 and 31.
32 Dustmann (2000); Castles (2006); Portes (2007).

inequality, they must be contested. For Rousseau, whatever causes man to leave a state of nature and enter civil society, private property and law create a conflict between rich and poor. Thereby man is corrupted only by his own delusions of perfectability and the harmful elements of his capacity for reason. Social contract, with a major focus on the artificial division of labour, is in significant part a negotiation of private property, away from the harmony of natural man.

Migrant labour markets have perfected the corrupting potential of private property arrangements. As the book progresses we will return to the market forces which unnaturally deflate the value and pricing of migrant labour. We will argue that it is not enough to explain discriminatory migrant labour value and pricing in terms of the poor public protection of property rights or wasted private protections, but rather it is much more fundamentally about how the market perceives the individual dignity of migrant workers and their property in their labour. Confirmation of this lies in the argument that devalued migrant labour would not be possible without the acquiescence of the migrants themselves. The implication of this justification is that impoverishment within sending countries, while not being the sole driver of migrant labour markets, is the essential context in which migrant workers struggle with each other for the dubious privilege of labour exploitation in the receiving labour markets. The terms on which migrant labour pricing is struck feed on the disempowerment of migrant labour as their labour force is commodified against the shadow of poverty and desperate survival obligations.

In a recent article discussing the current market trend towards *work on demand*, lack of job security, unpredictability of opportunity and the absence of genuine agency are identified as the dangers inherent in this developing labour market model.[33] If employees morph into independent contractors, the threat of a *Mechanical Turk Economy* through the monetisation of downtime has the article asking of conventional labour environments: what kind of private lives can we possibly have, what kind of relationships, what kind of families? However, at the same time developed economies thrive on migrant labour markets with undervalued workers, about whom no such fundamental life-style questions are considered, nor are measures of individual dignity valued even as a pricing base-line.

---

33 Manjoo (2015). An interesting comparison can be drawn with the insecure conditions of employment which fuel the EU job flexibility/economic growth policy discussed in chapter 6.

LABOUR PRICING AND WEALTH GAPS – THE SINGAPORE EXPERIENCE

The *Financial Times*[34] singles out the exploitation of cheap labour as both a key factor in Asia's recent economic growth, and in the wider perspective, the suppression of general wages which this distorted labour market feeds. Where migrant labour sustains construction and real estate development, local labour either eschews or is excluded from such an employment band. As a result the unskilled labour market for local workers is contracted, and the price of that labour is constrained through comparison with prevailing salaries in the construction (and domestic services) sectors where migrant labour dominates. On the other side of the market, real estate development is an artificially lucrative investment as a consequence of high margins of return ensured through suppressed labour value.

As the experience of many Asian transitional economies shows, these conditions overheat all levels of real estate commerce creating wealth bubbles, over-extended credit gearing and barriers to entry which produce conditions of unsustainable economic inequality and eventual social unrest.[35] It is argued that along with the advance of technology and the eradication of poverty, the promotion of *employment friendly* workforce regulation is crucial for contracting the wealth gap and creating a future for sustainable economic growth through a more balanced labour market where value and exchange are more aligned.[36] In her review of globalisation's impact on Singapore's socio-economic development, Amaldas speculates:[37]

> As the Singapore economy moves into higher value-added goods due to globalisation, the widening income gap amongst its population becomes the key political challenge. The rate of accumulation of human capital through education and training needs to keep pace with the rising demand for more skilled workers as the economy moves on to a higher value-added industrial structure. This will increase the wages of skilled workers relative to low skilled workers and increase the income inequality and vulnerability of local

---

34 Rhee (2012).

35 In Singapore this has recently manifested in anti-foreigner sentiment, focused on the assumption that migrant labour challenges local employability, and migration upsets established racial balance. Concerning the former it takes no account of the critical economic reliance on migrant labour in the present workforce frame. See Tan (2013).

36 Berg and Ostry (2011); Topel (1999).

37 Amaldas (2009).

> workers to the global trends. This suggests that education alone would be inadequate to manage income inequality in the future. Singapore may need more social welfare schemes to balance economic growth and the widening economic gap.[38]

To date the Singapore government's approach to income inequality has not involved significant structural workforce reform. On the other hand the government seems to manage the widening income gap not by reducing income inequality but preferring,

> … transparent attempts to reduce the real and imagined frustrations arising out of growing or high inequality. Managing may take various forms: national public discussions, ensuring equality in education and other opportunities, use of targeted and general subsides and various other forms of asset redistribution, the extent of redistribution being a function of political will, economic imperatives and stage of development.[39]

Despite this policy direction, and the continued ideological subscription to meritocracy, the Singapore government, following its recent 'national conversation' policy engagement, is selectively introducing mechanisms for transmitting gains throughout the economy and especially to the poor. Yet, as is later argued, without a radical repositioning of private property relations in Singapore, directed at the manual labourers and migrant workforce and the transaction of their labour, economic and social sustainability are at risk. As migrant workers and unskilled labour in Singapore only have their labour to sell, economic growth can only reach the poor if it increases the demand for their labour, by more realistically revaluing its price or providing complementary inputs that make their labour more productive.[40] In addition, a repositioning of law, as a determinant of private property relations that construct the workforce, can have direct influence on revaluing labour beyond skewed pricing through exploitative employment contracting.[41]

The Singapore migrant labour microcosm suggests a need to analyse current workforce practices and their economic attractiveness in generating selective individualised wealth, and promoting short-term economic growth, against even the domestic political realisation of this nexus as being economically and socially unsustainable in the medium-to-long-term. Consistent with this assertion that legal regulation repositioned to

---

38 Singh (2008), pp. 313–30.
39 Rao (1996), p. 360.
40 Amaldas (2009), p. 995.
41 Findlay and Lim (2014a), chapter 4.

promote socially sustainable property relationships provides a regulatory solution to this unsustainable nexus, this work next offers three regulatory conditions which, depending on their contextual relationship with law and property, can either promote or retard sustainability.

CONTEXTUAL CONDITIONS FOR AND AGAINST SUSTAINABILITY

This year will represent almost two decades since the Kyoto protocol in 1995, over 20 since the Rio Summit in 1992 and disturbingly distant is the creation of the Brundtland Commission (1983) whose subsequent report, *Our common future* (1987), defined Sustainable Development as: Development that meets the needs of the present without compromising the ability of future generations to meet their own needs.[42] It appears that we are now that future generation. But are our needs any closer to being met in even a market sense?

In proposing a guide for sustainable investment contracts the International Institute for Environment and Development identified the following issues:[43]

- Choice among, and framing of, contract models to maximise sustainable development outcomes, for example through promoting more inclusive business models in the design and implementation of an investment project;
- Tools to maximise the economic benefits to the host country, including public revenues and non-revenue benefits like investment commitments, technology transfers and infrastructure development, as well as local content provisions that shape the extent to which the investment project creates local employment and business opportunities;
- Tools to balance economic with social and environmental considerations: environmental and social impact assessments and management systems, safeguards in land takings, social investment requirements and legal remedies for groups adversely affected by an investment project;
- Stabilisation and renegotiation clauses, which concern the evolution of the contractual relation over time and may be used to reconcile

---

42 UN General Assembly (1987), para. 1.
43 Cotula (2010), pp. vi–vii.

the investor's need for a degree of stability with preserving host state capacity to take action in the public interest even if it adversely affects the project;

- Dispute settlement, including contractual provisions to regulate investment disputes that may arise under the contract and proper handling of disputes when they arise;
- Confidentiality provisions – acknowledging that although commercial confidentiality concerns may be at stake, openness and public scrutiny are essential to maximising sustainable development outcomes.

The list demonstrates a commitment to community inclusion. It is more than a celebration of law's collaboration in the autonomy of privileged interest (discussed in the context of dignity in Chapter 7). Maximising choice through inclusive business models, creating local employment and business opportunities, offering remedies for adversely affected groups, action in the public interest particularly through dispute settlement, and openness as the counterbalance to confidentiality each and all arguably represent more egalitarian legal regulation. In addition, these commitments speak to a more socially embedded market frame with a communitarian morality, reliant on and promoting mutual interests in a wider outreach. Choice in worker/employer negotiations is obviously empowering. As is discussed specifically in this book's later consideration of contracting, choice is nothing without essential knowledge regarding the contexts and constitutions of any choice preferred or imposed. The discussion of agency reveals how a denial of knowledge to workers disproportionately empowers agency influence and confuses the fiduciary relationships in favour of the agent/employer bond, at the cost of labour entitlement. These are not only considerations of rights compromised, but markets perverted in the cause of depressing labour value. In Chapter 4 where we examine the contract as a sustainable regulatory frame, and in Chapter 5 where we critically unpack law's role in agency, the significance of throwing a wider regulatory net over stakeholders' – now largely excluded from private property arrangements presently essential in market sustainability – exclusivity becomes the crucial justification for redirecting and expanding law's regulatory role. In order that the impact of regenerating law back to some of the central normative principles of agency and of contract can be evaluated, we suggest that the context of the market, its morality and the mutualities of interest which it expresses (and perhaps as yet excludes) need to be employed as analytical locations for the case study to follow. In addition, these locations provide the opportunity to view law as currently a force against market sustainability, and then to base the trajectory for its move into sustainability 'insurance'.

The frame of our analytical matrix[44] for understanding the forces which work towards and away from social embeddedness, and thereby economic sustainability, is designed as three Ms: markets, moralities and mutualities. Advancing our thesis that the legal regulation of private property relationships can be a positive force for sustainability and social bonding, by examining these forces against our three general themes, we anticipate a clearer understanding of how law (as a regulatory agent) should actively contribute to social bonding within situations where such bonding is disembedded. In the context of currently unsustainable migrant labour workforce markets we argue that the sustainability of workforce relationships crucially depends on positive social bonding, which law is presently failing because of regulatory capture or inaction. From this example, in order to understand sustainability in terms of markets, moralities and mutualities, we propose a useful measure of the outcomes of a sustainability project through a model role for law as a purposive regulatory agent with sustainability as its objective. In so doing the later analysis of migrant labour dependencies and vulnerabilities in particular, suggests crucial conditional interpretations of regulation which must move from individualised to mutual interests, advancing and not retarding positive social bonding within labour forces. Law is chosen as a regulatory agent with social justice at its normative core and discriminatory private property relationships as its contemporary labour market regulatory focus.

Markets

The resilience of the market as an idea, a place, a framework of exchange and mechanisms of interest enhancement depends on the social and economic interconnectedness of human beings from which exchange relationships grow.[45] Law as a regulatory terrain defines, delimits and determines these exchange relationships. As such, law retains a potential to reposition exchange relationships as forces for market sustainability. Market morality and stakeholder mutuality are platforms from which the

---

44 Which is introduced and developed in greater detail in Findlay and Lim (2014a), chapter 4.

45 Whether for primitive subsistence, or as the recent global financial collapse has shown, for corporate greed (revealed through excessive amounts of risk in order to gain 'free money' (Leith (2008)).

expressive and facilitative roles for the legal regulation play out.[46] Property rights ensuring either individualised wealth or sustainability as a general good, help standardise the form of products for market exchange (both tangible and intangible), being adapted for diverse, massive and frequent transaction; wage labour being an important example.[47] In the case of labour markets, the worker sells labour and the owner/manager purchases productivity under conditions essentially determined by private property relations (such as contracts), or by their absence which creates conditions determined by more predatory power relations if labour is in surplus. Migrant labour markets are attractive to the more powerful interests in an employment contract (and often to the state) because labour power is in surplus and transacted in conditions of poverty compulsion. The unbalanced and often discriminatory regulatory purpose of private property rights and obligations within the migrant workforce marketplace is revealed when considering the fictional instruments of exchange[48] which delineate ownership and entitlement provided by private property rights, from the transfer of labour power resources in arrangements which exploit labour surplus and exclusion from actionability (such as migrant workforces moving from underprivileged to more lucrative work opportunities).[49] It is well documented how the specialisation and division of labour cut across organic social bonding such that capitalist/labour relations become intensely distorted.[50] For migrant labour, its dispossession into environments of exploitation, moving from situations of deprivation, means that the host market feeds off and depends on fundamental social dislocation (see Chapter 2). In theory (or in labour markets which value labour power), law steps in to regulate such situations back to order for the benefit of private property value and exclusivity, or for the benefit of organised labour and collective bargaining. Law's failure in this regard, where migrant labour is concerned, is a consequence of exploitative and under-regulated workforce governance, and the incapacity of the market to correctly value labour power in situations of oversupply, the absence of organised labour representation and of collective bargaining in any balanced sense (see Chapter 2).[51]

---

[46] Morgan and Yeung (2007), introduction and chapter 1.

[47] De Soto (1993), p. 3.

[48] Dale (2010).

[49] Athukorala, Fukao and Yuan T. (2009).

[50] Silver (1994); Sirianni (1984).

[51] This is obviously so, when supply contracts and the market is forced to consider and compensate productive labour rather than always gear down to

In the context of private property relations within the labour market, it is not difficult to imagine how a similar transformation takes place when the categories of property multiply as market players try to distinguish a new and more valuable labour relationship from what already exists in market exchange. This is a destructive trend for social bonding if externally unbalanced market interactions lose connection with critical and essential social backgrounds and contexts, where sustainability is their primary value.[52] In migrant labour markets for instance, wage is not a measure of the objective or productive value of labour but rather of how little disempowered market players (comprising the supply of labour) are willing to tolerate.

Any convincing attack on disembedded market economies and their proclivities will first address the neo-liberalist conflation of the market's function as an analytical tool with its associated normative ideal (distorted by unquestioning acceptance of problematic variables such as competition and unregulated currency exchange).[53] For migrant labour markets, competition has been neutered by over-supply and poverty compulsion. The organic regulatory counterbalances which come with the realistic market value of labour have been disengaged and replaced by a mechanical rush to the bottom, being lowest tolerable wages and conditions often enforced by state prohibitions on industrial dissent, and immigration policies which create intense job insecurity.

Even if we seek to constrain law's role to facilitating the efficient allocation of scarce resources, it should not follow (if law is just) that the resultant market analysis has to be actualised into material benefit largely for those who profit from resources which are much more renewable (such as all resources with a focus on the productivity of labour power rather than raw materials).[54] Accepting (which we essentially do not) the retention of markets as the mechanism for determining who has the greatest need or who is able to produce the most value, it does not follow that owners/managers of the means of production, being protected through law by the existing scheme of private property rights, should receive as their personal income, monetary equivalents offset by the market's evaluation of labour force product, which does not materialise in the form of reasonable or proportionate wage compensation for that labour power. Rather, the prices arrived at through the operation of the

---

labour markets where capacity and productivity are lower, but labour value remains cheap.

52 Markova (2006).

53 Boettke (1994), p. 272; also see Findlay and Lim (2014a), chapter 3.

54 Rawls (2008), p. 350.

market can only retain their function as realistic or commensurate economic indicators used to derive a scheme of economic activities based on allocative efficiency, when they are determined consistently against features of social sustainability which value other things besides money and exchange. Where migrant labour is concerned this enhanced determination of value may well be an emphasis on the nexus between worker satisfaction, work security and productivity (absent considerations in the present 'free movement of labour' policy model).[55]

For migrant labour an equitable market price actualisation of wages is unlikely where the value of labour is overtaken by factors within and beyond the host market; within it could be the weakness or absence of legal regulation which would otherwise require fair payment practices or empowered inclusion in contractual bargaining, and external are the conditions in the home market which make migrant workers willing to tolerate exploitation or be powerless to resist it. In this state of learned helplessness the migrant worker is vulnerable to any market undervaluation of labour power.[56]

While the prices paid as income for labour power can be quantified in terms of the actual cost of renewing such resources, the prices imputed to consumption and production, unlike labour power, may have no distributive role because consumption in particular is both fragmented and sometimes indifferent to resource renewability. For instance, as mentioned in our later consideration of contracting and intellectual commons, the production and consumption of knowledge, released from copyright price may enhance renewability and general social valuing, but do nothing to redistribute the economic value of pre-existing knowledge commodification. Particularly for migrant labour markets, the link between renewability and sustainability, we argue, is crucial. In this sense we are not conceiving renewability as just the next worker when the last has been expended. More essentially, for sustainable labour markets with a mix of local and migrant workers, it is the renewability of orderly market bonding such as that which leads to trust and loyalty that we would argue is an important and viable project for legal regulation.

In the capitalist world order, the distributive role for inputs of productivity other than labour (such as natural resource allocation or managerial innovation) still exists, and more critically now in times of

55 Ruhs (2013).

56 Valuation here should not be seen simply in terms of wages, as a fictional exchange commodity wage alone cannot ensure sustainable labour market arrangements. Wider issues of worker bonding to the market must also be factored into the sustainability argument.

radical resource depletion. It is another regulatory role for law to ensure the efficient distribution of resources designed to direct these inputs and prevent any downward spiral denying income equity, maintained by a system of private property rights which risks market sustainability through the selfish exploitation of resources, particularly wage labour. Law's normative frame, as we see in the discussion of contract and agency (in chapters 4 and 5), is well designed to this task. Legal regulation towards sustainability can distinguish between the use of the market to organise economic activities efficiently, and to endorse a system of private property relations in which the worth of resources is only measured through the personal income of the owners by virtue of what are often coincidental rights of ownership. In such contexts law needs to participate in a remoralising of corporate advantage in labour markets and property benefit, if these markets and benefits are to be sustainable into the economic and social future. This re-directive role does not need a moral justification, though it has one, but in a market context may essentially achieve a mutual objective of market viability in a new sustainable form.

Moralities

Moralities are significant as a social bonding context. This view recognises more than the need for a *human face* covering the inhumanity of economic despotism. Arising out of the earlier proposed correlation between sustainability and social bonding, such social ties can be determined as sustainable or strained. Sustainability implies greater equity and that necessitates at least a consideration of social responsibility which is built on mutualised moralities. Mutualising morality does not necessitate a common stand on all moral questions. Rather, it anticipates that diverse views will congregate around the essential aspiration for a sustainable society, in which market economy may play an important role. A corollary to this is that disembedded market economies may be immoral because their emphasis on individualism and exponential growth for wealth is socially unsustainable. The move from individual to mutual interest is both motivated by fearful necessity and mutualised morality.[57] Where the wealth creation regulatory focus for motivating regulatory principle has time and again failed society, it is only through a remoralisation of market relationships that sustainable outcomes can be ensured. The morality argument for private property rights as it stands is limited in

---

57 Michnik (1990).

scope, and we see it mainly as providing these conditions for individualist advancement, which our analysis determines to be an unsustainable moral motivation.[58]

A facilitator of market remoralisation, and a bonding agent for market mutualities is trust. Trust is a major player in the regulatory game within more communitarian and subsistence world contexts. Social bonding relies on trust as a regulator in such contexts, thereby enabling society to maintain crucial mutualities of interest such as market sustainability. Realising that these mutualities can be sustainable even without the interference of law as constructed by and for the essential pre-conditions enabling economic order, explains law's role being where and when trust is lost. Contract arrangements, if they are to be viable as constructive market arrangements, rely on compliance rather than rigid recourse for breach. If trust does not underpin contracting, then the contract becomes a punitive regulator rather than a reassurance of market mutualities (see Chapter 4).

There can be no better example of a trust barren regulatory space than exploitative migrant labour markets. Within this set of arrangements, crucial trust deficits in private property market frames are agency relationships (or their constraint, even denial) wherein the worker has no genuine representation, and where the worker cannot play any actual role as a free and responsible agent (see Chapter 4).

Reflecting on *free and responsible agents*, conceptualised to describe individuals and corporate personalities interacting within the market and governed by contract law or agency, we argue against the self-centred and power-imbalanced moralities (or lack thereof) in systems where sometimes exploitative individualised ownership is supported by exclusionist private property rights.[59] Marketing migrant labour under capitalist conditions, is not a libertarian exercise of parity, 'clean hands' and unconscionability. At the most basic level of worker/agent/employer/state engagement, there cannot be said to be any individual, interest-free independence guaranteed by the freedom of contract in reality where participation is not equal and parity is only really normative. The surplus value assumed for labour if it is in abundant or non-discriminating supply, means that the bargaining value offered by surplus labour eventually dispossesses workers from the essential commodity necessary to sustain and maintain their labour power – that being a living wage. This outcome results from exchange/price disempowerment experienced

---

58 Boettke (1994), p. 274.

59 Rawls (2008), p. 324.

by workers who have no actionable way to anticipate or influence how much labour power they have to invest and gain returns from, in order to purchase commodities for their own subsistence, when price and cost are determined by markets in which they have no moral or practical purchase.[60] This disconnect between the normative guarantees of contract law, and the reality of labour price bargaining is another critical opportunity for the corrective influence of legal regulation principled on market sustainability rather than the protection of exploitative wealth creation.

In our earlier work we proposed the pathway to being *responsible agents* within liberated contract arrangements is that workers and owners need to enter into and respect *binding social agreements* which ensure compliance with orderly and amicable price and cost frameworks, guaranteed by the legally-endorsed certainty that the cost of breaching such agreements outweighs the benefits of doing so.[61] In order that legal regulation might return systems of commercial transaction, through trust-based contracting to the normative preconditions of contract law, the market has to value sustainability above the wealth creation and growth benefits for the powerful interests in constrained contract domains.

Mutualities

This field of analysis is critically reliant on achieving successful outcomes in market and morality arrangements. Currently law's role in negotiating benefit in labour force arrangements is very much dependent on the nature of the interests being advanced and the positions of power (or the lack of it) enjoyed by key stakeholders in these arrangements. All too commonly law, in the form of labour contracting, is not designed to achieve mutuality. Rather law protects the individualised property interests of those parties dominating the exchange environment. Regulatory mechanisms ensuring the mutualisation of interests should be mechanisms guaranteeing that productive and valuable workforce arrangements are attained and sustained. In the case of migrant labour it is the significant structural imbalances of power to contract and to negotiate and enforce mutually beneficial contract terms which makes employment contracts unbalanced regulatory implements. The powers of the employers, often enhanced through a patchy canvas of employment protection laws, is off-set by institutional impediments to the workers' bargaining

[60] Rawls (2008), pp. 326–7.

[61] Findlay and Lim (2014a), chapter 4. Also see Birmingham (1970), p. 284; Goetz and Scott (1977).

position. This imbalance mocks some of the fundamental principles (and fictions) of contract law, such as parity (see Chapter 4). For migrant workers, the poverty compulsion out of the workforce options in their home jurisdiction, and their uncertain residency status in the guest market (discussed in Chapter 2) further destabilises and disempowers their bargaining capacity. In such market conditions the contract is a regulatory device which implicitly or explicitly skews the more organic market forces which value labour. In addition the power differential between employer and employee makes the contract largely nonactionable from the worker's point of view when her meagre contractual protections are not forthcoming.

Polanyi intimates that organised labour is a mechanism which can redress contractual imbalance in workers' bargaining power.[62] The potential in a guild labour model offers the possibility of stronger and more diverse bargaining terrain, and if such organised labour mechanisms are available to migrant workers then the contract can be transformed into a mutualising mechanism. Unfortunately as chapters 2 and 6 detail, some state law specifically excludes migrant workers from this mutualising mechanism.

Positive market *mutualities* are social bonds forming market relationships, which in turn should maintain wider social sustainability through ensuring the essential social benefit of market outcomes. In the migrant labour force context, mutuality has been substituted by exploitation and simmering hostility. For the sake of medium-term market productivity alone legal regulation needs to intervene and create bridges and pathways for the mutualisation of common market interests which are both sustainability and productive market exchange.

Mutuality of interests can be determined and engineered by law through the establishment and maintenance of *binding social agreements* (as distinct from flimsy and one-sided contractual constellations). These arrangements are a new way of conceiving labour contracts and depend on inclusion and accessibility of private property benefit for ultimate market sustainability. We later touch on these as market sector contracts which benefit classes of market stakeholders (see Chapter 7).

How does law defer or deny the mutuality of interests that would make more available access to property and capital and thereby expand mutualised benefit (and economic social responsibility)? The mutualised advantage of more accessible property arrangements has to first be identified and then acknowledged along with the benefits that more

62 Dale (2010), p. 87.

distributive justice can bring, in particular the sustainability of both legal regulation and the property relations that it now normatively endorses. Therefore, with social sustainability as a core regulatory outcome, mutualities become the focus of law as social bonding.[63] It may be strange to apply the language of social bonding to labour markets which have for so long been adversarial and at times confrontational. We suggest that this negative mindset is a product of post-Fordist labour relations epitomised in the migrant work force context. If productivity is a genuine purpose for labour relations (and in certain contexts we doubt even this) then mutualities based on trust and shared benefit are much more likely to maximise the conditions and *wealth* of productivity than short-term exploitation and medium-term subjugation. Law can be a corrective agent in this shift of commercial consciousness. The stimulant towards this shift for reluctant market players is the eventually-realised risk of productive labour power drain.[64]

Having foreshadowed our argument regarding the need for a commitment to collaborative, distributive justice, regarding market knowledge and power (see Chapter 4) and other foundations of inclusiveness and shared progress – all of which fall squarely within the term general social good – the procedures or mechanisms to facilitate such shared outcomes require more concentrated analysis. The section to follow briefly returns to the dysfunctional, and socially disembedded features of Singapore's migrant labour force in order to give a location for law's failing as a regulatory mechanism for general social good within a transitional economy which has a clearly unsustainable migrant labour foundation. It identifies for later analysis (see Chapter 6) law's failure as a regulatory agent beyond the advancement of individualised wealth creation and exclusionist capital/labour relations. This discussion is a precursor to any argument for a shift in regulatory principle and a transformation in law's role when regulating a healthy and socially located employment market, and more inclusive and generally beneficial private property relations.

WORKFORCE REGULATION: LAW'S FAILING OR OPPORTUNITIES FOR REPOSITIONING?

Alleging failure of law's regulatory presence (or absence) in the migrant labour market, when measured against sustainable market arrangements

63 Rawls (2008), p. 351.
64 Akerlof and Yellen (1985); Boldrin and Horvath (1995).

and the outcome of a general common good, it is necessary to note how the migrant worker/agent/employer/government/civil society dynamic in economies such as Singapore relies on the maintenance of exclusionist and repressive private property arrangements. This reliance is made clearer through examining how law can address its failings when applied across the interests of all contracting parties, and thereby suggesting the need to include vulnerable stakeholders and make accessible to them law's protections as crucial conditions of the workforce market that at present are repressive and exclusionist against labour power's interests. In so doing it will be the absence of law perhaps more than its discriminatory protective dimension which is a feature of its regulatory purchase.

The contexts of disembedding migrant labour transition are sequential and recurrent. The labourer and the agent situated in his home country (the home agent) negotiate terms which are usually exploitative of the worker and his family sponsors, and even these terms are often eventually illusory. The worker embarks on a relentless passage of obligation wherein she is required to invest relatively large capital outlay for tenuous immigration status and employment contracts. The status of the home agent is certainly not as a representative of the worker's interests even in the negotiation of the original contract terms of engagement. For example, it is not clear in the practices of the Singapore agents or of any eventual employer whether or not the agency connections, from home to host jurisdiction, can be enforced by the worker in any legally recognised contractual conveyance. As Chapter 5 suggests, the whole purpose of agency law is to clarify the delegated role of the agent and to specify rather than obfuscate legal lines of responsibility which contract can ensure, and professional trust can reassure.

Market situations of social disembeddedness (and where as of now legal regulation is all but absent) in the migrant labour market involve the:

1. need for the prospective worker to pay home agency fees and travel costs on the uncertain promise of employment;
2. negotiations of contract terms with the home agent acting in their interests, and often with state oversight;
3. immigration status on arrival in Singapore being conditional on the existence and continuation of work contracts;
4. negotiation of contract terms with Singapore agents in the interests of the agent and the eventual employers;
5. reality after employment engagement, of the regular failure of contract conditions either in terms of the home agency, the practice

of Singapore agents, the industrial arrangements by the employer, each pitted against the reasonable expectations of the workers; and
6. residency vulnerability of the worker if in dispute with an employer or between employment contracts.[65]

Chapter 4 identifies contract law as a crucial platform from which legal regulation either advances or retards private property arrangements, in turn promoting or preventing sustainable market conditions. Legal residualism and regulatory reticence hallmark the manner in which employment law (and employment contractual conditions) in Singapore discriminate matters for contractual attention or legislative selectivity. The distinction drawn between *legislated matters* (matters relating to non-payment of salary or overtime wages, working hours and illegal deductions from the worker's salary)[66] and *non-legislated matters* (disputes relating to the working conditions, contractual conditions, the job scope, and the amount of salary),[67] can only be made sense of if the private property relations so regulated are skewed by legislated law away from the worker and towards employer/agency interest. The reason for this conclusion rests in the apparent illogicality of distinctions such that salary payment may have legal protection but not salary terms.

While the heart of law's failing here can be easily exposed through the disconnect between the normative guaranties of contract law principles, and the hard edge of industrial relations, normative cornerstones such as privity and parity of contract, lacking as they seem to be in practice, hold the key to private law rejuvenating more equitable and sustainable legal regulation (see Chapter 3). At present exclusion from contractual advantage and protection is the legal and intended consequence of contractual

---

65 (3) results in (6) because (3) means that the employer has complete power over the worker's eligibility to remain in the country (because the employer has total discretionary power to terminate the employment agreement). Thus if the employee is in dispute with the employer the latter can make litigation of the matter next to impossible through contract termination and the adverse effect that has on the disputant remaining in the jurisdiction.

66 Sections 21 (non-payment of salary), 27 (unauthorised deductions) and 38(4) (overtime salary) of the Employment Act (Cap. 91).

67 'Some 600 statutory employment claims (e.g. non-payment of salary or overtime pay, unauthorised deductions made from salary etc.) are processed every month, which are resolved through conciliation or adjudication by the Labour Court. More than 90% of such cases are settled within one month. For non-statutory contractual grievances related to the workplace (e.g. dissatisfaction with employment terms, wages, job scope), workers should raise the matter with the company or their unions who can take up their grievances.' See Tan (2012).

selectivity extended through the preferential positioning of employer interest, and the tolerance of perpetual breaches of limited worker protection through the state's blind eye or hands off approaches to inspection of enforcement. In addition, the exposure of power imbalances between contracting parties can identify the interests behind these disparities and open up possibilities for their reconciliation.

MUTUALISING THE DEGRADATION OF SOCIAL RELATIONS

Lacher highlights that the central thrusts of Polanyi's historico-cultural anthropology was how it distinguishes itself from Marxist and social-democratic political projects: by identifying as the problem of the market system the degradation of social relations, the destruction of the substance of humanity and its natural environment (as compared with targeting exploitation and low wages as the Marxists do).[68] With resistance to the profit motive and the self-regulating market at the centre of his writing, Polanyi formulates his expectation of a new great transformation (and thereby the conditions of reembeddedness as he sees it):[69]

> ... the market system will no longer be self-regulating, even in principle, since it will no longer comprise labour, land and money. To take labour out of the market means a transformation as radical as was the establishment of the competitive market. The wage contract ceases to be a private contract except on subordinate and accessory points. Not only the conditions in the factory, hours of work, and modalities of contract, but the basic wage itself, are determined outside the market. ... To remove the land from the market is synonymous with the incorporation of land with definite institutions such as the homestead, the co-operative, the factory ... However widespread individual ownership of farms will continue to be, contracts in respect to land tenure need deal with accessories only, since the essentials are removed from the market. The same applies to staple foods and organic raw materials, since the fixing of prices in respect to them is not left to the market. ... The nature of property, of course, undergoes a deep change in consequence of such measures since there is no longer any need to allow incomes from the title of property to grow without bounds, merely in order to ensure employment, production, and the use of resources in society.

Therefore, Lacher argues that reembeddedness has to go to the root of removing labour, land and money from the control of the market system.

---

68 Lacher (2007).

69 Polanyi (1944), pp. 259–60.

And this is envisaged by Polanyi to be achieved through a revision of the notion of property (and thereby private property rights) and the extent to which contracts override other more fundamental means of social bonding through regulation that preserves humanity. The disconnect between our summary of the legal regulatory terrain and migrant employment arrangements can at the very least support a conclusion that the state, often through fundamental misrepresentations of its regulatory objectives (see Chapter 2), aligns with the law it sponsors in advancing employer interests in the private property relations which determine the migrant labour market. The challenge for repositioning law outside this degraded sponsorship/servile relationship for law is to address market interest imbalance, even if for no other reason than medium-term market sustainability, by levelling out in particular, contractual issues of obligation, rights and actionability. Law needs to have a more holistic presence if it is to cover an expanded interest base. Its expressive function must clearly declare an interest in redressing imbalance. Its facilitating bite must be directed to:

- more detailed and objective legislative coverage with clear enforcement pathways;
- the determination of delegated authority with rigorous and transparent oversight powers and practice;
- a framework of independent arbitration and judicial review which is equal to other areas of law;
- dismissal and repatriation protections to enable actionability of protections by workers; and
- uniform insurance reporting requirements.

Regarding unsustainable migrant labour markets, in order to enable this transition in legal regulation there needs to be, as noted earlier, effective intervention at each critical stage of the work contract formulation. Typically this would involve:

- a claim of extra-territorial jurisdiction from the home (sending) to the host (receiving) states (or through bilateral arrangement) to ensure minimum conditions governing agency representations. In addition, both the receiving state labour agent and the eventual employer would be required to recognise a chain of agency in which each party was responsible for the crucial representations made to prospective employees up to and including the signing of the agreement. Host state agents would be required to act as the worker's agent, and not as the agent of self-interest and the employer;

- legislation stipulating minimum standard wage amounts and payment conditions, working hours, workplace conditions, and industrial health and safety;
- immigration conditions which would provide reasonable amnesty on repatriation if the worker is dismissed from employment while the worker is in dispute with the employer;
- creation of arbitration and adjudication facilities which are designed to resolve workplace disputes with equal rights and facilities for representation;
- creation of universal insurance requirements and facilities for labour organisation; and
- creation and implementation of an active inspectorate function with specific reporting requirements and detailed compliance and enforcement provisions. The inspectorate should focus on contract compliance and workplace conditions and not just on state licensing requirements. Attached to this should be a worker/employer complaints mechanism and public interest oversight. The inspectorate should have particular responsibility for agency practice, contract term compliance, workplace conditions and worker health and welfare.

Recognising the responsibility of law in enabling private property relations which fuel sustainable market failure, this chapter triggers an argument for redirecting the regulatory focus of law so as to reconsider the meanings and values of crucial market variables such as labour power. Central in this transition is law's expressive and facilitative influence which can move private property rights and obligations in the direction of sustainable social relations.

EPHEMERAL – PERPETUAL

One of the conceptual challenges when employing sustainability (as social bonding) for the purposes of regulatory principle is confronting the ephemeral/perpetual antonyms. In terms of both temporal and spatial considerations something may be ephemeral because it is transitory, transient, fleeting, passing, short-lived, momentary, brief, short, cursory, temporary, impermanent and short-term. As for perpetual we think about everlasting. Sustainability resides somewhere between.

Under the banner 'Ephemeral was yesterday, sustainable is tomorrow' a wine producer's website posts this about sustainability:

> In order to face the market evolutions and to respond to tomorrow's requirements, the wine coop signs up for the 3D process: destination, development and durability, which are the conditions for sustainable development. This process aims to evaluate the impact of the company's activities on the economic, environmental and social circles of the society ... (we have) launched an action plan with the objective of improving its societal performance.[70]

Borrowing from this mission statement, the analysis to follow looks to sustainability as a destination. Social bonding on its own is a process that can achieve beneficial or detrimental outcomes for individuals and communities. Bonding as enslavement within fundamentalist and exploitative cultures is not a *general good*. Therefore, when advancing sustainability as a regulatory purpose the argument must make clear what sustainable outcomes it prefers. For example, there are many subjective value judgements in constructing and determining political economy which will inform preferences for higher or lower taxation, or more or less rights for workers. Fortunately the normative frames of legal fields such as contract (Chapter 4) and agency (Chapter 5) clearly offer outcomes which define constituents of a common good. Development in a swathe of the sustainability literature is identified as the preferred futurist, even global economic terrain. There seems a resonant timidity to admit that social sustainability may not only sit incompatibly with contemporary development models, but it may be these models premised on exponential growth, which effectively diminish and even undermine sustainable outcomes. In the argument to follow, we embrace Polanyi's position that even with socio-economic development, economy must be subsumed within and supportive of social bonding towards a general good. Durability might be considered to be interchangeable with sustainability. The application of sustainable regulation and regulating for sustainability does not take durability as a given. This is where the ephemeral becomes the perennial. Advocates of sustainable development argue that the consideration of natural environmental factors when pursuing development, as well as economic and social factors, is vital in order to safeguard the ability of future generations to also enjoy an increased standard of living: what the Brundtland Commission referred to as 'meeting the needs of present without compromising the ability of

---

70 Cave du Marmandais website.

future generations to meet their own needs'.[71] Despite the obvious *North World-centric* science and rhetoric which argue that the environment and development are congruent, from the perspective of social sustainability many sustainable development projects fail the measure of reflecting and respecting the interests of the community where they locate.[72] Economic development is primarily prosecuted for the benefit of the modern state,[73] along with the supra-national interests of global commerce, and the legal instruments which enable development projects to consciously exclude the interests of local communities which not only fail to benefit in the development push, but are all too often sacrificed on the altar of growth.[74] Sustainable development may not be about durable sustainability where development priorities prevail over community sustainability inclusive of *general good*. Anthropology has done much to expose this disconnect and it benefits our analysis to follow which works from the premise that economic growth models promoting individual wealth creation are antipathetic to sustainable regulation.

> Anthropological critiques of sustainable development, in keeping with the discipline's general 'grass-roots' focus, are based on the argument that the inclusion of environmental concerns within the framework of development projects often results in the interests and expectations of external actors being served over those of the target communities. As we have seen, this is due to the way in which the inclusion of environmental concerns, preferences, etic over emic perspectives, and how, on a more practical level, this theoretical preference within the discourse results in environmental concerns being addressed ahead of the interests of the target communities. This, we have seen, is possible through the way the decision making and planning capacities of both the state and international donors are informed by the dominant discourse.[75]

UTOPIA OR RELEVANCE

Perhaps this juxtaposition can only be raised in an introduction as a caveat designed to instil in the reader the confidence to continue. We anticipate even at this early stage of our argument that some will be wondering whether the analysis can ever extract itself from the land of

---

71 Referred to in Smyth (2011).
72 Escobar (1995).
73 Scott (1998).
74 Brosius (1999).
75 Smyth (2011), p. 83. See also Edelman and Haugerad (2004).

dreams. Why would a hard-bitten employer or a pragmatic state policy-maker or a self-interested agent be induced into a paradigm regulatory shift which values market sustainability over shorter-term wealth creation? The answer to this lies in our work on sociability.[76] The sociability approach argues that despite differing pathways of interest, stakeholders can come together through the appreciation of shared risk (in this case the disappearance of a functional and profitable labour market), and work towards a shared fate outcome (sustainable market conditions in environments of finite resourcing and failing regulatory inoculation).

The larger question is why would law as a regulatory paradigm be amenable to repositioning away from the exclusionist protection of private property arrangements which has made lawyers wealthy for generations? To this we answer, relevance. The text that follows will give regular instances where as a consequence of its suspect alliance with the forces which undermine market sustainability, law is squandering its regulatory relevance. In these terms the question does not simply call on the sacrifice of self-interest but rather it predicts a call for survival.[77]

Relevance is a central evidentiary question for law in determining the tools of proof. However, as Ian Dennis observes:

> In contrast to all modern codes of evidence, English law has no authoritative or common law definition of the core concept of relevance.[78]

This absence of definition might reveal the attitude that *relevance* is such a fundamental legal determinant, and so common a question in the application of law that beyond the boundaries of common-sense it does not demand specification. Our application of relevance here is not relevance *in the law* but rather relevance *of the law*. In this text we argue that:

- a central justification for the current regulatory relevance of law is its relationship with exclusionist private property relations;
- the regulatory purpose of this relationship is to maximise and maintain wealth creation for a privileged few with access to enjoy these arrangements;

---

[76] See Findlay (2013), Preface, chapters 1 and 10.

[77] Note the discussion of the ebbing relevance of patent and trademark law in addressing the tidal wave of information piracy which is the crime of the younger generations world-wide. See Findlay and Lim (2014a), pp. 91, 115, 193.

[78] Dennis (2013).

- the global economic model of selective economic growth and individualised material wealth creation now appears to be unsustainable; and
- for regulatory paradigms such as law to maintain their relevance (in terms of a general *good and* a particularised social benefit as measures of *wealth* transform) it will be necessary for the regulatory purposes of these paradigms to prioritise social sustainability.

THE COMPARATIVE ENTERPRISE

In order to test the major allegations presented in Chapter 2, which there stand as no more than assumptions, it is necessary to look at the transnational transaction of migrant labour comparatively across regions with similar market dependencies but very different domestic, bilateral and regional regulatory patterns (see Chapter 6).[79] The labour migration pathways in both case-study regions (the EU and ASEAN) need to be traced from the perspective of home and host jurisdictions, and the ways in which regional regulation influences these. Chapter 2, as a scoping exercise, limits any comparative case-study analysis of guest workers across the EU and Southeast Asia, to considering the negative nexus between labour relations and migration regulation in contexts of employee rights and protections, employment disputation and worker repatriation.[80] At the outset, the chapter to follow interrogates the assertion that the forms of migrant status accorded to guest workers (for the purposes of their employment abroad) create varying potentials of discrimination and rights abuse. Even when migrant labour regulation includes laws which offer benefits to the migrant labour population through documentation and limited rights protections assuring such benefits, we argue these are predetermined by more fragile residency conditions for the 'legitimate' worker population than that enjoyed by citizen workers. Such vulnerability creates dependency relationships between workers and employers which are ripe for exploitation. It is the

---

79 In this respect the 'ASEAN way', of prioritising state autonomy and requiring concessional and empathetic regulation through compromise, is a long way from more interventionist EU regionalism.

80 The larger study presented in chapter 5 will widen the sites of vulnerability and dependency, and will consider the impact on both documented and undocumented workers. For the purposes of chapter 2, undocumented workers will only be considered in terms of their exacerbated vulnerability due to the denial of limited migration status.

human and the market consequences of this exploitation and the rights violations it facilitates, that prompted this research interest.[81] For socio-legal researchers, chilling is the realisation that the law is not simply failing to control, but is facilitating the crucial conditions of discrimination through the regulatory state (functional or fragmented).[82] Laws governing migration and repatriation enable further market discrimination. The second major theme in the chapter is a speculation on the role of private property interests as they promote and benefit from the market conditions that foster documented and undocumented migrant labour. We conclude that exclusionist private property relations, regulated through legal forms such as the employment contract or the work permit, advantage employers and enable them to exploit the vulnerable residency status of foreign workers for their market benefit.

Both the public (legislation) and the private (contract-centred) legal regulatory frames play important roles in the discrimination process, and each requires examination when analysing the dependency relations from market and labour force points of view. State-imposed legal market controls and contract-centred regulation (or their silence), crucially influence the employment conditions of guest workers and the marketing of their labour power. While migration and employment contract provisions could be vehicles for workers' rights protections, with foreign workers we see a tragic reversal of this potential in favour of enabling employers' market benefits (see Chapter 2).

Comparative analysis here must be dynamic in recognising the tensions between domestic regulation, as forming migration barriers for national interests to transnational labour supply, and regional regulation that endeavours to manage population flow.[83] Normatively locating such regulatory tensions within public international law and conventions, setting standards on the conditions of employment to be enjoyed by those in the labour force generally and more universally, is a discourse about action, but not a guarantee of actionability for all. For instance in the European context, international and regional law has developed considerably to cover documented guest worker employment as a migratory

---

[81] Findlay and Lim (2014b).

[82] Again further explored in Findlay and Lim (2014a), chapter 4.

[83] The intentions behind domestic and regional regulation here may be distinctly different, as the recent Swiss referendum on migration flow, and the EU's response, demonstrates.

process.[84] However, despite vigorous attempts at the regional level to ensure freedom of movement (for market benefit) that respects essential border protection, regulation of the conditions under which migrant workers are resident remains distinctly within domestic jurisdictions, and develops inconsistently as such.[85] This realisation reveals that the regulatory state migration focus is more concerned with domestic considerations of economic benefit and privileged citizenship, than it is designed to illuminate the discriminatory passage of migrant labour into disembedded labour markets, the uncertain and vulnerable status of their labour power within those markets and the perpetual fear of indiscriminate and arbitrary repatriation.[86]

Methodologically, recognising the significance of the regulatory state referent, the comparative interest at first instance should be with political paradigms. Initially, the focus is on one nation state to another in two different regulatory 'worlds', one selectively interventionist and the other largely divesting responsibility to other regulatory actors. At this level there will also need to be consideration of labour market 'transaction' from home to host jurisdictions. The next level of comparison is regional: clearly however with the consciousness that as regional configurations, the EU and ASEAN operate under very different constitutional legalities. Finally, the meta comparative level is how international conventions and regulations influence, if at all, each of the other two levels. The latter largely forms a normative restatement, and at worst a regulatory chimera in which rights are offered with no active, accessible and fair process for their enjoyment.

Declaring a political context for comparison should not conceal the essential market concern of our comparative analysis.[87] As much as they should be social, markets are essentially political as well as economic concepts central to the aggregated states[88] that form the objects of domestic contrast. Within the political configurations of the market there

---

[84] There are some distinct areas of failure here particularly when public and private legal regulation intersect over matters of agency. Barber (2000); Ford and Piper (2007); Anderson (2007); Ruhs and Anderson (2010).

[85] Kaur (2007); Parreñas (2001); Gibson and Graham (1986).

[86] NB the detailed case-study in Findlay and Lim (2014a), chapter 5.

[87] This does not mean that the paper is not concerned with social consequences. Consistent with our work on embedded markets (Findlay and Lim (2014b)) we do not advocate market analysis which is distracted from social context.

[88] This is a generalised comparative meant to include consolidated states with a generally stable political frame and viable, if unsustainable economies.

is the opportunity to consider, as we do, institutional, motivational and interactive paradigms governing market movement.

As previously indicated, the overarching purpose of the more detailed case-studies to follow in Chapter 6 is to employ private property relations and the conditions of discrimination and dependency they evidence and advance as an explanatory tool for understanding the regulatory failing identified above. Legal regulation thereby offers another comparative level, to test the assumption that the migration/labour nexus crucially advances exclusive private property interests. This will be achieved by theorising migration and employment status as a unique market context, highlighting the current regulatory conditions that exist for the advancement of exclusive and discriminatory private property interests through contract and agency arrangements (see chapters 4 and 5) against the more generalised market interests of employers within the host societies, and those migrating for work. Essentially it is a consideration of the 'marketability' of vulnerable and dependent worker power, and how in particular regulation as private property relations contributes to as well as controls these employment relationships.

CONCLUSION – HUMANITY OR COMMODITY

One of the irreconcilable tensions in the analysis to follow emerges from determining whether migrant labour is an issue of commodity or humanity. This consideration essentially predetermines the role of legal regulation in maintaining human rights frameworks, as well as ensuring sustainable markets of labour value. A sharp and critical examination of the humanity/commodity paradox is essential if we are to understand:

- the practical impact of rights protections for workers who both benefit and suffer from their enforcement;
- the reasons why regional and national priorities diverge when rights are expressed in discretionary enforcement regimes;
- the manner in which the recognition of citizenship rights and national social benefit fuel exclusionist migration regimes;
- how the free flow of labour which may enable essential corrections in market labour value is sieved through domestic political interests;
- how the economy of domestic states is critically supplemented by low-priced labour while the political/social dimension prohibits equitable inclusion in taxation responsibility, welfare benefit and communitarian responsibilisation; and

- why migrant vulnerability and dependence in disembedded markets feeds on and requires rights denial, and what this means for the regulatory reality of rights discourse.

Originally, this work claims that market sustainability and rational rights recognition are not incompatible in embedded market societies. This is neither ephemeral nor utopian. Avoiding the charge of some naïve claim absent of the political/social, this book advances the legal regulation of sustainable market relations as a starting point for making more viable and humane the exploitation of labour value. On the way, we will lay aside some of the fluff in rights rhetoric (see Chapter 7), and demand a reconsidering of the commodification of people, their lives and their suffering.

2. Private property relations and regulating the immigration–labour nexus

> Every actual state is corrupt. Good men must not obey the laws too well …
> Want of liberty, by strengthening the law and decorum, stupefies conscience.[1]

INTRODUCTION

Migrant labour markets are under-regulated world-wide. If the measure is legal regulation then the deficiency becomes even more marked. This lacunae is no coincidence. One of the intentions of this chapter is to demonstrate the external and internal market forces at work in creating unsustainable dependencies between key market players, with particular focus on how migration rules adversely influence the *health* of the migrant labour market. Whether it be against a framework of rights, or contractual obligations, or workers' health and safety, or migration registration and inspectorate it would be fair to anticipate that both public and private law fields would have an important regulatory function. The nature and extent of that function, and its dysfunctions, will be portrayed at key labour market crisis points, enabling the more particular focus on private law and property arrangements in Chapter 3.

There are two principle regulatory paradigms for migrant labour markets. Utilising employment contracting, agency and workplace conditions, the market acts as a regulator with the benefit in part of private law arrangements. Through mechanisms such as the domestic enforcement of international obligations, or the migration registration of worker *flows*, state regulation and its application of public law would feature. Both of these regulatory domains are lacking, we argue, so as often to favour the selective interests of propertied stakeholders and the market-oriented state. Below will be revealed the systematic devolution of state regulatory

---

1 Atkinson (1992).

responsibility when it comes to the protection of workers' interests. This drawback can be demonstrated in the:

- failure to give sufficient domestic legislative and administrative purchase to international and regional rights provisions;
- inconsistency of state regulatory involvement when comparisons are drawn between native and migrant workforces;
- selective interest of the state in regulating some categories of migrant labour against others (for instance domestic workers when measured against construction workers); and
- vigour of the state in enforcing residency registration conditions and worker levy fees, against a reluctance to enforce pay and condition provisions.

The market as a regulator over migrant labour relations is notoriously biased, skewed towards fast money to be made from deflated and undervalued labour pricing. It appears through the avenues of contract and agency (see chapters 4 and 5) that private law and its light touch facilitate the deferential interests of employers, and the state.

The intersection between these two general regulatory planes offers a unique insight into how law can differentially disembed native and migrant labour markets, home and host. The public law administrative regulation of labour migration registration and residency satisfies the state's political interests in discriminating the livelihood benefits of migrant workers, recognising and reflecting citizen suspicion and resentment. In addition, registration provides consolidated revenue, relieves the welfare and labour strains attendant on an aging population, and opens up investment streams in key economic areas such as construction and agriculture. In return the state allows employers and agents the benefit of private law largely as it suits them. The dangers to sustainability of this loose legal alliance will become clearer (in chapters 4, 5 and 6) after we address the market dysfunctions that currently prevail.

NEXUS

Research on labour law and migration regulation rarely intersects. When it does, the regulatory interest as evinced by the literature[2] usually centres on the formal requirements qualifying a foreigner to work. In particular, the migration status of the individual is primarily considered as it

---

[2] Wishnie (2007).

registers employment legitimacy and residency conditions prescribed by prevailing immigration and employment laws. Such a substantive, legalist perspective is built on the assumption that documented workers should comprise the guest labour force, and that the legitimacy of their labour status is determined by immigration regulations.[3]

What can be missed in this research direction are the vulnerable market contexts and relationships of employment dependency made possible by fragile residency status often exacerbated in the arbitrary protections offered through migration registration and its regulation. The selective application of employment protections contingent on migrant labour residency status creates a context of transience and a sometimes-unhealthy nexus between worker residency and employer discretion[4] that perpetuates dependency and vulnerability. We see the vulnerability/dependency intersection as facilitated by rather than ameliorated through conditional and often arbitrary migration status. In this sense temporary work permits as much constrain the quality of life as they provide authority to work. Market conditions develop to depend on undervalued labour pricing as a consequence.

At this point the reader would be forgiven for dismissing statements of the obvious. Historically, nation state migration registration has essentially been about exclusion and inclusion within the frames of citizenship, not cognisant of market conditionality. Beyond the days of slave trading, indigent labour pricing has evaded state protection from market exploitation. Temporary work registration should mean exactly that, and the residency conditions which follow will obviously create contexts (both in employment and lifestyle) that are transient and without protective conditions. We accept these observations. However, the kernel of our critical analysis is the paradox that migration registration, designed to regulate labour markets in a more orderly and transparent fashion, is exacerbating other market contexts of dependency and vulnerability that challenge and even defeat this regulatory constitution. As a result labour markets become unsustainable in terms of labour productivity and pricing.[5]

---

[3] Underneath these assumptions exist under-regulated or unregulated employment relationships that feature discrimination and exploitation as a consequence of vulnerable residency dependencies.

[4] Discretion exists to terminate employment for reasons that may not depend on employability, triggering work permit retraction and consequent repatriation.

[5] We develop this argument more fully in Findlay and Lim (2014a), by observing that low skilled and underpriced migrant labour operating in market contexts where work and residency conditions are transient, will neither have an

It is the objective of the following analytical frame to reveal that the regulation of employment through conditional migration status has become another factor in disembedding already exploitative labour markets. In addition, the regulatory techniques employed to ensure the rigidity of the migration/labour regulatory nexus, are producing often unintended destabilising market consequences, which must be considered in the development of temporary and transitional labour transaction.

Recognising its underlying interest in law's connection with exclusive private property arrangements, the discussion to follow will only engage meta issues such as rights to the extent that even at a normative level external interests strain the otherwise symbiotic connection between law and property. It is not the intention of the chapter to distance the solution for its unsustainability outside the market, and its mechanics which disembed from the social expectations that externalised rights might be seen to protect. In addition, the examination of market sustainability is not located in the perspective of disadvantaged workers, worthy as that may be. To do so might risk a pendulum shift which could swing past sustainability and onto the problematic contingencies of the counter-movement.[6]

TRANSNATIONAL LABOUR FLOWS

The following analysis does not shirk from the immediate negative consequences of labour exploitation as a market condition. Of course there is much comparative work on the exploitation of those without employment registration, an even more dependent and vulnerable worker population.[7] Transnationally, the undocumented worker phenomenon is understood in terms of the difficulties facing countries within different regions less able through effective migration policing to regulate the influx of migrant labour, and the strains this may present for maintaining appropriate and more universal employment relationships domestically and regionally.[8] In this dynamic sense the transition of labour force is determined as a migration problem requiring solutions from home, transit and host jurisdictions, rather than being addressed as a market variable.

investment in productivity nor complement permanent labour markets where productivity is said to be a factor in labour pricing.

[6] For a discussion of Polanyi's countermovement and its potential when employed towards the criticism of welfare dependencies, see Findlay and Lim (2014a), chapter 3.

[7] Stark (1986); Roberts (1997); Zegers de Beijl (2000).

[8] Bosniak (1991); Cohen (2006); Inghammar (2010); Sassen (1994).

The push-pull factors for unregistered migrants scoff at the regulatory focus on migration rather than markets.

In the European Union (EU) context, networked migration regulation has been advanced as the regulatory solution to the adverse consequences of liberalising the trade in labour services and their under-regulated globalisation. In this policy analysis regional and global labour market demands and itinerant labour power supply play out in a 'push-me-pull you' tension driven by undervalued labour pricing, insatiable domestic demand for cheap labour, reluctance in the permanent workforce to negotiate this demand, and voracious transnational labour trade. The *problems* in labour market migration are not viewed either in terms of disembedded market situations,[9] or economic and social outcomes of the regulatory conditions that enable market imbalance,[10] but instead are talked of as failings in cross border migration control, and deviant labour trading.

This chapter offers a more critical policy frame, questioning why networked migration regulation (slack or tight) is unable to resolve the social, economic and broad teleological inequities associated with the exploitation of migrant labour power leading to market disembedding.[11] To achieve this we consciously remove the analysis outside the regulatory state in favour of a critical market context[12] wherein the regulatory challenge has two dimensions:

1. because of the itinerant and 'under-visible' nature of labour migration, inconsistent legal and regulatory autonomies and ambiguities create for documented migrant workers a transition of vulnerability and dependency exacerbated by the market exploitation of migration status; and
2. because of the failure of employment registration through migration regulation to create appropriate, transparent and accountable employer/employee relationships in market economies unsustainably dependent on labour exploitation, an undocumented segment of guest workers is an inevitable and even more vulnerable part of the labour force.

---

9 Findlay and Lim (2014a), chapter 3.

10 Such as we will later argue private property relations can facilitate.

11 For a detailed discussion of our interpretation of the embedding, disembedding dynamic see Findlay and Lim (2014a), chapter 3.

12 The theorising for which is developed in Findlay and Lim (2014a), chapters 2, 3 and 4.

Labour markets, therefore, and their regulatory sustenance, we argue, provide a more valuable focus for understanding the ubiquity of migrant labour supply chains, particularly in comparative regional regulatory settings. Limiting any analytical and policy attention to state and regional regulatory competencies will eventually bypass the tragic antimonies degenerating migrant labour power through exclusive and discriminatory regulatory agendas. Equally distracting, we conclude, is looking across the documented–undocumented divide without interrogating the market imperatives that favour both conditions and how migration regulation inevitably enables the exploitation of both worker populations. It is important from an analytical perspective to recognise that the documentation dichotomy itself is a construct of migration regulation and is impossible to interpret outside that context, as we will later show regarding the negative consequences of inspectorate.

In order to avoid this regulatory blind spot,[13] researchers and policy makers should not ignore social and market perspectives, preferring instead some discussion of seemingly logical migration dichotomies. We address in other work the dangerous and destructive intersection between under-regulated labour markets and unsustainable market economies, where labour force vulnerability leads to worker exploitation, and unsustainable market dependencies foreshadow medium-term economic instability across all labour markers.[14] The interest of this chapter is to analyse the manner in which migration status, its determination, negotiation, maintenance and enforcement, generate vulnerabilities and dependency relationships which even vigilant and more uniform regional regulation cannot overcome. These are structural as much as policy and procedural considerations, and as such cannot be divorced from market dynamics, residency status being important in this regard.

At the outset of this analytical overview, we should address head on those who prefer to argue that the unavoidable regulatory imperative is migrant status through worker documentation. We will engage with this more simplistic position by appreciating the porous nature of the migrant status divide. In so doing we are not accepting the inevitability of the

---

[13] And we reiterate this will naturally occur when the research focus is the regulatory state rather than labour market conditions. For example, when structuring its responses to migration challenges such as people smuggling and human trafficking, the UK neglected the limited impact of its state policies seen against labour market pull-factors which provided the economic space for both regular and irregular migrants; see Geddes (2005).

[14] Findlay and Lim (2014b).

migrant/labour regulatory nexus but rather revealing through the endangerment of labour force value by requiring migrant registration, the often less-recognised discriminatory and unsustainable regulatory context of this nexus.

EMPLOYMENT DISCRIMINATION THROUGH MIGRATION STATUS

Undocumented migrant workers refer to those who take up employment illegally without meeting the requisite domestic residency conditions or obtaining conditional migrant status. Undocumented workers may enter the host country illegally or over-stay after entering legally on tourist visas or as irregular migrant workers. Illegal labour immigration occurs by evading genuine employment immigration clearance, often utilising the services offered by organised groups that engage in people trafficking.[15] Such transitional/illegal migration and employment status creates an initial dependency/vulnerability situation for the prospective worker wherein traffickers and unscrupulous employers collude to preferentially obtain undocumented workers, avoiding market restrictions effecting access to legitimate migrant labour, and obtaining more compliant, less protected labour at a cheaper price. Workers in these relationships generally carry a high agency burden with respect to traffickers, and risk the adverse consequences attendant on their illegal entry into an illegitimate workforce, which may be exacerbated by their obligations to people smugglers. Regarding the *ungovernability* of their employers and the unaccountable employment relationships forged once they enter illegal job contexts, these workers are exceptionally bonded due to their unauthorised, even clandestine migration status. It is one thing to be denied migration legitimacy and thereby be diverted into the black markets of labour and residency. It is another to exist in employment relationships without at the same time having even the most basic claims for decent and actionable work conditions from the boss, their supervisors or the state as a consequence of migration status distinction. Not only are these workers excluded from the minimum protections that conditional residency and employment contracts may offer, but also as participants in illegal residency and work arrangements they are constantly under the shadow of exposure should they resist discrimination or exploitation. The agency/employment context for these workers is set in

---

[15] CCTV.com (2007).

the illegality of their migrant status. That status (and its illegitimacy) creates the context for dangerously vulnerable dependencies.

Again, where undocumented workers secure employment initially through fraudulent tourist status, and over-staying, the vulnerability of employment relationships is a consequence of ever-present risks that their lack of documentation will be exposed and that by colluding in illegal employment they will be punished for violating migration and labour laws.[16] Perhaps the most vulnerable undocumented workers are asylum seekers and refugees who, even though sometimes allowed to seek employment pending the decision on their application via a provisional labour permit, often remain in work and residency even after the refusal of their application for legitimate migration status. The fear of exposure is exacerbated for this group, by uncertain or even denied citizenship and genuine concerns for personal safety if repatriation is possible.

However, it would be wrong to assume that these dependencies and vulnerabilities are cured through documentation. The fragile conditions of residency and permission to work, which we detail later, mean that documented workers live only marginally less exposed. It is the argument of this section that rather than providing regulatory certainty, where a worker stands on either side of the migrant status distinction is often only an extension of dependency/vulnerability contexts which the conditions of migration documentation (or their denial) confirm. Simply to focus regulatory attention on sharpening the clarity and impact of this distinction, without considering the relationship between migration discrimination and labour market inequities will not adequately address the negative aspects of migrant labour market conditions.

The next section briefly considers the argument that in addition to migration status regulation, opening pathways to more permanent migration status and employment integration will help manage dependency/vulnerability arrangements which enable migrant labour exploitation (and benefit the social demographics and population sustainability of the host nation – see Chapter 1). The other dimension to this policy approach is a clarification of migrant worker expectations when employment demand is temporary or constrained. There is no reason, we argue, that temporary workers should not, in an official market context at least, have standard employment and residency conditions for the period of their work permit.

---

[16] In Singapore, for instance, it is a routine sentence that worker 'overstayers' will be given three months in prison and three strokes of the cane, before being deported and banned re-entry.

TRANSITIONAL RESIDENCY STATUS – DOCUMENTATION TO 'LEGITIMATE' TRANSIENCE?

Temporary employment has been advanced by Germany[17] and by other developed countries within the EU as the balance between economically managing domestic labour demands and countervailing negative domestic attitudes to foreign labour force. Often the economic and political paradox between negative social attitudes to guest workers, and essential market benefits from their participation in the labour force boils down to concerns over national identity.[18] The common regulatory response has been exclusionist in offering determinate residency for labour, without confirming the general expectations of benefit which conventional immigration transition would allow, or regularised participation in employment markets would offer. As generally with the residency/work permit interconnection, the residency and labour vulnerability here arises from the conditions determining migration status – contracted employment on which limited migration status is dependent. If for any reason the employment is withdrawn then residency usually falls away.

The line between temporary and illegal employment is often traversed. Regularly, temporary employment morphs into illegal employment, sometimes as a result of the uncertainties of working conditions and residency futures when the employee:

- takes up more working hours/days than the permitted limited prescription in the documented employment status; or
- over-stays with the inducement that prolonged residence may de facto offer permanent residency if the host country values the duration of what despite its illegitimacy appears to be an otherwise normal employment relationship with a host employer. Seconded or project-tied workers seem to often follow this course.

On the other side of the employment divide, prolonged illegitimate worker arrangements may result in eventual legalisation of employment standing, again discriminated through residency concessions where undocumented workers have their employment status regularised through marriage with a citizen, the processing of an asylum application, or during general amnesty campaigns. For example, France has a long tradition of the *post hoc* regulation of labour migration through any or all

17 *Werkvertragsarbeitnehmer* in Germany, explored in greater detail below.

18 Pang (1991); Pang (1992); Amaldas (2009).

of these means, in recognition of the contributions made by migrant workers whatever their residency status.[19]

At this point it is useful to briefly refer to a particular scheme designed to formalise employment and residency status as they relate to migrant labour markets within the EU. Where such schemes contemplated possible transitions to more permanent migrant status, this policy presents an interesting comparative context with regulatory regimes in ASEAN (where this transitional phenomenon is very rare or indeed regulated against) (see Chapter 6).[20]

Migrant labour transition may be considered in two forms: transition from home to host country; and eventual transition from conditional work and residency to more permanent arrangements. Formalised transitional pathways can alleviate the vulnerabilities of temporary migrant status and the Damocles of unemployment-triggered repatriation. However, if the enforcement capacity of such regulatory efforts takes the form of random inspections which appear to be more concerned with illegitimate migration status, in preference to interrogating appropriate employment conditions, then workers will see the policy as furthering rather than reducing their vulnerability. Even where inspection-centred regulation prioritises work conditions, the uncovering of undocumented workers could lead to considerations of transition, but is more likely to precipitate repatriation. In the following programme, specific agency arrangements between the host and home countries have been designed to short circuit claims, after a designated residency and work period, to benefits more comparable with those expected by the native labour force. The potential damage that such discrimination can cause healthy labour markets is more than just a concern for migration regulation.

Werkvertragsarbeitnehmer or project-tied workers are used predominantly in the German building industry. Their employment context is compatible with worker subcontracting, but in this situation it is from home to host employment and across national labour contexts. The stated aim of the process is to promote cooperation between German and foreign companies, but it was also conceived by policymakers as a

---

19 International Centre for Migration Policy Development (2009), p. 39.

20 Examples of legislation in ASEAN include: Employment Act (Cap. 91) (Rev. Ed. 2009) (Singapore); Employment of Foreign Manpower Act (Cap. 91A) (Rev. Ed. 2009) (Singapore); Employment Agencies Act (Cap. 92) (Rev. Ed. 2012) (Singapore); Cambodia's 2011 Sub-decree 190; Law No. 39/2004 concerning the Placement and Protection of Indonesian Migrant Workers (Indonesia); Migrant Workers and Overseas Filipinos Act of 1995 (The Philippines); Alien Employment Act of 2008 (Kingdom of Thailand).

framework to reduce the need for foreign itinerant labour power in the domestic labour market and the resulting pressure it exerts on migration. As we have argued in our recent book[21] an over reliance on migrant labour not only creates disembedded market conditions but it strains social bonding when labour migration (temporary or transitional) is viewed by domestic workers as challenging employment and conditions.

Although built on an aspiration for reciprocity, the scheme managed to yield only a one-way traffic, with a heavy influx of foreign workers entering the country to perform jobs in Germany, and little return flow either from native or other transient workers. The demand for cheap labour and the difficulties in monitoring associated work conditions, in turn, allowed for large-scale abuses of the system: lower wages were paid to these workers than what was actually agreed, bogus contracts were concluded, quotas for the employment of *werkvertragsarbeitnehmer* workers by German companies were exceeded, and there were frequent illegal extensions of employment.[22]

This mutualised policy aspiration also reveals how regulatory directions which ignore market realities no matter how unpalatable will do little to achieve their aims even where these confront migration discrimination. In fact, distortions in agency and employment contracting regimes conspire with the market to defeat the non-market oriented objectives of the regulatory state, such as labour market equality.

REGULATORY PARADOX

The regulatory failure of these *shared responsibility schemes* seeking to engage home and host jurisdictions is rarely an issue of domestic enforcement. Directing regulatory purpose to uncovering adverse work conditions, while at the same time interrogating the legitimate status of migrant workers, is paradoxical in outcome and benefit.

At the international level, the ILO Labour Administrative and Inspection Programme is one scheme which has as its focus inspection as a crucial direction of enforcement. In reality, rather than providing some accountability over regulatory compliance by employers, inspectorate-based schemes often instil fear in the workers, becoming anxious as they do about the legitimacy of their residency status, more than looking

---

21 Findlay and Lim (2014a).

22 Similar excesses are common in the ASEAN region where it is not so much that enforcement has failed within formal migrant labour regulation programmes, but rather that such regulatory arrangements are weak or absent.

forward to benefits from inspection to ensure the actionability of contracted work conditions.[23] Even if on paper at least the regulatory regime is directed towards the protection of vulnerable migrant workers, undocumented workers, unrecognised by the migration conditions of formal transition schemes, will only be disadvantaged through inspection. Despite Article 3 of ILO Convention No. 81 on Labour Inspection calling for the protection of working conditions regarding all types of workers, including vulnerable workers, labour without permits will eventually fall foul of repatriation through domestic migration law restrictions.

Article 7 of ILO Convention No. 150 on Labour Administration recommends extending the functions of labour administration, with particular emphasis on inspection, to groups of workers who are not employed persons according to national laws – informal workers. This means that the international community prefers to no longer ignore undocumented workers, by shifting the scope of regulation to this illegitimate population as well. Unfortunately, market imperatives are fostered by exclusionist domestic migration regimes, against the transference of more equitable intentions into national legal regulation. The fact that workers in the informal economy, undeclared workers, usually earn less than formal workers and often perform compulsory overtime work with no incremental financial compensation, indicates that the dependency relationship which employers generate through manipulating illegitimate migration status is intended primarily for their commercial benefit, and is designed to ignore or defeat any formal labour force protections.[24] Such employment regimes thrive even at the risk of inspections because the profit through exploitation outweighs the cost of random sanctioning.

Undocumented workers and undeclared work have variously been referred to as underground or hidden labour, clandestine employment, *black* labour, moonlighting or, simply, illegal work. All these epithets are pejorative and to some extent at least discriminate against unauthorised workers as collaborators rather than victims.

---

[23] Situations of worker abuse and exploitation should remain under-policed and largely unenforceable in Singapore, even though the Ministry of Manpower in Singapore conducts monitoring and surveillance through random checks on employment status, and interviews workers and employers to test licence and contract compliance within other ordinary workspaces – a paradoxical approach to preferencing enforcement of migrant status over the employment conditions and safety of the workers.

[24] These workers may be deprived of social security benefits and may suffer from unstable living conditions because of their 'illegitimate' status.

According to the European Commission's (EC) Communication on Undeclared Work, undeclared work refers to 'paid activities that are lawful as regards their nature but not declared to the public authorities, bearing in mind that differences in the regulatory system of Member States must be taken into account'.[25] In direct terms this implies that while the labour might be contracted, the relevant authorities have not been informed of the employment arrangements which regulatory frames like migration conditions require.

Recent responses in the EU to the problem of undocumented migrant labour such as the EC's Employment Guideline No. 9 promote a punitive approach to undeclared work designed to control infractions through greater detection efforts (discussed in more detail in Chapter 6).[26] Considering that once detected, both employers and employees suffer negative social and market consequences, the detection and sanction regimes are likely to drive undocumented and undeclared employment arrangements further underground. Another effect of the regulatory approach is to increase worker vulnerability, and make more fragile and exploitative the employment conditions considering the fact that employers are exposed to punishment by hiring undocumented labour force.

Such inspection regimes activate sanctions including criminal prosecution. In France, for example, discovery of undeclared work can result in the prosecution of employers under criminal law: for subjecting such workers to inhumane working or housing conditions, by preying on a worker's vulnerability or situation of dependence, for obtaining services from such a person for no payment, or for a wage that is not commensurate with the value of the work performed. In most countries within the EU, criminal sanctions are available including imprisonment for employers and the forced departure of undeclared migrant workers. Both employers and workers can end up criminalised.

These measures, while designed to improve compliance with common employment registration conditions across the EU, however, appear to be largely confined to northern EU Member States. Today, even these states in recognition of the negative economic consequences of detection/sanction approaches are no longer relying as heavily on employer deterrence but are expanding their policy responses to include both carrots and sticks.[27]

---

[25] Communication from the Commission of 7 April 1998 on Undeclared Work (1998).

[26] European Commission's Employment Guideline No. 9.

[27] International Labour Organization (2010), p. 4.

If regulatory intervention is not going to exacerbate conditions of vulnerability and dependency exploitation, improving the enforcement of workers' rights and protections through more robust and responsive labour inspection regimes remains a necessary and important part of addressing undeclared work. If labour inspections are to act as a primary means of enforcing the rights of workers regardless of their undocumented status, these inspections must be accountable to workers' needs rather than migration expediencies and be carried out in accordance with a predictable criteria functioning as worker and employer expectations. In its 2008 Observation, the ILO Committee of Experts on the Application of Conventions and Recommendations underlined that no worker should be excluded from protection on account of their irregular employment status. Therefore, inspectors should not see their role as immigration police, but focus on the control of working conditions as the goal of these criteria. For any of these aspirations to receive worker cooperation there needs to be an alignment of migrant residency protections if undocumented status is uncovered. Rather than immediate punishment and repatriation, which is the Asian preference, undocumented labour can routinely be evaluated following discovery in order to determine possibilities for converting to legitimate employment conditions, where appropriate.

Within the framework of labour inspections, however, the problems of regularising discovered situations of non-compliance and compensating those whose rights have been violated remain commonplace. The difficulty is dissuading non-compliance on the part of the employer, without putting a worker's job opportunity or the profitability of the enterprise's survival at risk.[28] If violation of migration conditions (both by employers and workers) is deemed to be a strict liability regulatory offence it will be impossible to break the nexus between discovery and the punitive consequences of immigration breach for all parties, even when trying to ensure basic employment rights irrespective of documentation. The paradox remains that not only is the worker through inspection and discovery likely to lose employment placement, but repatriation or deportation are the natural results of exposing undocumented or unregistered status. This causal connection creates a double-bind for labour inspectors. As a rule these inspectors are supposed to protect vulnerable workers in situations where basic employment conditions are unsatisfactory. But because of the unavoidable consequent collapsing of employment relationships and the deportation of undocumented workers, these

---

28 International Labour Organization (2010).

inspectors are unable to redress in a meaningful way for the individual migrant concerned, errant employment conditions because through discovering and reporting their illegitimate status they lose both their jobs and residency.

An evaluation of this inspection-based approach however shows that sanctions appear to have been of limited effectiveness in the European experience. The same may be said for Southeast Asia to a larger extent; businesses will risk their employment of undeclared workers so long as the expected cost of the penalty is lower than the difference between the labour costs of undeclared and declared workers. In other words, sanctions are merely one element in the cost–benefit analysis.

If employers see the inspection risk as a cost of this labour market rather than as an inducement towards compliance and the improvement of worker conditions, then the regulatory consequences may simply exacerbate worker discrimination. Only if exposure through inspection could be separated from adverse residency consequences would the higher order purposes of inspection be prioritised.

COMPARATIVELY EXPLORING FRAGILE RESIDENCY STATUS IN THE SHADOW OF REPATRIATION

Considering the nexus between:

1. discriminatory migration regulation; and
2. employment exploitation of migrant labour force,

any critical comparative study of the migration/employment nexus works from the proposition that fragile residency status enables employment relationships of dependency which in turn work to undermine regulatory efforts to enforce uniform work conditions and fundamental employment rights.[29] The comparative paradigm examines the individual market and regulatory contexts producing the unavoidable consequence that when the exploitation of migrant labour is exposed either through disputation or

---

[29] The study is mindful of the importance of a rights-framework in analysing the employment of migrant workers. However, we are wary not to remain at a normative level in the consideration of workers' rights, preferring instead to focus specifically on the actionability of any available rights.

inspection, residency is at risk through the termination of employment relationships, or reporting on unauthorised migrant status.[30]

The limited objective for the empirical dimension in this chapter is to theorise the conditions under which employment failure (through discovery or disputation) triggers termination of residency and the adverse consequences that follow. If, for instance, residency is tied inextricably to employment contracts which are then tied to work permits, it is imperative to explain when and how this arrangement creates dependency relationships ripe for exploitation in legitimate and illegitimate foreign labour markets. The domestic and regional comparisons are as such, market focused and not concentrated on migration regulation or employment conditions as policy imperatives. Our interest in vulnerability and dependency has both regulatory and market dimensions. If migrant status and employment normalisation, through private law relationships and public law oversight, is exacerbating rather than alleviating these vulnerabilities, then market certainty and sustainability is at risk as are the employment 'rights' which the regulators wish to enforce.

Our comparative analysis, here and in Chapter 6, is centred on market conditions and the regulatory frames which influence and oversee these vulnerabilities. For instance, in considering a European example, that of Yugoslav workers seconded to the Netherlands, we see the importance of third-party accountability when directed towards vulnerability (reflect on agency discussions in Chapter 5), and are enabled to critique the absence of judicial oversight in ASEAN jurisdictions (see Chapter 6). In the European example the important impact of judicial activism around the rights of these workers is identified, notwithstanding the relationships of dependency that result from mainly contract-centred exclusionary provisions (in particular boilerplate clauses excluding rights to social security), as well as other unfair terms incorporated into contractual arrangements for their employment.[31] In Singapore, due to governance

[30] With construction workers in Singapore it is not uncommon that employers terminate work contracts for fabricated reasons if migrant workers dispute employment conditions. Regarding domestic workers, if they seek to terminate their contracts and to transfer to other employment arrangements they generally need the acquiescence of the original employer which if not forthcoming can lead to the termination of work permits, and repatriation. Both situations favour employers who would avoid any determination of matters in dispute.

[31] In the case of *Raymond Kohll* v. *Union des caisses de maladie*. C-158/96, Judgment (28 April 1998), the European Court of Justice decided that a national regulation which made the reimbursement of dental treatment abroad dependent on the prior authorisation of the competent insurance institution (situated in a

conditions which we discuss later, no such judicial oversight is likely or commonplace, and as a result regulatory transparency and stakeholder accountability is sacrificed.

A more sophisticated approach to comparative analysis here should not stop at identifying differences between regulatory instruments or activism. Specifically, when contrasting labour contracting and disputation consequences it is important to include considerations of the transition from home to host markets which the workers experience, and the social and economic conditions under which this occurs (see Chapter 6). The journey of exploitation involves crucial decision sites where regulatory activity or its absence is relevant in the progress of dependency and vulnerability. At the initiation of the contracting stage, for instance, migrant workers are always the weaker negotiating party. On from this initial stage, as a result of continuing immigration vulnerability and employment dependency relationships exacerbated through ambiguous agency regimes, employers are able to exploit *strong law* (such as immigration licensing and employment documentation) because workers feel powerless to enforce rights or bring disputes against their employers (in the Asian context, *soft law*) if they consider that they have been disadvantaged. This is exemplified in the Singapore context through the employer exploitation of the migrant labour force due to the arbitrary conditions governing work permits and the dependency on sub-standard work conditions which thrive under weak inspectorial regimes, and regulatory atmospheres of thin and largely inequitable employment law provisioning. Contrasting the EU regulatory context, despite relatively tighter employment, contract and agency law, both documented and undocumented workers remain open to exploitation, due to the fact that similarly arbitrary migration status (or work permit) conditions make residency status vulnerable.

A vital social disadvantage for foreign workers afforded qualified residency status is access to welfare which other workers in the market may enjoy. With migration/residency status inextricably connected to conditional and restricted employment, and migrant status being genuinely inferior to other migration contexts, temporary workers are commonly excluded from general employment benefits such as social security safeguards or entitlements for their family. Across comparative sites, and due to the conditionality and inferiority of their migrant/

---

particular country) violated the free movement of services. This created social protection for migrant workers such that patients could seek medical treatment in another EU Member State without depending on the discretion of their domestic insurance institutions.

residency status relative to the permanent labour force, foreign workers are uniformly disadvantaged despite the intrusion or otherwise domestic and regional employment protections.

REPATRIATION OF MIGRANT WORKERS UPON TERMINATION OF CONTRACT

Even for documented workers, as a consequence of the legitimacy of their residency being tied to the continuance of their employment relationship with often exploitative employers, dependency and disempowerment are characteristic of the market positioning of migrant worker power, with contract termination and indiscriminate repatriation an ever-present fear. Employers in Singapore are in a position to unilaterally terminate the employment relationship, thereby triggering a process of work permit cancellation and worker repatriation where legitimate grounds to further a dispute are raised, neutralising the threat that workers may pose in any possible abuse prosecution or disputation. These migrant workers are vulnerable to forced and often violent removal by repatriation companies or employment agencies[32] which each send back around 2,000 workers annually,[33] and are able to do so precisely because work permits are tied to the employment relationship which in turn is determined by employers ultimately for their material benefit. If the employer chooses to terminate the employment contract and further demonstrate employer control, it is their obligation (rather than that of the state) to secure deportation and worker repatriation. Should the employer determine the employment relationship, work permits automatically lapse. From this point, as agents of employers, repatriation firms operate to extradite these workers back to their home countries, acting with the authority of migration regulations which are essentially imposed by the state. The arbitrary and privatised nature of the deportation process provides practically no opportunity for the worker to effectively seek any arbitration of this action or of the precipitating dispute and the reasons for it.

---

[32] That such enterprises are registered by law and allowed a mandate that often constitutes activities which would otherwise satisfy assault and false imprisonment, is an alarming example of where state agencies entertain discriminatory physical and psychological abuse often of defenceless women, powers which otherwise would not be afforded untrained security personnel.

[33] Lim (2011).

At the root of this discriminatory exclusion lies two often racially motivated distinctions, between the comparative representation and valuing of guest workers and the local labour force, and between the migrant status of guest workers and that enjoyed by other classes of immigrant. By refusing to accept guest workers beyond their temporary contribution to the labour supply, while undervaluing of migrant labour power pricing in the general employment market, the dignity of labour is denied. Through the temporary residency status of migrant workers and the denial of access to welfare protections that follow if at all, these migrant workers are never accepted as worthy of benefits that flow to ordinary labour or residential citizenship. Such discrimination exists despite the economic and market reality in transitional and advanced economies that the guest labour force contributes often as valuably and productively to the market as do permanent resident citizen workers. Undocumented workers face *double discrimination* if their illegitimate residency status is enough in itself to fracture employment relations and trigger repatriation.

If the dependency/vulnerability context of migrant labour power is indeed exacerbated by migration regulation, then can legal institutions and the exercise of judicial oversight mediate this discrimination?

RIGHTS REALITIES AND THE ACTIVATION OF RIGHTS[34]

Protections for workers constructed within labour law depend vitally on the protection of their migration status. As we suggested earlier, employment regulation appears to be more compatible with regional and international harmonisation than is the case for migration regulation. Where one paradigm is more easily internationalised than another, what can be said about the universal *coverage* of rights conventions and agreements? With migration status selfishly guarded within the domain of national laws, sovereignty can become the challenge to the universalisation of norms for the protection of vulnerable workers in terms of their status. Migration exclusion is a fundamental of domestic political engagement and it is the fear of deteriorating material benefit and security (rather than appreciating the reality of short-term economic stimulus) that prompts citizen interest in migration protection. Immigration inclusion, temporary or otherwise, again is only justified in terms of

[34] This section should be considered against our later discussion of the limitations of the rights paradigm, in chapter 3.

economic growth and the benefit this offers for the wealth of the general population.

The chapter employs legitimate migration status as a context for discrimination and rights abuse through looking at disputation, discriminatory work permit conditions and repatriation under the *rights* lens. Can the same lens be turned on illegal migrant workers suffering the same exploitation but in conditions of greater vulnerability and exacerbated dependency? Should these workers who do not enjoy migrant status, but are no lesser contributors to the generally beneficial economic outcomes of their labour power, not be entitled to the same rights and protections simply because they do not come within qualified migration legitimacy?

The power imbalances in employment relationships render the activation of legal protections, or other less formal avenues of legitimate rights adjudication, difficult for documented workers and impossible for those without residency status. This is a consequence of law's role in protecting exclusionist and discriminatory private property relations, well evidenced through partial and often arbitrary migration laws. The motivation behind the nature and impact of domestic migration regulation is more likely to be a reflection of popular fears concerning the way that migration challenges the wealth and security of citizens, rather than being a rational reflection of the contribution to economic growth offered by migrant labour power.

DOMESTIC REGULATION CHALLENGING INTERNATIONAL LAW PROTECTIONS

After the Second World War workers originating out of Eastern and Southern Europe performed an important role in the rebuilding of the Western European economy. Labour migration then was partially regulated by governments through agreements on recruitment concluded with labour-exporting countries and partially through direct recruitment by employers. The phenomenon of migrant labour grew out of demands for labour at the national labour market level (what we see as a push factor), and the internationalisation of trade and multi-national commerce (a pull factor). Labour which was essential to market growth in domestic reconstruction became a stimulant in the regionalisation and internationalisation of these markets. Logically then market labour power would migrate as a consequence of regional and international need. However, nationalism supporting and supported by exclusionist migration regulation strained this natural flow, distorting labour markets and disrupting the pricing of labour power through conditional migrant labour residency regulation. Economic inequality state-to-state fuelled the development of disembedded labour markets.

Migrant workers are in principle protected by international legal instruments which cover a wide variety of issues. Three fundamental notions characterise the protections in international law for migrant workers and members of their families:[35]

1. equality of treatment between regular migrants/immigrant workers and nationals in the realm of employment and work (ILO Migration for Employment Convention, 1949, No. 97);
2. core universal human rights applicable to all migrants, regardless of status (established in the ILO Convention 143 of 1975); and
3. international standards for protection in treatment and conditions at work – safety, health, maximum hours, minimum remuneration, non-discrimination, freedom of association, maternity, and so on – that apply to all workers.

At the comparative level, the fact that migration regulation is at the first instance the province of the nation state challenges the capacity of regional and public international law to protect migrant work conditions for the common good, unless domestic law embraces these principles. In particular, the domestic legal distinction between documented and undocumented workers explored above exemplifies how the latter may be placed outside the reach and benefit of public international law protections. The comparison of regulation at the state, regional and international levels is enlightening in understanding the nexus because of the way in which immigration and labour regulations intersect.

Having explored how migrant employment arrangements are legitimated (or not) by migration status, and how the nature and conditions of this classification undermine the regulatory conditions of employment status, we now more specifically turn to the manner in which private property interests influence this dynamic. In addition, we will speculate on how market sustainability might complement social inclusion rather than exclusive private property relations.

The first theme returns to the private benefits of the citizen in the form of social security and the manner in which the denial of these benefits to migrant workers might be seen as undervaluing foreign labour force, as well as excluding this population from the civil society of the host state. In addition, reference to social security benefits here and their denial to

[35] International Labour Organization (2007).

foreign workers, makes paradoxically more palatable conditional migration status in the eyes of domestic citizen workers who fear the economic and social strains caused by waves of permanent migration.

JUDICIAL ACTIVISM AND THE POLICY OF EXCLUSION IN THE NETHERLANDS

In the European experience, the exclusion of migrant workers from entitlement to certain basic rights and protections, such as social security safeguards, has been addressed by the courts. In the late 1980s, the seconding of workers from the former Yugoslavia to the Netherlands in order to secure adequate labour supply involved the Dutch employers leveraging employment contracts with one of the (former) Yugoslav state employment firms, to divert labour power to the Netherlands for a period of usually two years.[36] After the expiry of their first contract, should a Yugoslav continue his employment in the Netherlands by entering into a normal employment contract with a Dutch employer, the worker became excluded from the Dutch social security system. At the same time, the worker was not covered by protections from his home jurisdiction because the employment relationship was deemed to have converted to a direct arrangement with the Dutch employer. As a consequence, the worker was not entitled to medical benefits and other ancillary social security safeguards from either jurisdiction.

After 1988, following two Supreme Court judgments criticising the policy of exclusion (in respect of the refusal of allowances for a child of a Yugoslav migrant who had worked in the Netherlands for 11 years, and another case concerning a Yugoslav migrant who had worked in the Netherlands for 15 years), social affairs ministry officials of the Netherlands and of the former Yugoslavia decided to conclude an interim agreement that excluded workers from the social security systems for a maximum of one year. The power of the court to protect the rights of these migrant workers was viewed by these governments as encroaching on the sovereignty of the home and host states.

In 1992, a Dutch labour court ruled for the first time that the labour contract of a Yugoslav worker posted in the Netherlands was governed by Dutch labour law, and therefore the worker in question was granted protection against dismissal provided by Dutch law,[37] with reference to

[36] Groenendijk and Hampsink (1995), p. 59.
[37] Groenendijk and Hampsink (1995), p. 60.

Yugoslav law, despite the fact that the employment contract originated in the home jurisdiction. This example of judicial oversight reveals that legal regulation is neither necessarily dependent on nor a consequence of distinctions between the contractual and welfare conditions of home or host jurisdictions.

Judicial interpretation may have an important role in determining the residency conditions affecting migrant workers beyond the narrow exclusions of contractual conditions however and wherever struck. These conditions, as the next section elaborates, are usually favourable to the employer and the state. Therefore, private property relations in contract form will generally disadvantage migrant workers, thereby leaving responsibility for amelioration to third-party judicial activism, if this is indeed available. It is such inequities which have required, in the Netherlands example at least, judicial intervention in order to rebalance workers' rights and legitimate expectations. Unfortunately, in jurisdictions such as Singapore, where judicial activism and the intervention of the judiciary to assert workers' interests particularly over the directions of the state are inconceivable,[38] no such rebalancing of unfair contractual arrangements is likely.

SOCIAL SECURITY PROTECTIONS IN EUROPE – DISCRIMINATORY APPLICATIONS

The EU has an advanced and complex social security web. The portability of these benefits is such that EU nationals usually enjoy full non-discriminatory access to universal social benefits, and for third-country nationals, equality of treatment is granted after a certain period of residence (no longer than five years).[39] However, the access for migrant workers to social security and social protection has become problematic particularly in high-income countries.[40] Various host countries restrict access to social benefits, partly to discourage unwanted immigration and partly to maintain the national social cohesion that is often seen as the citizenship foundation of these national welfare states.

[38] The 'one voice' doctrine dictates that both the executive and judicial arms of the government should share the same view. See Elias (2004), p. 95.

[39] European Union: Council of the European Union, *Council Directive 2003/109/EC of 25 November 2003 Concerning the Status of Third-Country Nationals Who Are Long-Term Residents* (23 January 2004).

[40] Van Ginneken (2013).

As touched on above, anti-immigration sentiment and economic predisposition has led to a somewhat perverse popularising of transitional and transient migrant programmes. Because of their temporary resident nature, migrant labour force programmes are preferentially regarded by those who fear waves of more permanent migration. Circular migration is also seen as taking better account of the interests of migrant workers and the wellbeing of the home country.[41] Demonstrated in the Yugoslav/Dutch collaboration aforementioned, through the conclusion of bilateral agreements between the host and home states, the home state social security legislation may be applicable to the host state regime and as such migration management is generally considered more palatable to the local workforce.

Interestingly, while the denial of social security benefits to migrant workers may habilitate this labour force in the eyes of the general citizen public, the desire of the latter to protect their private property rights in social security at the cost of a fairer labour market regime, perpetuates inferior social benefits for guest workers. So it is through the denial of employment-related rights and protections that migrant labour is made to appear domestically more agreeable in immigration terms. This nexus between employment conditions and migration sensitivities confirms our earlier assumptions about the debilitating nexus between employment and migration regulation, further working towards the vulnerability/dependency of this labour force.

RELATIONSHIPS OF PRIVATE PROPERTY AND THEIR IMPACT ON MIGRANT LABOUR MARKETS

Contractual arrangements governing the contexts of the migrant labour market regularly prove to be detrimental to workers in a variety of ways. The relationships of private property protection and advancement (as exhibited through contract and agency conditions – see chapters 4 and 5) which determine migrant labour market value often exclude or ignore important fundamental rights protections, and in so doing enable the interests of the employer and the state to prevail, even when international conventions express otherwise.[42] While it could be said in the

41 Gagnon and Khoudour-Casteras (2011).

42 For example, trade unions in Singapore that are established without government connection or sponsorship do not exist, such that no trade union is free from control by the government whose interests are often tilted towards

employment setting at large, labour force (migrant or domestic) is crucially influenced by private legal regulation through unbalanced contracting, the unique power divides prevailing in migrant labour contacting vastly exacerbate this common malaise. Both domestically and regionally, employment contract conditions (or their absence) are complicit in the operation of tendentious migrant employment relationships enabled by fragile work permits to exclude or undermine fundamental universal rights protections. An example of this is the determination of working hours, overtime obligations and leave days.[43]

There is a synergy in the regulation (or its absence) of migrant labour force contracting, benefitting private property arrangements and the market relationships that sustain these. Such regulatory contexts through private property arrangements are exclusionist and discriminatory, and other essential regulatory frames (such as migration and residency) being governed by similar market priorities and externalities work in tandem to protect such private property relations. Conversely, moving legal regulation away from this paradigm of private interest protection and more towards the promotion of social good will also allow for shifts in both migration and employment regulation to complement sustainable labour force market conditions. A key consideration here would be the creation of a flexible regulation system which would not be automatically triggered to repatriation, if workplace inspection found adverse employment arrangements resulting in worker displacement.

CONCLUSION

In a bid to protect one's national identity or the place of one's own domestic labour power, the wider economic, social and regional benefits of labour migration beyond the provision of cheap or even slave domestic labour can often be overlooked. Conversely, the consequences of taking

---

corporate employers in the balance between the rights of the workers and the investment injected by private firms.

[43] In relation to leave days, although there is a legislative provision for one no-pay rest day each week for foreign domestic workers, an exception envisaged by the law is that work on this mandatory rest day can be the subject of negotiations between the employer and the worker. In respect of working hours, although legislation does provide that contractual work hours should not exceed eight hours a day or 44 hours a week, any work in excess of these contractual working hours is simply considered as overtime work. And, in regard to overtime obligations, there is no limit on the overtime work permitted, merely that the employer and the worker may negotiate the resultant overtime pay.

purely a cost–benefit approach towards these workers can be disastrous. In Germany, the trade union IG Bau-Steine-Erden strongly campaigned against the employment of workers from Eastern Europe in the building industry, arguing that this led to unfair competition.[44] This position produced a tightening of the regime regulating the recruitment of foreign labour which in turn eventuated in the employment of undocumented workers in the country without the requisite labour permits and limited obligations. Because of the motivation to protect the private property benefits of domestic workers, without tempering the insatiable desire of employers to explode their private property windfalls in an expanding construction market, the labour market skewed towards the exploitation of the most dependent and vulnerable labour force.

In achieving principled and equitable labour market regulation, we argue, the first step is to move beyond the self-interested competition perspective and embrace the wider purpose of competition as the need for ensuring sustainable market conditions (discussed in more detail in Chapter 3). The benefits of labour migration for the host state stretch beyond helping that country overcome labour bottlenecks, but may also, if strategically managed, offer the improved vertical mobility for local labour power, and a sustainable period of transition where markets are technologising. Removing the conditions for exploitation, principal among these being discriminatory migration status, will lead to more balanced labour pricing and away from the phenomenon of unemployed (or under-employed) nationals coexisting uneasily with employed foreigners, and all the social and political dangers this presents.

Better understanding the intersections between public and private forms of regulation, and the manner in which both promote exclusionist private property relations, as well as their dynamics at the international, regional and domestic regulatory levels, can stimulate principled regulatory dialogues for the development of policy that better serves the protection of vulnerable workers along with the sustainability of fragile and disembedded labour markets.

This chapter represents only a sketch of a wider comparative empirical research exercise (advanced in Chapter 6). To take the discussion of its essential analytical themes further, the comparative dimension of the book's later empirical section will be more convincingly transactional by exploring the relative knowledge and power positions of market stakeholders and how they impact on each other. In the Asian region Singapore and Malaysia are selected because of their significant reliance

---

[44] Groenendijk and Hampsink (1995).

on migrant labour and laissez faire attitude to its regulation. The ASEAN regional approach is no less non-interventionist. Jurisdictions in the European Union, also heavily reliant on guest labour force, operate within tighter employment and contract law frameworks. The common thread in this chapter, which underpins an examination of different regulatory approaches with similar market intentions, is the way in which migration regulation creates contexts of vulnerability and dependency that disembed migrant labour market, thereby fostering exclusionist private property relations.

By examining the conditions governing the entitlement/status to work and residency, we see how the regulation of the migrant worker segments of the labour force exploits their fundamental labour value and replaces dignity with dependency, despite variations in employment regulation standards, domestic and regional. As a consequence, the relationships of dependency enabled by fragile residency status undermine regulatory efforts to enforce uniform work conditions and fundamental employment rights. As we will discover, it is the prioritising of labour as an undervalued market commodity for the benefit of exclusive private property arrangements that makes this so.

3. Private law, private property arrangements and inclusivity

> The law in establishing property ... has realized an abstraction, a metaphor, a fiction ...[1]

INTRODUCTION

As the previous chapter sets out, the empirical foundation of the remainder of the book is a comparative analysis of vulnerable migrant labour markets providing examples of law's disembedding history as a regulatory agent or shadow. The private property arrangements which operate and benefit from migrant labour are dependent both on discriminatory legal regulation and the selective advantages presented by laws' limited or even absent reach. This chapter explores more particularly the role of private law and introduces the fluid interactions between private legal arrangements and the more informal market negotiation frames which perpetuate the vulnerability and dependency wherein migrant labour lives.

Chapters 4 and 5 highlight contracts and agency as crucial private property arrangements through which legal regulation has deeply problematic influence over migrant labour markets. The relationships of dependency and vulnerability explored in the preceding chapter are given both form and substance though the interventions (and failings) of legal regulatory regimes such as contract and agency.

The critical analysis of the private property/private law nexus, however, depends on a more general identification of the private law field with which we intend to engage, as well as the current direction of legal regulation being a socially exclusive market force. In contrast with this, the chapter will later explore ways in which transformed legal regulation can indeed make private property arrangements more 'viable' within the wider critique that property, as currently employed in the process of

[1] Proudhon as discussed in Knowles (2004), p. 56.

disembedding markets, utilises law to legitimate market relationships and preferencing that in the medium term are unsustainable in jurisprudential and social terms.

Before outlining the approach to be taken in the application of private law as a repositioning regulatory interface, it is necessary to briefly explore our understanding of property.[2]

PROPERTY

In what the contributors refer to as a unique and very timely collection of essays, art projects and conversations, 'Undoing Property'[3] questions the sanctity of private property arrangements as commodities, against the growing interest in public domain, public access and intellectual commons. The intention of the publication is to enrich and extend existing debates about property and ownership into the future.

In their introduction the editors declare:

> Property shapes all social relations. Its invisible lines force separations and create power relations felt throughout the unequal distribution of what is otherwise collectively produced value ... What might a true negotiation of property or a practice of the commons look like today? ... Throughout *Undoing Property* we have argued for art as an embedded social practice, exposing many points of connection with the wider world. Looking realistically at where we are today, and acknowledging much still needs to change, we aspire to a more equitable system with a well-nourished commons and public domain, where the making of a collective culture is encouraged, acknowledged, rewarded, and protected.[4]

The *sabotage of debt* is exposed as part of the critique of private property arrangements advanced in the project. In this disembedded process, the need to access and activate the commodity benefits of private property often leads significant market stakeholders into crippling cycles of debt. Such financial dynamics of dependency not only evidence the exclusive nature of private property valuing which is discriminatory but reveal the process of commodification, access and activation which makes freer and more natural market engagement with property impossible and therefore

---

[2] In so doing we are greatly assisted by Edward Hyams' *Pierre-Joseph Proudhon: His revolutionary life, mind and works* (1979).

[3] Lewandowska and Ptak (2013).

[4] Lewandowska and Ptak (2013), pp. 20–21, 22–3, 26.

unsustainable.[5] The discussion of the agency bonding of migrant workers (Chapter 5) is a stark example of such market enslavement.

The 'cruel economy of ownership'[6] identifies stakeholder entrapment, compromised agency and the lack of choice possibilities as the eventual market conditions surrounding exclusive property alienation. Regarding the confinement of intellectual production, Szreder reminds us of Wallerstein's notion of *systemic bifurcation*:

> ... when old systems are not able to contain new dynamics: institutions of the past are faced with problems of the future. We reiterate already tested solutions while facing different challenges. But we spot glimpses of what might be in what already is, inventing responses on the move and testing them in action, without relying on existing manuals.[7]

Take as an example of this potential for change, the current dysfunctional and moribund agency arrangements in migrant labour markets discussed in Chapter 5. Ahead we show what needs transforming and suggest pathways for such change if market sustainability is to have the positive contribution of agency through facilitating repositioned contract relations (see chapters 4 and 5). We are left, however, confronted with the challenge, if the present situation is steeped in agent/employer self-interest, what would motivate these key stakeholders to embrace, or at least not sabotage such change? In our earlier work we proposed employing sociability theory, wherein even belated and reluctant recognition of risk would demand that different self-interests be mutualised to shift risk in the direction of a more communitarian fate for sustainable market relationships. With the entrenched market discrimination unequivocally evidenced through the exploitation of migrant labour, this process of sociability will require some regulatory prodding. In the book's conclusion we borrow and develop Szreder's notions of the labour of pollination, and the pollination of labour (see Chapter 7), to suggest how law might provide some stimulus for regulatory repositioning. These concepts could enable, in a market sense, the inevitable revaluing of labour power, both through forces external and internal to the market such as the:

---

5 Pasquinelli (2013).
6 Szreder (2013).
7 Szreder (2013), p. 50.

- recognition of social value in aging populations;
- need to increase the productivity of labour units in markets of diminishing resources;
- gradual and more general recognition that the denial of labour rights to migrants has negative ramifications for social order;
- political impediments to free worker migration, limiting legitimate labour pools; and
- transition in regional and global hegemonies giving more power and influence to home nation states,

producing natural coopetition among previously disempowered stakeholders. This movement in labour valuing we anticipate will generate, more likely with the assistance of transformed legal regulation of property arrangements (see chapters 4 and 5), greater extended cooperation in a more engaged market. Market mutualities in labour valuing will emerge out of risk to fate (focused around sustainability) as property arrangements become more solid and inclusive. What we will see in migrant labour market dynamics so reappraised are more intense, multifaceted and cooperative property exchanges, prefaced by more realistic commodification. The bumps in the road along the way should not be ignored. We are not awaiting labour resources to become scarcities in order for a more natural market revaluing of labour price. The transition in understanding labour as property, for sustainable markets into the future, is more than just considerations of wage equity. Labour force, in a generally developing and sustainable ascription to commons, will need to participate in a wider project of revaluing which may lead to a gradual decommodification of labour along with the development of new means of property exchange confirmed by law.[8] This will be the concern of the next book in this series.

Greater access to property benefit through intellectual commons is predicated on new images of property form, of its value and particularly of the manner in which legal relations provide both the meaning and utility for property. As Pentecost says about the revaluing of art:

---

[8] Take for example what Szreder refers to when valuing the labour of the artist, writer, musician, performer, as the cruel economy of attention: where the value of output as a commodity depends on broad critical acclaim which may have little or nothing to do with free access. He suggests that with breaking down copyright, while the profit value in art for some will be devalued, the more subliminal rewards to the artist will massively increase through open, common access.

> Artists' desire to cross disciplinary boundaries (like those guarding the sciences) is an expression of a desire to be part of some living thing larger than art. If we want to do more than supply diverse novelties to the bloomsday vault, we need to tune our efforts to the resonance of collective movements.[9]

The same could be said for intellectual property lawyers in particular, as they reject their conventional futile efforts to stave off the inevitable advance of commons, punishing few along the way for little purpose, and engage in creative and inclusive exchanges of private property arrangements and realistic licence pricing.[10]

PROPERTY AND VIRTUE

The juxtaposition of property and virtue might at first seem counter-intuitive. Historically many religions (beyond the Protestant ethic) decry that accumulation of property through wealth-generating usury as immoral. Recently calls for the remoralisation of the global financial industry gained credibility following the financial meltdown in 2009.[11] Amin suggests that the plundering of South World resources and its consequent impoverishment is not simply an immoral but an inevitable outcome of commodity exchange capitalism. Therefore, efforts towards the remoralisation of market economies which value wealth creation that in turn necessitates pauperism are little more than a mask for saving a market system feeding on itself.

Both Robert Owen and Montesquieu pointed out that a democracy depends for its survival on the virtue of its citizens.[12] If property is to be determined through accumulation then it is fair to reverse Thomas Jefferson's aphorism to 'all men are born unequal'. It would only be by preventing the getting and acquiring of property, and as Proudhon argued 'restoring to equality the inequality implicit in innate properties' (such as inheritance), that social justice, measured as greater inclusion for the property-less against constitutional concepts of universal access to, and the sanctity of, private property, might be achieved.[13]

Proudhon could not reconcile the inclusion of property into the four 'natural and unprescriptable' rights of man guaranteed by the American

9 Pentecost (2013), p. 90.
10 Northcutt (2007).
11 Amin (2011).
12 Hyams (1979), p. 5.
13 Hyams (1979), pp. 40–42.

constitution. He rejected the argument that virtue could be imbued in property by more equitable redistribution. For him, the *impossibility* of property meant that property *as we know it,* should not exist. How can this be in an age where property is power, and is this assertion no more than a manifesto for the destruction of markets per se?

In fact, Proudhon saw the coalition behind the use of property as its downfall:

> Adored by all it is recognised by none. Law, mores, customs, public and private conscience, all conspire its ruin and death.[14]

For Proudhon, a social system of absolute equality, in which all existing institutions would not only have a place, but themselves would become means to equality, had to exclude property or the sum of its abuses. Because of the appalling conditions of the majority of the *property-less*, many of whom make for the propertied the riches they enjoy, property is not only unjust, not only wicked, but clearly, impossible, through denying absolute economic equality, the only arrangement which was socially viable.

If property is *impossible* then why so, in any thesis which ultimately advocates market frames that are socially sustainable and that contribute to social viability, would we sanction the legal regulation of property arrangements? For us the answer lies in conceptions of property and their reconstruction. Proudhon argued that the distinction between possession and property gave rise to two kinds of *rights* in jurisprudence; the right *in a thing* and the right *to a thing*. The first form is particular, and the second common. From these forms derive rights directions – possession and ownership.

> In writing this factum against property I bring a petitory right (ownership) against the whole of society. I prove that those who have nothing today are proprietors by the same title as those in possession. But instead of concluding that property should be shared among all, I demand in the name of public safety, it should be abolished for all.[15]

In this Proudhon was invoking what he interpreted as valid social law that recognised and embodied truth established by observation and experiment. He relied in his argument against property on a conception of society that denied law, which represents the imposition of will by force or fraud. Law can be the insurance of property through force or

---

14 Hyams (1979), p. 39.
15 Hyams (1979), p. 39.

fraud, and is theft if, in order to deny general ownership in the protection of selective possession, the majority are dispossessed. Take for example, when the state or state agencies on behalf of particular commercial interests, compulsorily acquire real property necessitating the eviction of villages where the occupants have been in possession of the land and its benefits for generations. The state may have the legislative authority for such a requisition but in circumstances where the customary occupiers have treated possession as a natural consequence of collective *ownership* then the enforcement of supervening legislated private rights would in Proudhon's argument amount to proof of theft.

Interestingly, and this we will develop later at more length, Proudhon railed against domain of law in such terms:

> I am ready to treat but I want none of your laws. I recognize none, and I protest against any order whatsoever imposed upon my freedom of judgement by a political power which merely claims to be necessary. Laws! We know what they are worth: for the rich and mighty, gossamer; chains which no steel can cut for the poor and weak; and for governments, fishing nets.[16]

Even so, his idea of contract was as the only tolerable bond between free men. If economy can be organised around the reciprocal rights and obligations envisaged in the juridical term *contract*, then social justice can be embodied in contracting which takes the form of mutualised engagement without reference to statute.

> I want every citizen to be bound into society only by his free, contractual undertaking instead of subordination and obedience ...[17]

Nothing in this contradicts the presently accepted normative closure of contract law. It is the cognitive application of contemporary commercial contract that makes property arrangements often pernicious. Contract law principles are replete with equanimity. Contractual obligations based on mutuality (in the same way that they might be based on force or fraud) generate an environment of compliance where enforcement is not necessary in the vast majority of contract contexts. Like Proudhon's view, social viability is not offered through the possession, control and alienation of property, but rather the mutual arrangements of social contracting which consensually bond parties to an agreed outcome. Where the analysis to follow diverges from the Proudhon position is in

---

16 Hyams (1979), p. 185.
17 Hyams (1979), p. 186.

the conviction that law, reimagined, does have a place in assisting sustainability under particular market conditions of morality and mutuality.

Proudhon can be seen to parallel some of Henry Maine's 'status to contract'[18] and Spencer's 'militant to industrial society' arguments.[19] For them the process of society is one of evolving government to contractual agreement, wherein contract replaced the need for government and contract is empowered through mutuality rather than externalised authority. In taking individual responsibility for one's life, people will interact via contract and exchange. In this vision contract must be a totally self-assumed obligation. That said, in order to contract in a federalist governmental sense, and in a manner which grows from individual liberty rather than externalised legal authority, there needs to be substantive equality of contract. These assumptions are again well grounded in contemporary legal principles. They are radically absent in the market practice of migrant labour arrangement which we later detail (see Chapter 6).

Hayek deploys a similar idea of the society that enjoys commutative justice through the liberty to contract and to create voluntarist rights and obligations.[20] Proudhon, however, would have scorned any distributive 'spin' which might be placed on the outcomes of such commutative connections.

> Hayek concludes that in a free society there will be distribution in accordance with value rather than moral merit: that is in accordance with the perceived value of a person's actions and services to others. Despite his rejection of a patterned conception of distributive justice, Hayek himself suggests a pattern which he thinks justifiable: distribution in accordance with the perceived benefits given to others, leaving room for the complaint that a free society does not realize this pattern.[21]

Where Hayek's liberal interpretation of the role of contract in social ordering radically diverged from the Proudhon position is in the necessary role of the state as an enforcement agent. Hayek's vision of justice takes the common law rules of justice as a given and state institutions like the courts as playing a vital role in effecting contractual arrangements that are themselves just.[22] It may be wrong to assume in this

---

[18] Graveson (1941).
[19] Offer (2000).
[20] As discussed in Weale (2013), chapter 5.
[21] Wellman (2002), p. 252.
[22] Touchie (2005), chapter 1.

argument that the value of legal rules can only be determined through consistency with wider legal rules or with the system itself. It would be more convincing to argue from a minimalist social perspective that there are more fundamental social preconditions which give the legal rules for contract their social value. As these are ignored in legislation or process, then the social viability of these new creations are in question.

Despite Proudhon's dislike of communism and of distributive justice, he had no affection for an unregulated market. Proudhon believed it was identification of the appropriate regulatory forms, beyond the mutualised freedoms of a utopia justified by pseudo-scientific norms or 'objective' laws of social evolution that confounded much of the utility of earlier libertarian or socialist political economies when they are directed against contemporary internationalised market economies. Proudhon identified competition as a mechanism which complemented his ideas of social mutuality and individual freedoms. As we know from the recent experience of internationalised mega-market economies, competition may produce regulatory outcomes both unintended and unsustainable for market viability in the medium-term.[23]

SOCIAL SPONTANEITY AND COMPETITION

> Monopoly is the natural opposite of competition. This simple observation suffices, as we have remarked, to overthrow the utopias based on the idea of abolishing competition, as if its contrary were association and fraternity. Competition is the vital force which animates the collective being: to destroy it, if such a supposition was possible, would be to kill society.[24]

These comments can either be interpreted as relating to the institutional frameworks of the market economy, or more generally as a characteristic of a *federalist* economy, which Proudhon grew out of his mutualised model of governance. The relationship between understandings of economy and competition is crucial in any argument where competition can have a socially liberating potential. For instance, the present concentration of economic power and the internationalisation of the market economy are:

> Not just the result of 'bad' government policies, or 'market failures' ... the shift from proprietary (or entrepreneurial) capitalism to the present internationalised market economy, where a few giant corporations control the

23 International Labour Conference (2007).
24 Proudhon (1846), p. 272.

> world economy, did not happen ... as the outcome of a reaction to great market failures of the nineteenth century. It was competition which led from simple entrepreneurial firms to present giant corporations. The market failures are not a God-given calamity ... it was competition which created the need for expansion, so that the best (from the point of view of profits) technologies and methods of organising production (economies of scale) are used. It was the same competition which led to the present explosion of mergers and take-overs in advanced capitalist countries, as well as the various strategic alliances. In this problematique, it is not possible, within the existing institutional framework of parliamentary democracy and market economy, to check the process of increasing concentration of economic power.[25]

This critique logically could lead back to the conclusion that competition as a market morality, is more reliant on virtuous, viable and inclusive social frames than it is on market freedom or legislative protection. Even competition among freely associating groups of workers (imagined by both Marx and Proudhon) can lead to new inequalities. The market itself cannot achieve equality here, since differences in productivity will lead to variations in competitiveness which in turn produce inequalities at the macro-economic level, even if exchanges are more equal at a micro level. The question then arises, what mechanisms can be sustainably introduced to eliminate market inequalities while at the same time sustaining market viability? Does the answer lie in some contractual ideal of association?

> Not until hierarchy has scored its triumph in the early world and begun its journey into class society, did equivalence, equity and contract begin to form the context of human relationships. The quid pro quo of exchange and its ethical balance sheets were simply irrelevant to a community guided by the customs of usufruct, complementarity and the irreducible minimum.[26]

Is it fair to criticise philosophies founded on individualised ownership, self-interest, contractual market relations, and distribution based on ability rather than need, as little more than conventional middle-class contentions? Whether Proudhon and anarchists, libertarians or statist-socialists would have it otherwise, society currently exists in various contexts of market economy, internationalised and domestic. The state and its laws have powerful regulatory potentials. The shadow of the state over the market prevails. In any new regulatory project, even one which continues to celebrate the virtues of competition, a challenge worth investigating is the other side of law and its regulatory influence in social arrangements which intend contractual inclusivity.

---

25 Fotopoulos (2000), p. 8.
26 Bookchin (1991), p. 320.

PRIVATE LAW AS WE SEE IT

The flexibility of private law has enabled it to fulfil multiple roles in market economies. In *Contemporary Challenges in Regulating Global Crises*,[27] we explore how law could be said to be implicated in the recent boom and bust cycles of the international financial market. The critique of legal regulation post global financial meltdowns has focused on the failings of public law and its state instrumentalities. Little scholarly or policy attention has been invested in: a) how private law enabled the exchange and commodity flows that risked financial sustainability; or b) what manner the processes and instruments of private law were so often bypassed in the commercial preferencing of other less formal arbitrational arrangements.

A simple way of appreciating private law is as that legal province which protects and enforces private rights.[28] Yet as we have seen in the earlier discussion of migrant worker/agent/employer/state intersections, even strong externally imposed rights discourse will have an obfuscating effect if access to pathways of action are not ensured, or available in ways which do not endanger the commercial viability of all too often radical power imbalances. If rights protection means ensuring the rights of the propertied against the just claims of the property-less, then it is little more than an alternative arena of oppression. In this regard the intersection between public regulation and private rights (empirically engaged in Chapter 6) reveals opportunities for the state to stimulate or to responsibilise private property arrangements, flexibly constructed and contained through private law.

Another way of viewing private law is through considering whether the normative framework promoted reflects some externalised mandatory measure, or is rather a structure of privately created norms largely or only relating to the beneficial entitlement of parties selectively included on the basis of their claims to property. Proudhon took this to be reflected in the distinction between property being exclusive or inclusive, measured against notions of ownership versus possession. If ownership was recognised as universal across society then the exclusivity of possession would fall away and there would be no need for the law as its protective agent.

In property arrangements so internalised within a private law regulatory world (the self-regulation of private law) legal regulation is not concerned with, or premised on, some dominant protection through the

27 Findlay (2013), chapter 7.
28 Michaels and Jansen (2006).

organs of the provident state.[29] This private law *pecking order*, as with rights protection in the non-state realm, is concerned with transaction and transactability. The alienability of property is facilitated through law rather than its universal access or beneficial use. Traditionally, the role of law in limiting private property rights (through contracts, patents, trademarks, copyright and so on) has contributed to the value claimed for that property arrangement, and the boundaries of wealth creation it provides.

Private law does not deny transacting parties their access to the levers of the law. It is claimed, for instance, that the freedom to contract enables financial innovation even to the point of 'legal engineering'.[30] Private law has facilitated, if not enabled through their creation, the sometimes chimerical transaction instruments which have generated phenomenal wealth for the few in global financial markets while at the same time endangering the viability of those markets, their clients' interests, accountability standards and ethical probity.

Access to the levers of private law has not been dependent on claims of legitimate use, public policy or merit.

> Instead what private law can offer in an uncertain world boils down essentially to two things: contractual certainty and dependable property rights in a clear system of property entitlement.[31]

Judicial oversight has its place in the legitimation of both public and private law (see Chapter 6). However, unlike judicial review of state administration which in many common law countries has become more interventionist in recent times,[32] the role of the courts in managing relations fundamental to private law regulation is more nuanced and respectful of the independent integrity of property arrangements. Private law facilitates the workings of the markets by offering participants proprietary rights which have traction in a predictable fashion. Private law's facilitative function in the market parallels its responsive capacity when property arrangements in markets dysfunction. To the extent that private law represents equitable rules it has at its power vehicles for the vindication of property rights rather than a complex framework for creating proprietary entitlements.

The prevailing commercial reluctance to employ private law responses to market crises might be seen as much to do with the *light touch* of

---

29 Beck and Levine (2004).
30 McBarnet (2010).
31 Bridge and Braithwaite (2013), p. 363.
32 Yeh and Chang (2009); Dixon and Ginsburg (2014).

courts in minimising intervention into private commercial arrangements, risking negative influences on conditions of profitability.[33] In response to what have come to be known as *self-help* remedies, judges have demonstrated a reluctance to overturn the contracting parties' perceptions.[34] Commentators have expressed concern at the courts' selective use of private law at the cost of certain fundamental principles which underpin the market.[35]

> Five years after the collapse of the Lehman Brothers group and the nadir of the global financial crisis, it is apparent that private law not only underpins the financial markets but also that it helped weather these unprecedented events. A closer look at this undervalued aspect of the response to crisis has shown that the flexibility of private law, but also that it will not take care of itself … It would be misguided to assume that the task of absorbing long-term lessons of the crisis for private law may simply be left to the courts; the continued robustness of private law requires a more proactive approach in other constituencies.[36]

The chapters which follow, through examining the role of contract and agency in the disembedding of migrant labour markets, take up this challenge. Private law has in part represented a compromised regulatory terrain if one considers the manner in which property arrangements facilitate the vulnerability and dependency relationships which we will show, undermine sustainable labour markets in the medium-term. In the labour market context, the regulatory influence of private law is likely to complement other regulatory regimes designed to balance risk with damage control. This interactive approach represents the paradox of private property as a market agent: enabling property arrangements which profit from risk, and offering limited regulatory capacity not so much to restrict risk but to mop up the aftermath of excess. In this duality lies the selective nature of private property and wealth creation – for the few at the cost of many.

PRIVATE PROPERTY AND WEALTH

Despite the accepted consternation over how to convincingly define private property, what governs its activity is less debated. Jeremy

---

33 Cazes, Verick and Heuer (2009).
34 Kuhner (2014).
35 Bridge and Braithwaite (2013), pp. 397–8.
36 Bridge and Braithwaite (2013), p. 399.

Waldron in 'What is Private Property'[37] interrogates the private property system and discusses the sophistication of social rules which manage its operation. Waldron identifies scarcity, access to control, the nature of material objects, and types of property and ownership as significant variables in understanding private property as a crucial feature of modern wealth measures. Associated with transactions such as government largesse, the marketing and alienation of private property are crucial for understanding the pathways to wealth accumulation.

In his paper 'Dis-embedding and Regulation: The paradox of international finance',[38] Sol Picotto describes the new world order of 'financialisation' in terms of:

- liberalisation – the breaking down of barriers to provide wider pools of financial capital;
- a shift from relationship-based to market-based finance; and
- financialisation – the rapid growth of financial sector profitability linked to the escalation of financial transactions and speculation.

He charts the connection between risk and regulation, debunking the assumption that risk depended essentially on absent or light regulatory frames. Risk in turn can be seen as an inherent feature and consequence of private property arrangements and their valuing. In so doing the analysis explores the public/private intersection in the state's support for failing firms. Again this speaks of paradox. In an economic model which rewards through profit and punishes through insolvency, the bail-out regulatory push runs clearly contrary to fundamental market principles. Wealth is disconnected from property in ways such that bank capitalisation (or the absence of it) is passed over in favour of subsidisation and massive debt relief not offered at anything like this scale to failing and disaggregated South World states and economies.

Picotto along with other critics lay blame for the asset bubbles which precipitated this enormous wealth redistribution of public to private in the context of deep-rooted contradictions of an unstable growth model which rested on widening income inequalities both national and international, along with the vain meta-attempt to maintain western hegemony. On the upside, Picotto heralds a reshaping of the world economy out of the ashes of reckless financial dealings and wealth creation:

---

37 Waldron (1985).

38 In Joerges and Falke (2011), chapter 7.

Coupled with a rebalanced international economy based upon paying realistic social wages to workers in the new economic growth poles of Asia, Latin America and even Africa, as well as reducing income inequalities in the developed countries, a more sustainable pattern of economic growth could be possible. If one lesson is clear from the latest financial crisis, it is that banking and finance cannot be allowed to remain the province of unrestricted pursuit of private profit, in Polanyi's terms 'marketised'. It must be recognized as becoming highly socialized, the transmission belt between social savings and investment, and its institutionalized structures should begin to reflect this. The lessons for regulation are that it is not the amount or the degree of regulation that are crucial, but the form that it takes. Financial regulation should be aimed at underpinning the social functions of finance, rather than its 'marketisation'.[39]

ECONOMIC INDIVIDUALISM AND INDIVIDUALIST ECONOMIES

The individualist vision for theorising global economy has strong political and moral purchase, even though in a number of liberal democracies it does not predominate, and in some more autocratic governance frames it is preferred. The parable goes that individuals can get what they want so long as they are willing to pay for it. Freedom is said to equate with user-pays choice options. This also holds for the supply side of market exchange such that individuals should be able to produce whatever they can materially profit from irrespective of whether it is essential or even necessary in terms of social sustainability. The worker exploitation which backs up such product preferencing for a materialist, commodity-focused consumer demand has been referred to at length in what has gone before. Its negative impact on labour pricing and worker dignity is established.

> There is no higher authority – king, pope or the planning minister – to tell individuals what they should want and produce. On this basis, many free-market economists have argued that there is an inseparable link between the freedom of individual consumers to choose and their broader political freedom. Friedrich Von Hayek's seminal critique of socialism, The Road to Serfdom, and Milton Friedman's passionate advocacy of the free-market system, Free to Choose, are famous examples.[40]

Paradoxically, it is assumed that the morality of individualism stimulates choices only for ourselves that result in the maximisation of social

39 Joerges and Falke (2011), p. 179.
40 Chang (2014), p. 175.

welfare. Market morality and mutuality, internally or externally generated, are unnecessary because when individuals behave as ruthless maximisers of utility then the market is both profitable and productive, benefitting all.

It cannot, however, be assumed that economic freedom ensures political freedom and vice versa. As the international financial meltdown following 2009 demonstrated, empirically the unrestrained pursuit of individualised wealth creation and economic growth do not benefit the masses. If the moral and practical justifications for the individualist perspective are so specious why are they given such wide economic credence? The answer remains political. As with our challenge to the assertion that a bad job is better than no job, the individualist position:

> takes the underlying social structure, such as property ownership or worker rights, as given, not questioning the status quo.[41]

Property arrangements underpinning market dysfunction continue unchallenged and unchallengable. Therein lies individualism's demise when considered along with the essentials of market sustainability measured against stronger social bonding and individual integrity (as opposed to wealth accumulation).

COMMODIFICATION OF LABOUR – LABOUR AND VALUE FORM

It could be said that the abstraction of work, through the obscuring of individualised purposes for labour with requirements such as utility and productivity, denigrating the belief in the ability to act beyond the confined constraints of the 'job' has become fundamental to capitalism's mechanisms.[42] We live in a digital era awash with 'playbour'; where the movements of labour and of consumption become blurred. It is a world where large quantities of unremunerated labour, or productivity not recognised as labour operate as if to preserve the specious freedom of non-contracting agents.[43]

Value, in this world, is more and more based on speculative profit generation. For example, monopolistic social media platforms such as Facebook adopt a profit model converting relationships and shared

---

41 Chang (2014), p. 176.
42 See Vishmidt (2013).
43 Terranova (2000).

information into capital, and uncertain as this may be, advertising revenue is returned on its promised outcomes. This in turn, Lanier suggests,[44] drives down the value of labour across the board through the fractionalisation of work (in terms of time, space, place and sociality) which erodes traditional modes of resistance to labour exploitation. In the mechanical marketplaces for migrant labour, requesters can source the cheapest available registrants and develop their migration and employment terms without human interaction at the first instance.

The valuation of property such as labour once it has become commodified also depends on monopolistic models of ownership. In the case of migrant labour markets which are explored later in the book (Chapter 6), labour is not in any viable economic sense owned by workers. It is agents and employers who are the more influential interests in labour commodification, and through contracting take over the virtual and actual rights of transactability. The prefigurative imperatives behind our argument for a transformed role of legal regulation in managing labour market arrangements, builds from the antagonistic realisation that workers have not only been denied fair value for their labour, they have also been dispossessed of ownership over the service they offer.

Again, however, the concerns associated with labour as property are not contained within value or ownership contests alone. Even if migrant labour could be set free from exploitation in pricing and transactability, there remains the question of how in new market arrangements the value of labour might be more sustainably imagined. Importantly attendant on any discussion of new remuneration models are the current processes whereby workers' disposable incomes continue to be diverted into unsustainable social or economic cost forms, thereby pressuring the subsistence component and exacerbating the vulnerability and dependency situations in which these workers find themselves. We will look at this briefly in the context of remittance obligations back to families and communities which the worker deems as their economic responsibility. Along with this drain are the disproportionate costs imposed by agents and employers when it comes to bonding, and the provision of living staples such as housing, insurance and communication costs.

Fortunately for the cause of transition, and the reconsideration of property, we live in a technologised age, where the influence of technology over social relations provides new and practical possibilities for envisioning and organising other new forms of collective value and benefit. An example of this is the liberating possibilities available through

---

44 Lanier (2014).

instructing and making more accessible to migrant workers the techniques and potentials of information technology (IT), social media and the intellectual commons across the internet. Unfortunately it is regularly the reverse experience for migrant workers in that the use of inflated and exclusive mobile communication facilities, further diminishes worker disposable income and enslaves them more acutely to the sabotage of debt.

As Polanyi identified in his analysis of fictional assets, money is an example of abstraction, but with real effects.[45] The enslavement of wage labour for many migrant workers is a very real consequence of their limited access to a fair monetarisation of labour value. This application of money to the vulnerability and dependency conditions of migrant labour can be exacerbated by the fees and charges extorted through the negative incursions into the market such as agency and remittance trading.

> Ultimately the power of abstraction is to make us believe that our power to act has been severed from the conditions of that power, that is, from the contradictory and oppressive structures that allow us to have any kind of voice at all. This then generates both a deathly pragmatism of action and the equally torpid reproduction of the same, which activism can leave untouched. The abstract conditions of our experience whether reflected in art, forms of immaterial property, or production, cannot be separated from the analysis that allows us to interpret it *(in this text's case, the market)*. They are one and the same and they have to form the substance of our politics.[46] (emphasis added)

It is important to remember that the 'property' in migrant labour is alive. Property removed from the humanity of labour is little more than a legal regime that is in differing degrees appropriate or inappropriate for the managing of public and private goods. Ownership of property in this sense is not a fact but a legally endorsed tool for the management of goods. As Stadler rightly points out regarding the notion of 'belonging':

> The two meanings of belong both relate to what we call possession, but these are curious, elastic ideas of possession. The first is our private possession of things, which are taken by law or force out of a kind of natural commons that would exist without property. We keep them, process them, so that they lose their own future, becoming solely an extension of our own, the owners, the one they belong to. The second, when we belong to a group, obliges us to cede our autonomous, unconstrained liberty and take on the rights and

---

45 Discussed in Findlay (2013), chapter 3.
46 Vishmidt (2013), p. 169.

obligations towards others. We are possessed by the group, linked by a shared resource and its future and its well-being.[47]

As our critical exploration of the nexus between migration and employment regulation indicates (Chapter 2), these two legal paradigms conspire to remove migrant workers from both their home and host communities. It is one of the most profound consequences of the commodification of their labour in markets where they are essentially constrained from creative participation, that these workers are property in a context on not 'belonging'. The way in which law can regulate to remedy the alienating potential of migrant worker commodification is by adopting a formula which Ostrom (et al) generate for effective common pool resource management:[48]

- establish clear boundaries;
- confirm proportional value;
- ensure collective choice; and
- enable nestled enterprises.

It has become necessary in an age where migrant labour is returning as the reluctant salvation of many crumbling demographies and dependent economies, to reconceive the place and shape of such labour within property arrangements.

> The difficultly in fully grasping today's property relations – conceived as increasingly immaterial – through traditional concepts of selfhood and objecthood is generally acknowledged. It has almost become a truism that the proliferation of 'new technologies' has come along with substantial reinterpretations of the meaning and the effects of ownership and control.[49]

More conventional interpretations of private property arrangements in capitalist markets would have these as a:

> … complex array of interconnected processes and relationships through which political rights, social membership, knowledge production, and the related spheres that constitute personhood are increasingly brought within the ambit of the capitalist marketplace.[50]

---

47 Stadler (2013), pp. 179–80.
48 Ostrom, Gardner and Walker (1994).
49 Schneider (2013), p. 197.
50 Maurer and Schwab (2006), p. 8.

In the case of migrant labour markets, from the perspective of the worker, the property in their labour is no longer (if it ever could be) the mirror image of a self-owning *self*. In migration contexts these workers are not given the role of responsible subjects to negotiate their place in markets of reciprocal production and reward. The distortion of labour markets where vulnerability and dependency maintain their labour value attractiveness, the relationship between property and personhood has been pummelled by profit margins. The machinations of migration and market frames are:

> … reifying living beings by abstracting them from their concrete qualities, capturing their forces, arresting movement, and then remobilising the stagnating entities as disciplined items in controlled environments.[51]

It is clear in the fragility of these labour markets that even where legal protections (usually of employer/agent interests) are present, property establishes imaginary social relationships between the owner and the *self* of a thing. In migrant labour markets even conventional ways in which private property relates to the division of labour in industrial capitalism have become misaligned. The social divisions which marked out labour in industrial capitalism have today become radically applied and distorted on a global scale, empowered by poverty on the one hand and mass migration on the other. Beyond national-interest-based migration regimes, in a market sense, there is developing a pressing need (as Europe is presently facing) for a new model of organising workflows and more meaningful hybrid divisions of labour. This challenge connects importantly to considerations of the *dignity of the self* which are introduced for much more expansive consideration at another time, in the book's conclusion. The law must have a balancing role in generating truly relational value if the property arrangements in migrant labour markets are ever to be sustainable.

CONCLUSION – HYBRID FORMS OF LEGAL DISCOURSE

The advocacy for law as a sustainable regulatory device should not be confused with pleas for social contract. We elaborate in Chapter 3 how the sustainability of markets is not guaranteed merely by broadening contractual franchise, valuable as this may be, but rather it is necessary to

---

[51] Schneider (2013), p. 198.

fundamentally reposition contracting outcomes towards the solidarity of social bonds, and away from individualism. The analysis to follow will, in the context of employment contracting and agency, test the conditions wherein the contractual element gains ground over the discriminatory authority of legal regulation as it currently intersects with property arrangements, and profoundly challenges the mutuality at the centre of most social contract theorising. It is not enough to see the power imbalances of current employment contracting simply overpowered by hard bargaining driven by the citizen with the state, or by the state on the citizen's behalf. To retire to such a position would require the belief either that the state is motivated by the common good or does not have property interests in the market which are separable from those of society at large. Any such naïve interpretation of the role of the regulatory state drifts us back to the confusions which we have otherwise criticised.[52] The citizen needs some certainty that she receives in return from the state what she has sacrificed to it, and as discussed in the examination of the employment/migration nexus in Chapter 2, this is an unbalanced outcome.

Where is the role of law in this? It will be advanced that law can be viewed free of the state and state interests.[53] Law can work towards a contractual facility wherein parties undertake equivalent and reciprocal obligations to one another, and each reserve unto themselves a measure of rights, liberty, authority, and eventually property that is currently conceded through vulnerable and dependent property inequalities. It could be said that under existing notions of social contract the individual gives up a greater measure of freedom (such as with residency registration) and authority than the part she reserves, sometimes on the anticipation that illusive benefits will eventually accrue in some more balanced fashion, or that inequality is tolerated because the alternative to distorted social contract may be perceived by that party as a worse outcome (chartered by poverty). The 'brute engine' of state authority can be modified through law so that an optimum allowance of contractual liberty can be reconciled with an expedient measure of order, against which positive social ordering can proliferate. The contract in a viable market, sustainable through greater social embedding avoids on the one hand an excess of liberty leading to chaos and on the other the excess of discriminatory authority leading to oppression and poverty. The state

52 Findlay and Lim (2014), chapters 1 and 7.

53 In the context of freedom of religious beliefs and neutral laws see Marin (1991).

through law can initiate the conditions in which equitable movement can emerge, but if law takes over then politics can withdraw.

In the later proposed repositioning of regulatory principle, the market as a field for social sustainability will operate under the expressive morality which presently is evidenced in the principles of contract law. These principles require and retain market mutuality which develop rather than derange essential social bonding.

That said, there is much in what Collins draws from Teubner's view that the law remains normatively separate from other regulatory systems even if it retains the potential for cognitive interconnection:

> Legal operations, by their very operative closure and, as a matter of principle, cannot reach out into domains of non-law. As a result law can only reconstruct its environment internally through closed self-referential operations. This internal reconstruction of the external world is never identical with the events as they happen in the eternal world. Even if their substance appears to be identical they are different because they are non-contextualised ... Calculations of costs and calculations of power, policy arguments and scientific constructs ... all become strange hybrids which are now, however, the sole responsibility of the legal discourse.[54]

If this conclusion is so, then it is a challenge for market regulation towards social sustainability to better understand the qualities of hybrid forms of legal discourse which can essentially reposition private property arrangements. We have throughout this chapter implied that the current collision of private law with public regulation[55] (where the state employs private law in basic social ordering) offers potent possibilities for how the influential normative frame of private law contracting can assist in market remoralisation. Indeed contracting can offer a modernised approach to the social embedding of market relations that might appear as the antithesis of conventional contract thinking, invoking:

> ... obligations based on solidarity rather than voluntary undertakings; it recognises groups as a form of human association rather than being composed of a collection of separate undertakings; and it resists strict and finite measures of social obligations. Embeddedness in personal relations based upon history and social ties tends rather to exclude contractual thinking, to treat it as an inappropriate and dysfunctional understanding of events and relations. In this context, the interference between contract thinking and norms based on ties of solidarity is one of conflict and competition, with each communications system providing opposing evaluations of conduct ... But the

---

[54] Collins (1999), p. 55.
[55] Discussed in Collins (1999), pp 46–52.

> communication system of contract is never entirely closed, for it incorporates a set of standards drawn primarily from the conventions of the local market or particular trade which flesh out the full context of those undertakings.[56]

This chapter follows and is dependent on the more detailed discussion of how the nexus between migration and employment law (or its inadequacies) has generated relationships of vulnerability and dependency, migrant worker to employer (Chapter 2). The discussion above leaves us ready later to speculate on why contract and agency have facilitated this market reality (chapters 4 and 5). The purpose behind the critique of law's complicity in vulnerable property arrangements has a very specific social edge. We want to ask how through the example of the discriminatory commodification of labour, law is assisting in rather than confronting these property arrangements which are socially unsustainable for both home and host markets.

---

56 Collins (1999), p. 28.

4. Substantive inequality to contract?

> Normally, like planets circling a star, political philosophy and the law of contracts affect each other's path without their orbits ever coinciding.[1]

INTRODUCTION

Contracting is the making and keeping of promises. The images of contract as a relationship of liberty and social mutualisation, discussed in Chapter 3, rely on contracting serving two ideal functions in providing a guarantee of: a) equivalent exchange, and b) liberty, since contractual relations are voluntary and free from coercion. In such a setting of mutuality (legalised or otherwise), contract characterises a new form of social sustainability. Almost mystically, justice is conceived in contractual bonding as reflected through equal liberty to contract and the shared and consensual adoption of individualised obligations.

The common law principles of contract law represent similar contextual and functional arrangements. In searching for the core elements of contracting principle it is easy to be distracted by the proliferation of commentary which deems principle to be process. The normative foundations for contracting are what should explain the essential steps in the process which keep it in line with this central principle. The governing intent behind contracting is that people should only be bound to promises which they entered into having the capacity to consent, the knowledge of what it is they are consenting to and that their consent is actual and not unjustly procured.

This chapter has two clear intentions. First will be the exploration of the dissonance between contracting principle and the practice of contract law, as it has evolved along with the emergence of fictional assets.[2] The examination of this contradiction is the more straightforward task. Of greater theoretical interest is the application of trust as a regulatory

[1] Collins (1986), p. 137.
[2] Findlay (2013), chapter 7.

motivation with the power to reposition the contract in law as a device for social-embedding and sustainability (introduced as a notion in Chapter 3).

THE PROMISE OF CONTRACT

Theories of contract have their essential connections with the law's treatment of harm. In this respect Charles Fried's *Contract as Promise*[3] introduces the question of whether contract law, especially when this area is equated with the enforcement of promises, is in tension with John Stuart Mill's 'Harm Principle'.[4] Fried offers an important corrective for those who disparage the role that the connected values of autonomy, will, consent and promise, plays in contract law.

> Regarding the implications of the Harm Principle for contract law, there are limits to which the prescriptive Harm Principle could be directly relevant to contract theory, as theories of contract law are best understood as descriptive, explanatory or interpretive. However, the Principle might justify the law's approach to contract remedies. Additionally, the applicability of the Harm Principle is less clear when contract law is viewed from the lens of "Contract as Promise," seeing contract enforcement (at its best) as a resource available to people to increase their liberty, allowing people to make a certain kind of commitment that would otherwise not be possible, rather than as a duty imposed upon them.[5]

The harm/promise juxtaposition suggests a fundamental divergence in the attitude to contracting. As a promise the contract is no more than the iteration of intentions to comply with representations made. From the harm perspective the contract provides recompense for breach of promise and the consequent loss.

There is a second level for interpreting this juxtaposition of promise and harm. If contracts are tools for constraining the reach and implication of promises, particularly from the benefit of those over whom the promise has effect, then contract ring-fencing generates harm to those who do not have legal status as parties. For instance in the arranging of migrant employment, prospective employers contract with agents in order to engage workers on terms beneficial to the employer and the agent but not to labour force and as a consequence labour is devalued. The *promise*

---

3 Fried (1981).
4 Mill (2010), chapter 1.
5 Bix (2011), Abstract.

between agent and employer is about the services offered by the prospective workforce, but except through discriminatory employment contract terms which may eventuate, the worker is excluded from the realistic rewards of her labour having no genuine or influential standing in the agency contract. The counter argument is that to blame inanimate contract frames instead of selfish and obfuscating agency is misdirected. We blame both. Contracts need parties and human enlivening. Agency and contracting in the migrant work environment are now inextricable and both have potential in the repositioning of legal regulation under a fair fiduciary umbrella.

Looked at in these terms, and recognising in the employment/migration setting that contracts cantilever off each other in a daisy-chain of obligation and benefit, the harm/promise relationship can exponentially disadvantage powerless participants. Migrant workers offer themselves up for market exploitation when entering the migrant flow as vulnerable parties. Law needs to intervene at the pre-entry point if market sustainability is to be anything but a remedy for inevitable exploitation.

Because contracting may be different in its manifestation of promise and its interaction with harm, the expectation of one grand theory to explain its existence and its action is unrealistic. For our purpose in this chapter we can restrict our interest in such theorising to the nexus between contracting and private property arrangements. In their discussion of contract theory as a possible unitary domain Schwartz and Scott[6] observed:

> Contract law has neither a complete descriptive theory, explaining what the law is, nor a complete normative theory, explaining what the law should be. These gaps are unsurprising given the traditional definition of contract as embracing all promises that the law will enforce. Even a theory of contract law that focuses only on the enforcement of bargains must still consider the entire continuum from standard form contracts between firms and consumers to commercial contracts between business firms. No descriptive theory has yet explained a law of contract that comprehends such a broad domain. Normative theories that are grounded in a single norm – such as autonomy or efficiency – also have floundered over the heterogeneity of contractual contexts to which the theory is to apply.[7] Pluralist theories attempt to respond to the difficulty that unitary normative theories pose by urging courts to pursue efficiency, fairness, good faith and the protection of individual

6 See Schwartz and Scott (2003), pp. 521–2.
7 Benson (1989); Barnett (1986).

> autonomy. Such theories need, but so far lack, a meta principle that tells which of these goals should be decisive when they conflict.[8]

It is useful to extract and classify the nominated pluralist expectations for contracting, listed above, when trying to understand contract as a facilitator of property relationships; efficiency, fairness, good faith and the protection of individual autonomy.

The *efficiency* school would have contracts as interpretative devices which enable the maximisation of profit in conditions that are stable and certain for business parties. The exclusionist and discriminatory capacity of contracting through the limitation on party status and benefit not only restricts but calibrates property in a profit sense and its value through the constriction of transaction and alienation. Powerful parties profit, powerless parties disproportionately provide benefit, and the contract ideology of equity and informed consent is hostage to information deficit and bargaining imbalance.

In a critique of autonomy and efficiency theories of contract, Trebilcock concludes that both theory types are 'valid in their own right', but without a 'meta-theory that weighs and ranks these various values', both values should be pursued in different social contexts according to the relative competency of different legal institutions to perform effectively.[9] This is a far too narrow and normatively dismissive attempt at reconciling two motivations for contracting which are crucially interdependent. In recent times contracting in a legal context has had the principal incentive of maximising individual wealth creation. Contract disputation employs the law pitching one party against the other in order to distil prevailing autonomous profit advantage (or to limit autonomous loss). Efficiency does not contest these autonomous modes provided it is not viewed in a societal or communitarian sense. So long as efficiency is measured against individual wealth creation and economic growth, legal battles over prevailing autonomous profit or harm are only bumps in the road.

Fairness and good faith,[10] as with individual autonomy and efficiency, pair up around common *general goods*. However in the case of fairness and good faith, the drivers are comparatively social rather than predominantly economic. If contracts are viewed as the reciprocal exchange of assumptions of legal obligation,[11] we sense the social but are beguiled by the circuitous reasoning that contracting is about the acceptance of

8 Eisenberg (1982); Eisenberg (2000).
9 Trebilcock (1993), p. 248.
10 Eisenberg (2000), pp. 243–4.
11 Coote (1988), p. 183.

liability under changing circumstances. It is not enough to see contract principles distilled from a collection of responses to contract violation, if we are searching for common considerations of fairness and good faith. The challenge in genuinely engaging fairness and good faith as actual rather than legal concepts in contracting requires revolutionary repositioning in contract scholarship (although not as if we remain on a normative plain):

> If the theory fails to provide such an apparatus (for lasting conceptual change) then we are left essentially with data in the form of case-law but with no real way to interpret its significance. In effect we need some apparatus in order to make a comparative comparison with what went before … to lay bare the core moral issues and to expose the argumentative techniques used by lawyers to deal with them.[12]

Fairness can drive judicial considerations of scope and inclusion in contracting which prefer *benefit*, rather than *form* prevailing. In the case of *Walton Stores* v. *Maher*[13] the High Court of Australia held that words and conduct during negotiations gave rise to liability, even though no contract eventuated and no tort was identified. The theme of this judgement is that 'promise' and contractual obligation are more governed by notions of fairness and good faith than autonomy and efficiency. The then Chief Justice, in explaining the uniqueness of the decisions, explicitly sought out social location:

> Independence of Australian contract law will become more pronounced as Australian judges shape the common law of contract to accord with Australian circumstances, needs and values.[14]

The ideas to follow, as with the analysis of agency after this, lay out the normative closure of contracting and suggest intersections with regulatory potential. From this position the analysis progresses to explain why things are not as they seem. In so doing, the chapter is not only a revelation of failed principle or cynical legal practice. Rather, in demonstrating the contradictions characterising the cognitive transition of contracting, it is intended to explain the current facilities on offer through contracting which so construct property arrangements in such ways that the markets in which they feature (like migrant labour markets) are disembedded and unsustainable. Achieving this, the chapter builds a

12 Drahos and Parker (1990).
13 *Waltons Stores (Interstate) Ltd* v. *Maher* (1988) 164 CLR 387.
14 Mason (1988).

platform for the strategy to redirect and reservice these arrangements utilising contracting repositioned towards sustainable market conditions.

A critic might call halt and demand to know how exclusive and discriminatory contracting challenges market sustainability, when it could be argued that these private property arrangements are at the heart of contemporary economic growth models. Our response is twofold:

- economic growth has its eventual dénouement where market resources are finite, and productive labour force is not inexhaustible; and
- social growth disentangled from economy requires much more than labour commodification for markets to satisfy inevitable social need.

Accepting for the point of argument that current contracting modes challenge rather than consolidate market sustainability, access is here identified as the key to change. Information and the power that knowledge brings are crucial to opening up access and consequential benefit. At present the law is more exclusionist than it is inclusive both in terms of party status to contracts and the quarantining or property benefit such as through intellectual property protections.

CONTRACTING

> Even if we discover that law plays a marginal role in the establishment of habitual trust, that conclusion leaves open the possibility that it could be improved so that it might provide better assistance. The general question becomes what kind of law is best suited to this task of regulating markets and contractual forms of association, and how might its success be measured and evaluated?[15]

To consider the contract as a legal form is to undervalue its dynamic possibilities as a regulatory process. Contracting relies on the minds and actions of parties. Later we will suggest how these are constrained by factors external to the contract (see Chapter 6). From the making of an offer and its acceptance contracting takes on a voluntary flavour. Even so, external interests predetermine contracting such that the bargaining position and power of parties and the differential value they place on

[15] Collins (1999), p. 6.

contracted outcomes challenge any simple notion of voluntary contracting and equal terms.

Before the nature of contract can be considered, preceding questions of capacity may require resolving. Depending on the jurisdiction, all parties need be at least of a certain age before they can enter into a contract. All parties must have the mental capacity to understand the contract's terms and non-performance consequences. Someone who is intoxicated, under the influence of drugs or coerced into signing can move to have the contract set aside in court.

From the contract being a conversation, the law requires bonding agents. The settling of consideration is the practical glue which from the outset might also provide an indication that neither the 'morality' nor 'mutuality' of contracting parties is sufficient without the addition of real risk in the consequence of breach. Consideration is something of value to make a mere promise enforceable. It must be sufficient for the purpose but need not be objectively adequate. Consideration must move from the promise and generally at least binds the parties, unless additional interests can be brought within the contract through some rights created in consideration.

Even at this stage, with offer, acceptance and consideration, the contract may not be considered legally complete. The contract must be intended to be binding. In most commercial relationships this is presumed. However, many social arrangements do not amount to contracts because they are not seen as intended to be legally binding. Equally, many domestic arrangements, such as between husband and wife, or between parent and child, lack legal force because the parties did not intend them to have legal consequences. For instance, in *Balfour* v. *Balfour*,[16] a husband who worked abroad promised to pay an allowance of £30 per month to his wife, who was in England. The wife's attempt to enforce this promise failed: the parties did not intend the arrangement to be legally binding. In addition, the court held that the wife had not provided any consideration. This example not only suggests a divergence from contracting as a commercial rather than a *just* property arrangement, but it might exhibit inequitable liberties to contract, and questionable equivalence of exchange measured as it was in preferring commerce over family obligation.

In this very brief overview of contracting it is not intended to spend time on matters of form, beyond noting the potential for these to undermine the principled contracting conditions referred to previously.

---

[16] *Balfour* v. *Balfour* [1919] 2 KB 571.

The general rule is that contracts can be made informally; most contracts can be formed orally, and in some cases, no oral or written communication at all is needed. Thus, an informal exchange of promises can still be as binding and legally valid as a written contract. A contract written on a cocktail napkin is just as sound as one drafted in a lawyer's office if all the required elements are included.

The terms of contracts are fields of formalisation where inequalities arise. Terms can be express (written down in the agreed form) or implied. Once the express terms have been identified, there is the question of interpretation. The document setting out the parties' agreement should be understood objectively: it is not a question of what one party actually intended or what the other party actually appreciated to have been intended but of what a reasonable person in the position of the parties would have understood the words to mean. The starting point for ascertaining the objective meaning is the words used by the parties. These are interpreted according to their meaning in conventional usage, unless there is something in the background showing that some other meaning would have been conveyed to the reasonable person. Terms can be implied from the facts which appear in the contract, from laws and statutes, and from general custom or usage. The interpretation of the latter obviously offers opportunities for discriminating between the rights and obligations of parties from more than a literal legal standpoint.

Contracting has its finality. There are four ways a contract can be brought to an end: expiration, termination, vitiation and frustration. Fortunately for the utility of contract as a regulatory mechanism primarily reliant on trust, contracts largely expire within their terms. Breaches of contract, failure of contractual conditions, or a breakdown in contracting arrangements create conditions of loss out of which the mechanisms of enforcement or the compensation of damages may be available.

ACTUAL CONSENT

In the earlier discussion of migrant worker contracting arrangements (see Chapter 2) one of the essential issues which determine the relationship between potential employees and agents, and workers and employers, is whether parties either understand what they are agreeing to, or are in a position to agree in a truly voluntary fashion. This consent requirement boils down to whether the consent of the less powerful party is informed and actual. Both these conditions on contracting imply power and knowledge.

In order to confirm that both parties agree to the contract of their own free will, a party's genuine consent is an essential element of a legally binding contract. Genuine consent to enter into a contract can be affected by a number of issues. For example, during the contractual negotiations, there may have been:

- *Undue influence* – this exists where there is an inequality of power between the contracting parties which results in the weaker party entering into a contract with the dominant party. Where the weaker party cannot be said to have entered into the contract voluntarily because of the influence of the dominant party, the influence is said to be 'undue' and the court may set the contract aside.
- *Mistake* – mistake has occurred when the parties have agreed to different things, or where there are such different beliefs that the contract was never properly understood, and the contract may be declared void. Mistake is a complex area of contract law and one where judges have traditionally been largely unsympathetic to someone who argues that he or she has made a terrible mistake. As a general rule, being mistaken about some aspect of a contract will not provide a party with a right to escape contractual obligations – even if that mistake is fundamental.
- *Misrepresentation* – is the giving of false information by one party to the other before the contract is settled, which induces them to make the contract. If the contracting party relies on a misrepresentation and suffers loss as a result, the contract may be nullified or damages claimed.
- *Duress* – is defined as actual or threatened violence to an individual to obtain a contractual promise. If it is established that consent is obtained through duress then the weaker party may choose to avoid the agreement.
- *Unconscionable conduct* – deals with unfair or oppressive transactions between dominant and weaker parties; it therefore overlaps with duress and undue influence.

Each of these factors or events may mean that consent was not freely given by one of the parties and that party may therefore be able to avoid their contractual obligations, if in fact the consequence of such determination is not more deleterious to the weaker party than simply accepting the violation of condition. For instance, as the nature of dependency relationships tragically reveals (see Chapter 2) despite a realisation that consent on behalf of the worker may not be actual, it could be to her fundamental disadvantage to have even an unconscionable contract terminated for lack of power or knowledge if that leads to a severing of the employment arrangement and consequent immigration repatriation. Damages would be unlikely to compensate for the loss of work and residency ongoing, added to the complication of a loss of jurisdiction following repatriation. This is the enforcement dilemma which is so keenly felt even if the less powerful contracting party has access to justice under contract regimes.

INTENTION TO CONTRACT

Similar to the above considerations of actual consent, there is much criminal law theorising on the nature and extent of intention which is particularly relevant to understandings of contractual equity and empowerment.[17] Anthony Duff has an interest in the manner in which what he refers to as the 'Principle of Double Effect' constructs the moral concepts of intentional action.[18] In seeking to discover how an agent may relate himself to the effect of his action, Duff focuses *on judgements of responsibility*; decisions made or accepted by the agent and influenced by internal and external discretionary determinants (some within the agent's control and others well outside it). The decision process ranges from a direct intention to bring about some consequence, through knowledge that the consequence could occur, onto consent to its occurrence. Even if the occurrence is foreseen and not desired there is some necessity for empowerment through understanding and some degree of control by activating outcomes. In this power paradox lies a more simple distinction of intending a result or bringing it about intentionally.

Duff insists that ascriptions of intended and intentional agency belong with ascriptions of responsibility and demands for justification.

> The criteria of intentional agency as to a given effect are also the criteria of responsibility for that effect: and they involve not just the agent's knowledge of and control over that effect, but the significance of that effect in the context of his action as providing a reason for or against the action.[19]

---

[17] A foundation of much of the thinking to follow can be seen in Kenny (1975).

[18] Duff (1982).

[19] Duff (1982), p. 4.

Take this into the situation of migrant employment contracting. If the worker is without sufficient knowledge she is denied control and disempowered from reasoning the consequences of her actions. The employment agents, home and host, are active in denying detail and proliferating confusion, while at the same time hiding behind an uncertain chain of delegation. The eventual employer has the knowledge and the control in order to determine the contracting outcomes but denies responsibility through claiming the significance and reasons for his actions in economic self-interest, not challenged or delegitimated by the contract's regulatory frame. The utilitarian measure of an increase in happiness grows (for these preferred interests only) exponentially the further the contracting is removed from the employee.

> ... an agent's judgement of his own agency and responsibility for an effect of his action will thus depend on his judgement of its significance, and will reflect his own values, attitudes and interests.[20]

In order that we do not leave this consideration of intention and responsibility stranded in a realm of inequality and subjectivity, it is necessary to move to the judgements and descriptions of observers. Law and legal regulators can offer important observational roles in the determination of significance and responsibility beyond sectoral self-interest. Observers can agree that:

- someone is or is not an intentional agent;
- their actions are or are not significant (against empirical measure);
- they should therefore hold some responsibility (or not) against a moral measure.

The *Principle of Double Effect* is especially important in evaluations through absolutist moralities which hold that some action is absolutely wrong or absolutely required, whatever the consequences. In such measures the moral critique can be both directed against *actions* and *outcomes*. The more that an agent, through empowerment and knowledge, has control over actions and consequences, the more that moral gaze is rightly shone in his direction. If legal regulation is the mechanism of moral gaze, then repositioning contractual responsibility through the law might have more effect if it contains and constrains the self-interest of the employer and the agent, rather than generally speaking of the rights of the employee to contractual fairness.

---

[20] Duff (1982), p. 5.

The impact of legal regulation over employment contracting requires calling into account those who deem or deny the responsibility for their actions and outcomes, and act intentionally or intend their actions. Whether as moralised agents or moralising observers, critics of the regulatory potential of contract law, in demanding equity and fairness, identify as an impossible flaw this need for subjectification by the law in a counter-intuitive generalist mode such as contracting.

CRITICAL CONTRACT LAW

In her seminal essay on the deconstruction of the contract doctrine[21] Claire Dalton engages with contracting in terms of contradiction and indeterminacy. To set up the critique the argument paints a model (and perhaps ahistorically) laissez faire contracting environment against which is reflected the neo-classical liberalism of the Reagan-Thatcher economic era. Through the application of stark polar analysis Dalton is able to celebrate the fundamental contradiction approach that is at the heart of much of the critical legal studies movement.[22]

> The dilemma facing liberalism is that any moral and legal code it might generate for individuals is capable of being subverted because it relies on conceptual dualities that are themselves unstable due to the presence of dangerous supplements (the disfavoured pole in the duality, such as taking care of ourselves and taking care of others).[23]

For the critical legal studies position where the essential tension is between the self and the other, there is a disbelief in conceptual or instrumental schemes like contracting as being sufficiently neutral to convincingly determine which consensual values we should regulate and which we should predominate, what self-interested behaviour is intolerable and what is not.[24] For the crit, if contract law is about the voluntary association of individuals in liberal societies, what is it that sets up contractual dichotomies favouring one side and not the other? Dalton sees these explained by problems of power and problems of knowledge. In the case of knowledge for instance, the liberal position is that law should only enforce the actual knowledge on which the contract is based. But how is that to be established when we know in the migrant worker

---

21 Dalton (1985).
22 Unger (1983).
23 Drahos and Parker (1990), p. 35.
24 Dalton (1985), p. 1000.

employment contract context it is difficult to determine what choices have really been made and what meanings have been communicated and received? The law tries to mask these profound knowledge uncertainties through the unsatisfactory application of reasonableness testing and objectification.

The converse of law's objectivity is the critical scholar's challenge to subjectify the legal subject. When, for instance, a migrant worker is confronted with some form of contract document and they sign it, the law assumes that they do so exercising informed consent. In reality, due to their relative position of market powerlessness workers are without the essential knowledge and experience of the contracting ritual to either satisfy or challenge such a legal presumption. When it comes to the power problem, it divides in Dalton's critique between the power of the state over the market (say through legislation to ensure more informed and equitable contracting) and the power of one individual over another within the market. This forms a very useful conceptualisation of what we present in Chapter 2, as the state's role in creating a subjugated migrant worker market through migration, residency and permit regulation (public law), followed by the employer's beneficial construction of employment arrangements by contracting (private law).

Attempts via legal regulation at reining in power imbalance, from a critical perspective, will run into the problem of knowledge. If we are to enliven 'free will' or 'choice' through better balancing market power, regulation faces the problem of determining individual intention. Reflect on the paradox that migrant workers may favour the conditional certainty of employment in sub-standard conditions rather than endanger that employment as a consequence of regulating up standards and obligations in workplace environments. Unconscionability is therefore preferred to the risks inherent in parity, unless regulation both protects against adverse employment consequences of empowerment and fosters that empowerment through essential knowledge sharing and actionability.

From the critical position, reforms in form (for example, enforcing uniform contracting) without understanding the complexity of substance (such as the impotence of contract conditions to protect the vulnerable) can be both counterintuitive and counterproductive. The answer to this dilemma may better emerge out of supplemental shifts in form acting with the injection of individualised substance. So, in the case of employment conditions and migrant work, the state could be more strenuous in valuing labour and then, within a more realistic labour pricing frame, the worker and the employer could discount and negotiate certain working conditions but not beyond a proper boundary again set by the state or independent agencies.

SYMMETRICALLY INFORMING PARTIES

The knowledge deficit/power imbalance continuum identified in critical legal scholarship may not in labour markets be corrected through an injection of more information at critical decision sites. What is necessary for worker empowerment when knowledge is the currency will be the understanding of information by parties across an agreement, and its implications.

Contracting vocabulary is contentious when employed to exclude certain parties from informed consent. Vocabulary itself is complex in the contract setting. It not only refers to the nature of language but to intended meaning and even sub-optimal sets of vocabulary that can be determined and applied ex post facto.

Complicating the issue of contracting language further, and its impact on understanding and relative bargaining power, is where there are conscious asymmetries. In this respect certain parties may deliberately confound understanding through proposing language which is either ambiguous or designed to be understood in ways that are influenced by externalities to the contract. In these circumstances law's regulatory function (and that of any necessary judicial interpretation) demands more than ensuring vocabulary and its adequate supply. The interpreting function of regulation directed towards more general stakeholder empowerment is equally important. In this regard contracting regulation supplies solutions to problems of understanding, rather than only or primarily providing recourse where conflicts as to meaning produce damage.

> The public good aspect in supplying solutions to problems implies that problem solving default rules should be created. But there is a distinction between supplying governance modes or dispute resolution schemes and the solving of particular problems. The former sets of solutions can be highly general, and applicable to a wide range of commercial behaviours ... [despite the impediments posed by the heterogeneity of large modern economies, and of asymmetric information flows in contracting, it is necessary in a regulatory sense] to develop a theory of what the state should do regarding contracts and then to specify which legal institutions should perform which substantively desirable functions.[25]

[25] Schwartz (2000), pp. 108–9.

CONTRACTUAL CERTAINTY AND INDETERMINACY

Harking back to the discussion in Chapter 2, the vulnerability nexus between migration and employment regulation creates the current market necessity for a disempowered labour force through conditional residency and routine inspection. Labour force in this context constitutes the dislocated party in employment negotiations, and as such the relationship between contracting and indeterminacy needs reviewing against sustainable market aspirations if communal fair dealings rather than individualist exploitation is to emerge as the prevailing contracting *morality*.

> … indeterminacy is produced … by the same dualities that structure the rest of our life and thought, and effect the very development of our cultural values and understandings, then indeterminacy must exist at all these levels. Our seeming ability, nonetheless to understand and predict (in a historically contingent fashion) the particular links that decision-makers construct from the testimony submitted to them, requires us to search for other explanations.[26]

The framing of indeterminacy, therefore, is essentially social. Our application of indeterminacy here is somewhat different to the critical legal studies position that legal doctrine is never able to provide a determinate answer with respect to a given factual situation. Building on that circumspection however, in the contracting case, law has developed to employ the indeterminacy for some as a determined benefit for others. The relationship between employer preference and the initiation of migrant labour repatriation is a telling example (see Chapter 2).

Returning to the legal regulation of migrant labour working conditions it is impossible for law to predict how the regulatory relationship will be received in each instance, or even the objectives that it may achieve for all. On the other hand, the indeterminacy of legal regulation here reflects and contributes to market adjustments (such as the explosion in undocumented labour) that ensure determined and even predictable benefits for some employers who are favoured in private property arrangement through the use of migrant labour.

Predictably the law's attempt to modify its own exploitative potential by employing concepts of reasonableness and duty of care will propagate indeterminacy. This outcome is an obvious if regrettable consequence of the manner in which the courts through interpreting contractual rights and obligations have balked at allowing the public sphere to enter and

---

26 Dalton (1985), pp. 1009–10.

enjoy the private. The judicial view of the world is often as powerful a determinant of inclusion/exclusion as might be legal logic, interpretative possibility and law's reformative reach. Drahos and Parker suggest that through the preferring conventions concerning rule use, there exists the possibility for a more determined application of contracting law, and the opportunity to predict which *pole or supplement* may be selected in certain conditions, and how even the *dangerous supplement* (such as revaluing labour pricing) might be entertained for wider sustainable *goods*.[27]

Contradictions and selective choices through contracting, we agree, stem from more fundamental antimonies within liberal thought. Conventions can and do operate to cure indeterminacy and unconscionability provided the *community of rule users* deploy them in what we call for as a sustainable manner. Sight lines to ensure probity in the creation and application of legal conventions include that they should:

- displace rather than entrench inequitable self interest;
- create duties compatible with the normative principles of contracting; and
- reoccupy the space left from interest repositioning with conditions fostering the *general good*.

The necessity that law can facilitate change whether certainty or uncertainty is the outcome, provided that *general good* is the motivation, should be an argument for convention-based broad thematic vocabulary rather than nit-picking legal disputation over terms in the name of predictability. A stimulus for law taking a more inclusive approach to contractual meanings and understandings should grow from the appreciation of trust relationships between the contracting *self* and the contracting *other*. Trust bonds and resolutions are not achieved through resort to dangerous supplements alone without consideration of the fundamental poles around which contracting develops.

> … the making of fundamentally different conventions for handling the conflicts between self and other; … by direct resort to dangerous supplements rather than the manipulation of favoured poles … should be that nothing is inevitable or determined, whether by precedent or by forces of economics or morality … but it can be changed when its basis of thought is made clear.[28]

---

27 Drahos and Parker (1990), p. 41.
28 Drahos and Parker (1990), pp. 48–9.

COMMERCE AND MORALITY

Returning to our '3 Ms' analytical matrix, is it realistic to expect *morality* in our current market models where mutuality of interests is overshadowed by individualism, or is it appropriate to demand of law to police *market morality*? Talking of a recent period in Australian common law, Paul Finn observed:

> Contract law is in evolution, if not (to some) revolution. The unconscionable dealings doctrine is resurgent; consideration is under siege; privity has taken a mortal blow; the mistake rules are being revitalised with their limits as yet unsettled. The implication and interpretation of contractual terms seem set fair for some reappraisal; relief against forfeiture is in a state of expansive uncertainty; and the last word has not been said about penalties. The doctrine of good faith in contract performance is now squarely upon contract's agenda ...[29]

Despite resistance, the judicial appreciation of modern contract law in jurisdictions such as the USA, Canada, New Zealand and Australia is requiring the interpretation of standards of conduct that the law needs to extract from persons in conditionally voluntary dealings with others. This development in legal regulation through contracting is more than a shift in the ideology which informs legal doctrine.

> Associated with this is an emerging tendency to formulate some range of doctrines, not in terms of distinct, limited and discrete rules of behaviour, but as generalised standards of conduct which in a controlled way are instance-specific in their application.[30]

Such an observation is consistent with the earlier discussion of conventions governing contracting for principle rather than individualised interests. Opposition to this direction would return the law to the twentieth century individualism and self-reliance protected through law. To sanitise their preferred position, the critics suggest convention or instance-specific broad doctrines challenge certainty. However, if predictability rests on the exploitative outcomes of legal and moral autonomy conflated then it is a high price for rejection of good faith and fair dealing.

The sense of a new direction for contracting as legal regulation is evidenced through judicial language as well as a new and heightened

---

29 Finn (1989), pp. 88–9.
30 Finn (1989), p. 90.

standard setting for commercial engagement.[31] Finn relates this back to communitarian social bonding and what he calls *the neighbourhood idea* and what we would prefer as sociability. Neighbourhoods are unequal contexts at best, and contracting can exacerbate or relieve this prevalence.

> A rather simple impulse seems to inform a major theme (though not the sole one) in the expanding neighbourhood idea: it is to afford some measure of protection from unfair treatment when, in a relationship, a person is in a situation of vulnerability. Such a position may arise for example from disparities in information possessed [return to Dalton's power and knowledge conundrum], from personal circumstances and/or relative positions [antimonies exacerbated by migration law for migrant labour], from powers formal and informal, the other possess to effect prejudicially [how the state disposes its responsibilities to employers/agents in migrant employment contracting], or from a course taken in the other's encouragement, or without demur [agents in migrant labour contracting having now clear fiduciary responsibilities]. Each and all of these possibilities occur, and occur commonly, in commercial business dealings.[32]

CONCLUSION – CONTRACTUALISING SOCIAL LIFE

> Can we explain how the law of contract is both fundamental to the social system, and yet almost irrelevant to most daily market practices? How far, if at all, do laws and legal institutions contribute to the construction of habitual trust?[33]

The possibility by the use of contracting to reposition law's regulatory role in private property arrangements is not achieved through the development of *contract-lite.* General conventions rather than strict rules of interpretation, and abeyance to fairness alone will not in the end defeat the armies of self-interest who have employed contractual exclusion to their massive economic benefit. Even the hope of commercial remoralisation may be too-little-too-late.

> Commerce is founded on relationships with others, and this is the heart of the matter. And if this be acknowledged and if it be accepted as a worthwhile value to afford limited protection to the vulnerable, then an accommodation – a balance – must be struck. To harken back to a golden age, to the law of the late nineteenth century, is to give almost complete primacy to one interest and to accept that casualties to that interest should be accommodated because of

31 Mullins (1992); Gennaioli (2006).
32 Finn (1989), p. 97.
33 Collins (1999), p. 5.

> its importance. We may be able to afford this in economic terms. But there is a moral cost. And would its acceptance be socially deleterious?[34]

The answer – it will be catastrophic!

Contracting is not only a form of regulation without instrumental objectives. It is a failing of the fairness principle that it does not oblige consideration of welfare goals or distributive potential outside the words of the agreement. For too long the socially sustainable possibilities of contracting regulation have been hamstrung by legal thinking, that contracts cannot shape behaviour. In this regard Stapleton is wrong in the assertion that:

> Contract doctrine does not 'row' or 'steer' freedom of private ordering. It merely lays down minimum construction requirements for the canoe that the coxless pair will use![35]

Maybe consistent with the quaintness of the Oxbridge analogy employed here, as we have argued above, presumed prerequisites of freedom to contract, and bargaining equity are no more worthy of protection through contract principle and practice than they are realistic features of contracting in disembedded market frames.

We respect the position of lawyer reformers, with one eye over their shoulders towards the 'big end of town' and its power to recant from more principled practice, who talk of the need for balance, for protecting the vulnerable, for addressing the subjectivity of the case, and for interpreting contracting against a broad convention lens of fair dealing. That said, we warn, it is not enough to talk rights without addressing law's power through private property arrangements to systemically discriminate.

There is a grave risk in balancing contracting interests and protecting the weak stakeholder that we forget either those who have through ignorance and powerlessness no real purchase over their contracting position or those who through market contexts of vulnerability and dependency no longer can claim an actionable ownership of the value they might contract. And then there are the populations that should be parties to contracts in which they have real and general interests, but from which they are barred. These are the weak that any new approach to contracting as a rejuvenated regulatory form must confront and comfort. How is this to be achieved?

34 Finn (1989), pp. 98–9.
35 Stapleton (2004), p. 129.

In responding to the challenge of private property repositioning we take as a foundational task the requirement to meet and engage with those who Finn describes as now possessing the primacy of interest. Unless contracting *substance and form* do not return to equity in practice, then the notion of voluntary contracting is little more than a middle-class domain. The substance of the law and the current judicial interpretative fashion in some jurisdictions at least is available for this redistribution of genuine rights. The first place to start is for the law to require essential knowledge on which actual consent would be tested, and its transparency, so that parties can understand what they are consenting to and its consequences. But this attack on the knowledge deficit does not tackle the power imbalances that defuse any genuine equity in activating contractual protective frames.

The central reformist platform, in our sustainability model of contracting, is open access. Some might rejoin that if access to party status is more generalised then this would undermine the potency and enforceability of contracts and their regulatory (and even market) value. Not so. In the history of contract law there is nothing to be said that the more exclusive the interest coverage the stronger the promissory bond. In our view it is confusing to essentially conflate how the value of the interest is calculated against how it is protected.

The power/access connection is at the heart of the contracting regulatory transition that we envisage. In the short space available a complete strategy cannot be proposed but an example is offered, within two confines that should mean such a transition is neither destructive of regulatory form nor reliant on radical expressive re-formulation:

- the structural characteristics of contract law can be employed in order to achieve selective empowerment and enlarged access, while
- inclusion within contract benefits contextualised through more transparent information/knowledge exchange will lead to the revaluing of general good.

Take the contract condition of consideration as a tool for regulatory repositioning. In the employment contracting environment, prospective and engaged migrant workers are not afforded significant contractual standing (if they have standing at all) as a consequence of the devaluation of their labour price which is valid contracting consideration. It is necessary both for external regulatory mechanisms such as the state and public law and internal forms such as the other contracting parties and private law, to initiate and accept labour price revaluation and its recognition as sufficient consideration to allow for access and active contract participation and benefit. Such reconciliation defends the charge that both public and private law are complicit in market disembedding.

POST SCRIPT – INTELLECTUAL COMMONS

For contracting, the example of free software licences that aim to set up a positive commons (that is, innovations in algorithms belonging to all), is evidence of unlimited access to knowledge benefit where previously this was the exclusionist realm of copyright, trademark and patent law. It would seem clear in the domain of global knowledge sharing that about the only way to resist the privatisation (and the commodification and profitisation) of the intellectual commons by means of restrictive intellectual property is through contractual arrangements of the kind that the Free Software Foundation have created for software. This regulatory inclusive exercise for contracting conceives of the property in knowledge as the province of trust rather than the avenue for exclusive commercial gain.

The role of law in the face of intellectual commons has been recalcitrant. Non-disclosure agreements between software designers, manufacturers and distributors have endeavoured to thwart the open access movement. Again, free access may not mean without commercial cost. Free software does not mean *non-commercial.* Selling copies may be consistent with open access if prices are so calibrated not to exclude stakeholders with genuine use claims from use benefits. Also, being paid for services or development is acceptable. Not everybody is a programmer: if the software is free, any programmer can make custom modifications for anybody else to enhance the benefits of access.

The 'free software movement' is against the term intellectual property on the basis that it confuses different aspects and laws, in treating abstract entities like material objects. Through this process the law has employed contractual exclusion in order to artificially calibrate the price of 'property' to reflect some ephemeral and infinite conception of knowledge enhancement. These contract-protected private property arrangements perpetuate wealth for those who already are wealthy enough to comply with the price barriers of knowledge commodification.

When it comes to open access literature, the question of rights waivers is as significant as are concerns about who stores the information, on behalf of whom and for what purposes. The Budapest Open Access Initiative, which made 'open access' the term of art for this kind of literature (February 2002), put it this way:

> There are many degrees and kinds of wider and easier access to this literature. By 'open access' to this literature, we mean its free availability on the public internet, permitting any users to read, download, copy, distribute, print, search, or link to the full texts of these articles, crawl them for indexing, pass them as data to software, or use them for any other lawful purpose, without financial, legal, or technical barriers other than those inseparable from gaining access to the internet itself. The only constraint on reproduction and distribution, and the only role for copyright in this domain, should be to give authors control over the integrity of their work and the right to be properly acknowledged and cited.[36]

As Stuber says of open access literature, the economic imperative can be faced and settled without endangering access, if law can assist rather than frustrate access for the general good.

> The economic prerequisite for OA is to find the means to pay for the physical and legal prerequisites. If the work is not yet digital, then one cost is digitization. If the work is digital but not yet online, then another cost is putting it online; sometimes this is the high cost of lobbying the recalcitrant, not the negligible cost of FTP'ing a file to a web server or moving a file from a closed online directory to an open one. Permission is sometimes the least expensive part of an OA project, and sometimes the most expensive. In any case, permission is only necessary, not sufficient, to create OA.[37]

To promote open access, contracts will require a diffusion of value. Scholarly publication for example, has traditionally meant that the author stakeholder receives a pittance in royalty returns on book sales, while the publisher governs price and hence reader access in order to protect their disproportionate profit margins. However, viewed from the eyes and interests of the author stakeholder,

> The royalty-free nature of journal articles also explains why scholars would not be hurt if copyright law were dramatically reformed to restore balance between copyright holders and users. Or, to see this from the other end of the stick, publishers who pretend to speak for authors in defending the current imbalance in copyright law speak for authors of royalty producing literature. Authors of royalty-free literature have very different interests.
>
> Scholars have an interest in disseminating their work to all who can make use of it. They want the widest possible audience. That is the best way to be noticed, read, used, and cited. For royalty-free literature, enlarging the sphere of fair use serves the author's interests; for royalty-producing literature, it invades the author's interests. Having relinquished royalties, authors of

36 Budapest Open Access Initiative website.
37 Stuber (2006), p. 2.

> royalty-free literature have no need to protect a revenue stream, so they have everything to gain by consenting to OA and nothing to lose.[38]

Stuber explains the momentum behind online knowledge access in the age of the internet as both within and beyond conventional commodification. The challenge is for contract to adapt to accommodate rather than to misalign with this eventuality.

> An online, open-access intellectual commons in research literature is growing from many sources for many reasons. The incentives and economics differ from genre to genre, discipline to discipline, and decade to decade. But ever since texts have been stored in bits, which makes it possible to produce perfect copies at virtually no cost, and ever since the emergence of a global network of bit-switching machines, which makes it possible to share these copies with a worldwide audience at virtually no cost, the trajectory has always been up. There's no going back.[39]

---

[38] Stuber (2006), p. 5.
[39] Stuber (2006), p. 23.

5. Agents, pirates or slavers

> If the machine of government is of such a nature that it requires you to be the agent of injustice to another, then, I say, break the law.[1]

INTRODUCTION

It is not simply that law should be more involved in the sustainable regulation project. Regarding migrant labour markets, populations on the move progressively encounter crucial decision sites in their search for a better life. Engaging at these decision sites (discussed in more detail in the following chapter) could be expected to be the state, private market interests or civil society contributing to a regulatory environment where sustainable market relationships and outcomes are advanced. The regulatory reality reveals both a lack of regulatory activity and, where it may be present, an unbalanced operation of regulatory responsibilities (see chapters 2 and 6).

The hypothesis that more outcome-oriented and more interest-balanced regulation will better produce a viable market framework leading to socially sustainable bonding, necessitates promoting regulation for migrant labour force beyond a humanitarian endeavour.[2] Healthy labour markets cannot be confused with the exploitative commodification of cheap labour value, which in fact contributes little to the social sustainability of home and host nations.[3] Even so, the monetary motivations of migrant workers should not be sublimated into a sustainability push that, because of short-term negative economic consequences, can endanger the legitimacy of the regulatory strategy from the perspective of those it is most designed to protect. In calling for the repositioning of law (through contract and agency) so as to improve decent work opportunities and conditions, there is the short-term market risk, or even the likely consequence that labour pricing should move up to a more realistic value. The complexities and idiosyncrasies of labour pricing are explored in

1 Thoreau (2005), p. 9.
2 Backer (2007); Bratland (2004).
3 Cawthorne and Kitching (2001).

more detail later (see Chapter 6). At this stage it is important to specifically anticipate that if the regulation of contract and agency comes at such a market cost so as to ratchet up the price of labour (or this is the contrived response of employers explained in Chapter 6), in a market where pricing (wage) protections are not strong, and the supply of alternate underpriced labour remains, then improvements in wages will be met with a drift away from existing migrant labour preferencing. In the short-term such a development can paradoxically deny improved wage benefits to workers in work, as it disinclines bosses to employ a registered migrant labour force. These 'regulatory' negatives from a transient worker perspective are challenges to the overall rights-based regulatory strategy that is advocated medium-term. Beyond the short-term, through employer reconditioning to narrowing profit margins on the back of worker exploitation, pressuring worker empowerment to be more strongly positioned at any bargaining table, and tighter efforts at minimising access to *black* and exploitative labour markets, the hip-pocket negatives may be ameliorated and the market made more responsible.

The next chapter recognises this immediate market dilemma, but in terms of social sustainability, particularly for countries with aging populations and declining birth rates, migration in general is one of the critical components in rebalancing socio-demographics into the future.[4] Labour markets and their viability are crucially wedded to this reality. It is not with her heart on her sleeve that the German Chancellor has been recently so strident in her attacks on Britain's efforts to restrict migration movement across the EU. The Chancellor, clearly cognisant of the demographics of her country now and into the future, is counting on ready access to cheap migrant labour and through domestic law and its selective regulatory inaction has created laissez faire market conditions even inconsistent with EU labour force equality provisions.[5] Chapter 6 startlingly reveals how the commitment to free labour movement represents a regulatory policy ruled by economic growth imperatives above worker rights and job security in domestic or migrant labour contexts.

This chapter has two purposes. First is, by exposing the exploitative potential of agency in migrant worker arrangements, to make clear the case for regulation towards market sustainability. Second, rather than

---

[4] Interestingly in some closely culturally managed states such as Singapore it is not a preferred common approach. This could be explained by the aversion among civil society in general to migrants based on problematic perceptions about challenges in the labour market, sub-standard socialisation, and eventual overcrowding and drains on resources/infrastructure.

[5] Wintour and Traynor (2014).

radical surgery for the employment agency sector, the chapter offers ways in which, through a restoration of equitable fiduciary spirit, the original responsible agency frames can return to the migrant labour market.

It is also intended here to provide a bridge into the more detailed empirical work in the chapter to follow. The methodological structure in that chapter will comparatively interrogate some crucial decision sites in the migration progress of workers from home to host markets. Important in managing the decisions made at many of these points is agency.

To commence this analysis, we return to a consideration of labour pricing and the pivotal role played by agents in its artificial positioning. We want to emphasise that a sustainable labour market can rest on fair labour pricing, but in a world dependent on differential labour value, and diminishing opportunities for well-paid wage labour, sustainable markets must look to evolving other social bonds of value.

LABOUR PRICE SETTING: TOWARDS DECENT WORK

Structural regulatory reforms, particularly directed towards responsible, balanced and transparent agency arrangements, we argue, can advance the sustainability of labour markets through involving a reconsideration of labour pricing which will not necessarily endanger the relative but rational economic attractiveness of this labour force. In addition, such reform should have the consequential effect of opening up labour opportunities that are artificially constrained at the bottom of the employment ladder due to the general undervaluing of migrant labour.

In his report 'Fair Migration: Setting an ILO Agenda', the Director General observes:

> It is crucial to recognize that the first policy response to this situation must be to promote decent work opportunities in countries where they are currently inadequate. The UN post-2015 development agenda is an opportunity to give renewed impetus to the shared responsibility to promote decent jobs and social protection everywhere. There is *no corresponding responsibility on any one country to compensate demographic shortfalls in any other. This is what gives meaning to the idea that migration should be an option available to individuals and not an obligation imposed upon them.* It also gains force from our knowledge that international labour markets do not respond perfectly to pricing signals. There are many reasons why people prefer to stay at home even if a higher income and better conditions could be had elsewhere.[6] (emphasis added)

---

[6] International Labour Office (2014), pp. 6–7.

Decent work is not just about better pay. The precarious features of migration registration regularly require migrant workers to accept job opportunities that do not recognise their professional qualifications or work experience obtained beyond the host jurisdiction. The more active representation of workers' *marketability* through committed and truly representative agency engagement might be one pathway to rectifying their artificial denigration of value.

At the outset of discussing agency/law relationships in the context of migrant labour force, there is a stark contradiction. Particularly in the Asian dimension of our empirical case studies to follow it is an absence of legal regulatory influence that marks out the *ungovernability* of agency. Despite this lacunae it is worthwhile examining the potentials of law's influence in migrant employment agency even if only for the recognition that the legitimacy it provides will come with the price of some minimal accountability.

The pressure for agency reform is both internal and external to market arrangements. Employers, particularly until recently in the EU, have tried to avoid agency engagements due to high service costs (a transition discussed more fully in Chapter 6). This aversion against agency is shifting in an employment and migration climate where it is becoming more complicated to negotiate the transfer of migrant workers across the external barriers of Fortress Europe. Workers have always resented what they see as high agency bond fees for little truly representative service. From the workers' perspective they are indentured to the employer's agent. This reluctant requirement has led to informal networks of information transfer from migrants in the host country with experience of the pitfalls in the process, to potential migrant workers back home.

There are two particular analytical drivers for this chapter which will assist in the formulation of strategies directed towards sustainable work-force market arrangements. The first addresses the nature of dependency contexts identified in Chapter 2. It is argued that if traditional agency relationships can have stronger enunciation in the migrant worker market frame, then staged agency responsibility can be more clearly apportioned and the conditions for improved autonomous and efficient contracting will follow. The second theme is that of transition. As noted already, in our comparative empirical endeavour (see Chapter 6) migrant labour flows are examined home to host, and important decision sites present fertile comparative contexts for understanding the *push-pull* effects of globalised labour marketing. This chapter sets the scene to interrogate what role law plays in facilitating these often exploitative flows and how that influence can be redirected with sustainability and viability as dominant principles and market outcomes.

TRUST OR SUBMISSION?

Agency, like contract, is another area of social engagement depending more on trust than enforcement. The theme of *good faith* is prominent. In migrant labour agency practice, however, we see precious little evidence of trust bonds for the general good. Oxford University's International Migration Institute recently published 'Migrant Workers and Labour Agency: Social actors or submissive players'.[7] The abstract of the paper noted regarding a shift away from prevailing market agency arrangements:

> … migration leads to high levels of clustering in the low and unskilled segments of the labour market followed by limited progression thereafter. Involvement in classical collective labour movements is low but other daily strategies are employed to navigate the labour market mostly involving individual agency. Recognising these processes of mostly individual agency targeting self-improvement has implications for understanding the limits and potential of wider labour struggles seeking to tackle structural exploitation of migrant labour within destination labour markets. In addition, looking at distinct migration corridors, linking different origin and destination countries, also puts in evidence the specific contextual frameworks that shape migrants' agency in particular labour markets.

On accessing labour markets and agency influence more specifically the paper concludes:

> The recognition of individual-level agency is important to understand the nuanced processes of labour struggles (Cumbers et al. 2010: 57) but also to grasp the extent to which migrants may be willing or encouraged to join larger (collective) labour demands and calls for a further understanding of 'labour consciousness' and its implications for labour agency (Bergene 2010) in migration processes. In addition, when looking at labour's agency it is important to think not only of 'how much' or 'in what way' but also 'whose agents' are involved in contexts of uneven power relations (Coe and Jhordus-Lier 2011: 216, Gregson 2005: 29) and potentially with conflicting interests (for example national workers vs immigrant workers, older vs more recent workers, etc). Who is empowered to contribute to changes in particular structures? How are the disenfranchised and most vulnerable groups able to contribute to change and develop agency capabilities, for example in articulation with other, more powerful, groups?[8]

---

7 Pereira (2014).

8 Pereira (2014), p. 16.

This quote sums up just the sorts of questions that the analysis of migrant employment agency within disembedded labour markets should be confronting. In particular, it challenges the specific direction of the agency relationship (and by implication any conflicts of interest which arise out of dual agency commitments common in these markets). The research agrees that even with the development of individual agency arrangements, migrant workers are submissive players rather than social actors when it comes to taking charge of their livelihoods. Despite any pre-existing academic, professional and work experiences, due to their *contexts of reception,* large percentages of this labour force cluster at the bottom of the occupational ladder. Such disconnects suggest:

> … the overwhelmingly conditioning role played by structures in the destination countries in processes of labour market incorporation. These include the labour market itself (particularly of labour demand or employment practices) but also immigration regimes or structures available to migrants for example for the acquisition of language skills, recognition of qualifications or further education. Simultaneously, the analysis provided here reveals that migrants are also able to perform the 'social actor' role and to act in ways that enable them to gain access to more qualified positions in the labour market, with time of residency, namely by investing in further education and language acquisition; and negotiate more favourable labour market positions within the same occupational levels … negotiations take place at the micro-scale of migrants' working lives which impact on their subjective experiences of employment, and agency is exerted in more nuanced ways than has been generally acknowledged (exceptions mentioned by Cumbers et al. 2010: 54), thereby constituting mostly individual agency through reworking and resilience (Katz 2004 in Coe and Jordhus-Lier 2011: 216). Collective labour agency articulated either through community based institutions or origin country structures or in association with destination country social and labour movements is less evident …[9]

This is a story of workers 'doing it for themselves' often against the exploitation of private agencies, inadequate access to community agency, and the woeful failing of state representation for their interests. If formalised agency relations are failing the migrant labour market from the perspective of labour power then, without the generation of positive legal environments, the potential for agency through *resistance* will grow. Along with the redirection of contract, our challenge for law as regulation is the facilitation of a more (pro) active role for labour as an agent shaping the economic geographies of capitalism.[10]

---

9 Pereira (2014), p. 17.

10 Bergene, Endresen and Knutsen (2010), p. 4.

AGENCY – THE FIDUCIARY WHEEL

Contract is not the only supposedly private consensual relationship woven into the common law. Agency and trust are two significant fiduciary relationships. It has been argued that as a vehicle for empowering and protecting otherwise weak contracting stakeholders, agency for instance, enhanced by equity and reinforced by prudent confidential relationships, can provide fertile ground for regulatory repositioning.[11]

If agency establishes a fiduciary relationship then the agent is required to recognise duties of prudence. In so doing the questions emerge: duties to whom, prudence regarding what?

In the progression of labour migration, detailed in the empirical comparisons to follow (Chapter 6), agency is a force for denying any general fiduciary environments, favouring agent self-interest and employer exploitation. As co-conspirator, the state fails to require through law even similar agency obligations that might be imposed in the transaction of real estate, or the responsibilities of company directors. Why should this be so?

In the agency literature fiduciary duties are often discussed primarily in terms of agency cost and the risks associated with breach of duty.[12] There is little need for such consternation when examining relationships between agents and migrant workers. Duties of agency in this employment context and at all its increments remain unclear and often unstated. The migrant is largely disempowered and deeply obligated (financially and for the perpetuation of residency) so that even if breaches in any duty were apparent they would either not be actioned or the migrant would not have effective standing in any of the limited avenues of recourse. It would be similar to suggesting that the slave or the indentured servant only had to have identified a breach of duty and the law would spring into action, or even more unlikely, the light of fiduciary loyalty would require the agent to *do the right thing*.

Gloomy as this might sound against the most basic power/obligation analysis we are not inclined to dismiss fiduciary bonds as a possible pathway for law to bolster the emancipating power of agency. There is a somewhat unrelated school of thinking interested in agency and trust protection; that is the safeguarding of equitable trusts. In the quest for dignity laid out more specifically in the conclusion of this work, we intend to borrow this notion for another purpose – agents as the

---

11 Rounds (2009).
12 Alexander (2000); Sterk (2005).

protectors of essential trust relationships on which sustainable labour relationships must be built.

The analysis later in this chapter will locate such an aspiration beyond utopia. If the regulatory principle of social sustainability is accepted then:

- the conventional role of the agent as the 'go-between' bridging stakeholder interests can be active in requiring fiduciary compliance with negotiated terms, and accepting the challenges posed by any conflict of interest; and
- the law can require of the agent a responsible exercise of their duties to either or both stakeholder parties, above and beyond agency self-interest.

It is not so difficult to suggest a principled framework whereby fiduciary consciousness should guide agency relationships and obligations. What becomes more challenging is tackling interest issues that would undermine or compromise higher order fiduciary considerations. In the more recent development of agency law, fiduciary bonds are grounded in loyalty to the principal. This has sometimes provided a smoke-screen for doing the principal's bidding no matter what. In the migrant employment setting, however, where the relationship between employer and principal can arise quite far along the migration process, and much has been committed by the time it is struck, then there have been many other interests at work on the agency frame, and some of these at least may neither be to the benefit of the worker nor the employer. Agent self-interest looms as a significant impediment to the activation of uniform fiduciary bonds.

Another, and perhaps more equitable and potent representation of fiduciary duties in the context of agency, is trust, and the generation and maintenance of trust relationships. Generally, two-party agency arrangements would not operate successfully outside a general climate of mutual trust. In two directional agency bonds (common in the migrant labour setting) the trust pendulum has swung in favour of the agent–employer side. Even in a practical sense this presents dangers for the agent in a medium-term commercial sense and for the two-directional relationship all along. The more that workers are unable to trust agents and see the fees they charge as a tax rather than an impost for valuable service, the greater will be the push to avoid agency facilitated migration or to develop individual agency arrangements. Regarding the agent/employer engagement, the commencement of relationships with the worker based on a trust deficit eventually will impact productivity and workplace stability, even insidiously. Therefore, fiduciary roles embraced by the agent as a trust mediator will have very clear benefits for all parties which are as yet not realised.

AGENCY LAW AND RESPONSIBILITIES

Agency is a legal relationship that is crucial to any modern legal system because most contemporary global commerce is carried out by *agents* working for their *principal*. The law of agency covers both personal *and* business activities which principals authorise and agents perform on their behalf, and for the interests of third parties. The formalities of a contract or consideration are not necessary in order to have an agency relationship, though they are very often present.

Agency is a *conductor of liability*. It represents an agreement by one person (an agent) to act *for* a principal at the principal's direction and control. Agency law is concerned with any principal/agent relationship, in which one person has legal authority to act for another or others depending on the extent of their legal engagement and subsequent duties. Such relationships arise from explicit appointment or by implication.

Agents are firstly responsible to their principals and then to third parties such as potential employees in workplace arrangements. In migrant worker facilitation, the agent is not simply operating with the worker as a third-party stakeholder. In the migration process there is commonly a chain of agency through which, particularly with domestic workers, there may be no relationship initially connecting the eventual employer with the worker, when a host country agent liaises with a home country agency to attract a *stock* of labour that then may be made available to employers who shop for services through this stock.

Concerning the principal, the agent needs to:

- perform duties delegated
- act loyally
- demonstrate obedience
- comply with duties to account
- act with care and skill

If these responsibilities are forthcoming then the agent can expect reciprocal responsibilities from the principal. In terms of the agent's (and through them, the principal's) responsibility to third parties these are somewhat further removed and may be dependent on contractual terms. Generally, however, they involve duties to:

- perform contracted terms
- act fairly and in good faith
- not commit tortious damage or harm against the third party
- not make fraudulent representations
- not misappropriate funds not belonging to the principal or agent consistent with any express or implied terms

From these responsibilities generate duties that are mutual, and which, unfortunately, if directed towards exclusive private property arrangements, may not be governed by fiduciary principle.

AGENCY RELATIONSHIPS

The law of agency is based on the maxim *he who acts through another is deemed in law to do it himself.* Because of the commercial emphasis in agency dealings, agency practice has tended to be committed to a narrow range of commercial self-interests, including that of the agent. Through the acts of the agent, the principal and a third party may be brought into a contractual relationship.

The agent may have the power to dispose of property of the principal to a third party. Generally the agent's acts have such effect because the principal has authorised the agent to do the acts in question and the agent has agreed. The agent in a sense becomes an extension of the principal and is therefore capable of altering the principal's legal position either by binding him to a contract or effecting a binding disposal of the principal's property.

The principal may authorise the agent to perform a variety of tasks or may restrict the agent to specific functions, but regardless of the amount, or scope, of authority given to the agent, the agent represents the principal and is subject to the principal's control. More importantly, the principal is liable for the consequences of acts that the agent has been directed to perform.

An agency relationship is created by the consent of both the agent and the principal; no one can unwittingly become an agent for another. The intent of the parties can be expressed by their words or implied by their conduct.

Conventionally, if the analogy is drawn with a real estate agency, the agent acts on behalf of the owner of property in order to introduce them to potential buyers. With migrant labour markets, unless the agent is engaged by an employer to seek out labour from a host country, it could be assumed that the worker has her labour as property and the agent links this to the potential employer/purchaser. Were these to be the conditions of the agency arrangement then the agent clearly acts for the worker/principal, generating the responsibilities which this relationship should require. Not so in practice. Due to the earlier discussed (Chapter 2) disempowerment of migrant labourers from the first stage of the agency chain, and the eventual dispossession of their ownership of their labour, the agent is more likely to eschew responsibility to the worker, preferring to act as an independent subcontractor in the labour market process.

AUTHORISATION AND DELEGATION

Agency, like the principles behind contracting, relies on trust. The agency arrangement is said to be created through the voluntary agreement of autonomous parties. A voluntary, *good faith* relationship of trust, a fiduciary relationship, exists between a principal and an agent for the benefit of the principal. This relationship requires the agent to exercise a duty of loyalty to the principal and to use reasonable care to serve and protect the interests of the principal. In theory at least, an agent who acts in his or her own interest violates the fiduciary duty and will be financially liable to the principal for any losses the principal incurs because of that breach. This translates into a deeply problematic web of responsibilities in migrant labour agency contexts. Agents are more likely to see workers as having binding responsibilities to them, and through disempowerment, rarely put themselves out to ensure the best interests of the worker after the contract has been signed.

Perhaps the most important element of a principal/agent relationship is the concept of control. The extent of the principal's control over the agent distinguishes an agent from an *independent contractor*, over whom control and supervision by the principal may be relatively remote. An independent contractor is subject to the control of an employer only to the extent that she or he must produce the final work product that she or he has agreed to provide. Independent contractors have the freedom to use whatever means they choose to achieve that final product. When the employer provides more specific directions, or exerts more control, as to the means and methods of doing the job, then an agency relationship may exist.

If host agents are perceived as independent contractors then they still retain all the obligations in the contract connection discussed in the previous chapter. Again, as a consequence of worker disempowerment and their knowledge deficit in the contracting situation, agents regularly obtain inordinate financial advantage, due to the largely deregulated environment in which they obtain and offer labour force.

The agent's authority may be actual or apparent. If the principal intentionally confers on the agent express and implied powers to act for him or her, the agent possesses *actual authority*. Certain powers, being a necessary part of the express duties of the agent, are implied. When the agent performs any or all of these duties, whether express or implied, it is as if the principal has done so in their own right.

A more complicated situation arises when the agent possesses *apparent authority*. In this case, the principal, either knowingly or even mistakenly, permits the agent or others to assume that the agent possesses authority to carry out certain actions when such authority does not, in fact, exist. If other persons believe in good faith that such authority exists, the principal remains liable for the agent's actions and cannot rely on the defence that no actual authority was granted.

This scenario rings true in the context of migrant labour agency. Particularly large-scale migrant labour employers know from experience that host and home agents regularly misrepresent the terms and conditions of eventual employment. Even so it is rare to find an employer sanctioning an agent for this practice or specifically instructing against it.[13]

The scope of an agent's authority, whether apparent or actual, is considered in determining an agent's liability for their actions. An agent is not personally liable to a third party for a contract the agent has entered into as a representative of the principal so long as the agent acted within the scope of her or his authority and signed the contract as agent for the principal. The agent may be sued by the other party to the contract for fraud.

Many migrant labour employment contracts contain terms endeavouring to specifically exempt agents and principals from the impact of more general legal obligations. Under these provisions, workers can be forced to indemnify the agent/principal for what might otherwise amount to legal liability or obligation.

UNDISCLOSED AGENCY

A major difficulty in migrant labour agency transactions is determining who provides the agent with authority and for whose benefit they may be

[13] Tan (2013a).

employed. To advantage the employer in later disputes over work conditions and remuneration it may be beneficial for employers to conceal the nature of agency and the terms on which it is struck. In addition to such obfuscation for commercial advantage, the employment agent acts in an agency web or chain, rather than a direct line of delegation:

- Host agents engage potential workers on terms which they independently represent or which can be conveyed down to them from future employers and the agencies in the host jurisdictions.
- Agencies in the home country bargain with agents in the host, and can even establish cross-agency arrangements to their mutual advantage.
- Host agencies can take over agency arrangements with the workers on arrival and seek contractual benefit from the worker.
- The host state, through agents, can negotiate migration arrangements with the home state and the constraint on transferring benefit.
- The host agent can take on the potential employer as a principal and generate strong conflicts of interest between their agency obligations with workers, and those with the employer–contractor.

Under the law of agency, there is a peculiar feature known as *undisclosed agency*. Essentially, where an agent enters into a contract intending to do so on behalf of the agent's principal, provided the agent was acting within the scope of the agent's authority, the principal may as a general rule sue and be sued on the contract even though the principal's existence (and not merely his identity) was unknown to the third party.

The doctrine has been criticised[14] for enabling contractual benefits to be claimed by a non-contracting party against the third party who was altogether unaware of the existence of the undisclosed principal. The privity in contract is obviously challenged by such undisclosed obligations.

In undisclosed agency contexts, the initial contract is one made between the third party and the agent in the agent's personal capacity. Since the third party believed that he was dealing with the agent, and the agent did not contract in a representative capacity, the agent apparently assumed personal liability under the contract. The agent may therefore sue and be sued on the agreement.

---

14 Ames (1909); Barnett (1987); Higgins (1965).

This arrangement could pertain to both home and host agency in migrant labour transactions. In terms of the issuance of work permits by the host state, agents' engagement of labour preceding successful placement is premised on the eventual labour contracting, which may present a contract arrangement in addition to any struck earlier in the agency chain. In such circumstances there is uncertainty, often to the employer's advantage, about what contractual terms prevail. The assumed independence of the host agent in particular may go some way to explain the powers they can exercise over migrant workers in terms of their migration status.[15]

Undisclosed agency has been justified on the basis of commercial convenience. Often, persons act for someone else without disclosing this fact. This is not necessarily attempting to perpetrate fraud but because the existence and identity of the principal may be of little importance to the other party. It might also be that the agent sometimes acts on his own account and sometimes for others, and it is impractical to segregate these various transactions. The agency web here (where the agent can be engaged by another agent, by a worker, and with the intention of engagement with future employers) considerably complicates hierarchies of duty and responsibility in the migrant labour market.

Agents might not disclose a prevailing obligation to a principal because the agent does not want the other party to bypass his or her commercial involvement through negotiating directly with the principal. In other situations, a principal may not want the market to know, for business reasons of any direct involvement in a transaction, and therefore employs an agent to appear to be acting for her/himself. The confusion that this process of concealment presents for inexperienced and ill-informed workers further contributes to their market disempowerment.

UNCERTAIN AGENCY TRIANGULATION

The supervision hierarchy in many agency/worker/employer relationships is far from clear or conventional. This uncertainty, particularly from the worker perspective, is exacerbated when:

- there are several agents with which the worker will have contact performing different roles along the chain;

---

[15] The status of the home agent is certainly not as a representative of the worker's interests even in the negotiation of the original contract terms of engagement. See Findlay and Lim (2014a), p. 201.

- onshore and offshore agents do not clearly operate in agency relationships one to the other;
- agents appear to be acting more in their own commercial self-interest as sub-contractors;
- agents operate with different legal and informal agreements, revealing various levels of clarity and specificity;
- jurisdictional divides mean that the relevant laws applicable to agency services and arrangements may not be consistent along the chain; and
- the eventual employer expects that terms negotiated by workers and agents at different decision points along the migration flow will not eventually be binding in any finalised employment arrangement.

As Collins observes about agency realities in employment settings when compared with more conventional principal/agency bilaterals:

> In my view the model proves too simple to provide an explanation of efficient properties of many of these business relations. A more sophisticated explanation recognises the fact that the business relation is better characterised by the presence of two principal and agent relations. These contracts have been dubbed 'symbolic contracts' … In these contracts there is a crossed principal and agent relation: each party both acts as the agent for the other, and as a principal in its own right.[16]

Even this elaboration of agency relations and obligations leaves concealed the imbalance for workers, through market disempowerment, where they may never be so positioned as to claim the benefits of a principal. What arises in these market contexts are asymmetries in the agency supervision/responsibility requirements governing an agent. Regulation needs to intervene to correct the imbalance not only to limit agency opportunism but rather to address lop-sided governance structures.[17]

AGENCY CHAINS AND PATHWAYS OF TRANSITION

This section is a precursor to the more detailed comparative examination of crucial decision sites along the migrant worker journey (focusing on

[16] Collins (1999), p. 239.
[17] As discussed by Collins (1999), p. 241.

migrant domestic worker experience),[18] developed in the chapter to follow. For our purposes here we aim to specifically identify the role of agents at these points, as they create private property relationships and in so doing offer opportunities for regulation. Brief reference will be made to different jurisdictional contexts in EU and ASEAN Member States. These examples will also benefit from broader elaboration in the upcoming chapter and will be looked at in terms of more stakeholder influence than agency.

Stage 1: Before the Move – Role of the Migrant Domestic Labour Agent

Apart from using their own contacts, migrant workers rely on intermediaries such as agents, recruiters, smugglers, consultants and so on to facilitate their progress through migration employment pathways.[19] Within the migration industry,[20] migration agents broker scarce information about migration routes, job opportunities or the means of integrating into the host society.[21] As most of the information needed for this transition is difficult to obtain by prospective workers unless they have contacts in the host situation, and many of the administrative requirements for migration residency and labour licensing are complex and designed for agent intervention and management, agents expect to be paid fees from the outset for passing on information.

The first experience of agency for the aspiring worker is with migration agents in the home country. Elrick and Lewandowska propose a three-staged migration framework to highlight the varying significance of the migration agent as worker experience of the migration chain develops.[22] This is in some limited degree an example of worker empowerment through access to knowledge and understanding (discussed in more detail in Chapter 4). The first stage is of 'agent-domination', where migration is facilitated by agents who passively or actively recruit prospective workers. Agents are usually more proactive at the very

---

[18] Migrant domestic workers have been selected from the main categories of migrant labour employment due to the commonality of market demand across the market sites, and the similarities between sending nations and the work profile required by receiving employers. In this selection we recognise the constraint on the analysis in not covering large commercial labour employers and their considerable economic/political influence.

[19] Elrick and Lewandowska (2008).

[20] Castles (2007).

[21] Elrick and Lewandowska (2008), p. 722.

[22] Elrick and Lewandowska (2008), p. 727.

beginning of a new migration outflow,[23] trying to win over potential employees by personally visiting the villages to advertise their services and the benefits of work abroad. More passive recruitment is where potential migrants who know about the agents' existence contact them directly.

In the second stage, the role of agents diminishes as pioneer migrants start to develop their own networks in the destination country. Some pioneers become agents, setting up their own businesses to exploit their competitive advantage over other migrants (this being largely prohibited in ASEAN host states).

The third stage is where migrant networks mature and migrants are able to access the knowledge of other migrants from their community without being charged a fee. However, agents remain important, as workers need to negotiate the complexities of foreign migration documentation.

According to Singapore's Ministry of Manpower (MOM), there are about 1,000 active agencies specialising in migrant domestic work for the Singapore market.[24] While there are no statistics on the prevalence of the use of migrant domestic workers' agents for employment facilitation in that jurisdiction, it is uncommon for migrant domestic workers (MDWs) to be employed without the help of an agent, and the state openly endorses the use of migration agents through press releases and published guidelines.[25] The Singaporean agencies usually work with their counterparts in the home countries, enabling local recruitment. In this preparatory arrangement we have arguably two levels of agency; home migration agent to worker, and host employment agency to home migration agents.

Some Singaporean migration agents also work with illegal, unlicensed or unregistered recruiters based in the sending countries. These illegal recruiters are paid their cut of the transfer fees upfront, while the receiving agencies deduct the total sum in monthly instalments from the MDWs' salaries, which can amount to as much as eight out of 24 months of the MDWs' employment contract.[26] This extortionate practice has led to recrimination in some home jurisdictions.[27] Obviously extortionate agency placement charges present a regulatory opportunity for the home

---

23 Massey D. et al (1987).

24 Ministry of Manpower, Singapore website, Employment Agency Search.

25 Ministry of Manpower, Singapore, *Your Guide to Employing a Foreign Domestic Worker*, p. 19.

26 Dancel (2014).

27 In 2013, the Association of Licensed Recruitment Agencies to Singapore (ALRAS), a group which represents 120 of around 150 Philippine recruitment

state to crack down on Singapore agents using home recruiters that rely on these crippling *spotters fees*. No coordinated state-to-state approach for controlling initial agency charges is currently in place across ASEAN and therefore the first stage of exploitation spills over into the worker's obligations once employed in Singapore. Workers can face introduction/identification fees, home transfer charges, and all on top of the placement fees that Singapore agents will require of them. Such a major financial burden at the stage of the migration process when workers are least able to carry the cost creates multi-levelled dependency relationships. In particular, new migrant workers are in such vulnerable positions arising from identification and transportation costs at home that they are willing to accept any employment conditions which host agencies have on offer for their labour value.

Despite decades of migrant labour flow into Singapore, the migration network has not been enabled through regulation to 'mature' and market controls are set against this outcome. For example, the MDWs cannot become agents in their own right as they are refused residency and work permits when they cease to be employed as MDWs. This limitation on labour mobility acts against migrant labour organisation, collective empowerment and labour bargaining. Without a critical mass of MDWs who are working long-term in Singapore, the (informational) value of the MDW agent cannot be replaced.

In Singapore MDW agents have to be licensed under the Employment Agency Act (EAA). For renewal of their operating licence, the agents have to be registered by either of the two accreditation bodies, the Association of Employment Agencies (Singapore) or CaseTrust. Both of these bodies are in reality self-regulating associations. Four key amendments regarding agency legitimacy were made to the EAA in 1984, involving tighter accreditation requirements for the agencies, fee caps and refunds on agency fees paid by MDWs, and changes to the licensing framework for agencies and the security deposit framework. Offences and penalties have also been enhanced, such as increasing the penalty for unlicensed agencies from a maximum fine of SGD 5,000 to a maximum fine of SGD 80,000 and/or up to two years' imprisonment for first-time offenders. The problem with the direction of these regulatory initiatives is that they continue to rely on the probity of the agencies and their

firms that supply MDWs to Singapore, suspended sending of MDWs to Singapore to press for a ban on placement fees. It resumed business a month later after it received commitment from 60 per cent of some 300 Singaporean agencies that they would stop taking placement fees or keep them to two months' worth of salary from the MDWs. See Dancel (2014).

associations, which are regularly called into question by NGOs with an interest in migrant labour. If the state is to divest crucial work condition obligations and management to a group which have proved themselves to be self-interested stakeholders, then the self-regulatory association oversight requires responsibilising at the very least against a code of conduct which workers can consult and upon which they can take action in situations of breach.

In Malaysia, the state also relies on MDW agencies as significant actors in bringing in MDWs for local families. However, the regulation of MDW agencies is loose. While MDW agencies have to be registered under the Private Employment Agencies Act 1981 ('PEAA'),[28] the state does not require these agencies to be certified in terms of subject matter knowledge.[29] Though the PEAA states that fees charged for local placement should not exceed 20 per cent of the initial month's pay, this is not applied to MDW agency fees, which can be up to a few months' worth of the MDW's salary.

Additionally, the state seems ready to accede to the agents' requests, even in situations when the agents' position is contrary to an agreement between Malaysia and another country. In 2011, Malaysia and Indonesia signed a memorandum of understanding to lift the moratorium on the supply of Indonesian domestic workers which was imposed in June 2009. The memorandum of understanding included a cap on the fees charged by MDW agents and minimum conditions such as minimum monthly wage at SGD 320 and a mandated day of rest per week.[30] However, the Malaysian state subsequently allowed local agencies to charge a fee that was higher than the agreed amount, causing Indonesia to reactivate a ban on sending its women to work in Malaysia as MDWs in 2012.[31]

Stage 2: Entry into the Receiving Country – Status of the Migrant Domestic Worker

Migrant domestic workers enter Singapore and Malaysia via a *front door policy*; gaining residency to work on contract in a defined job for a specified number of years.[32] Under this policy, governmental regulations

---

28 Act 246 (Malaysia).

29 To be registered, the agency need only provide proof of registration as any other businesses. See Department of Labour, Malaysia website, Issue of Private Employment Agency Licence.

30 Ahmad, Zolkepli and Yuen (2013).

31 Aruna (2013).

32 Yamanaka (1999), p. 479.

designed to manage immigration flows require employers to pay a levy upon hiring each employee, and a security bond to ensure her exit upon completion of the MDW contract.[33] While the MDW is protected under general laws, they are largely excluded from the regulatory coverage of the relevant employment acts (discussed in more detail in Chapter 6).

As noted above, compounding their regulatory vulnerability and market disempowering, MDWs are prevented from joining the mainstream labour market beyond the specific job justifying their work permit (unless a transfer to a comparable position has been specifically approved by the migration/labour authorities and is further contingent on securing residency outside the terms and conditions of their original employment engagement).[34] At the expiry of their work contract (or its termination) migrant domestic workers must leave Singapore within seven days,[35] and are not guaranteed other residency permits outside the original work permit conditions even if they are married to a resident or citizen. Such policies it is argued are effective in regulating the MDW population numbers, while favouring employers' interests in times of economic downturn, or where the employer and worker may be in dispute.[36] In addition, state regulatory intervention is more about revenue raising and residency enforcement (along with the prevention of labour mobility and residency permanence) than it is the protection of minimum workplace conditions.

In the European experience, migrant domestic workers from other parts of EU enter Germany, for example, to work as MDWs on special work permits. These are highly regulated and limited in quantity.[37] Germany and new EU Member States came to an agreement in 2002 that citizens from these emerging jurisdictions are allowed to perform domestic work (but not care work) in Germany for three-year periods.[38] It appears that the proportion of households subscribing to this scheme is insignificant relative to the estimated number of MDWs employed by German

---

33 Grugel and Piper (2007), p. 77.

34 Yeoh (2006), p. 31.

35 Wong (1997).

36 Yeoh (2006), p. 31.

37 Helma (2008).

38 This agreement was made between the German 'Zentralstelle für Arbeitsvermittlung' (German Federal Employment Office) and the new EU Member States in 2002. These MDWs from Eastern European states work 38.5 hours per week and they receive monthly wages between EUR 1,000 and EUR 1,400 before tax.

households through other means, such as Au Pair arrangements and unregistered employment.[39]

Specifically, migrant domestic workers from non-EU states enter Germany to work, perform cleaning and child caring work as Au Pairs, utilising a visa which is ostensibly meant for cultural exchange.[40] Apart from the Au Pair culture, other MDWs enter the country on a tourist visa or apply for student visas and *over-stay* after its expiry. Such visas only provide the right to reside in Germany and do not allow for employment aid. Therefore, this black market labour force operates totally beyond the regulatory web of registered migrant labour, and is even more open to exploitation due to the suspect nature of worker's residency and employment status, along with more general age, gender, language and residency dependency issues.

Overall, if MDWs form part of the legitimate/registered work frame (more likely in ASEAN jurisdictions than EU states) then the regulation of the legal status of the MDW is through migration and work permit strictures creating the vulnerability and dependency relations discussed in Chapter 2. These relationships are uniquely likely to involve exploitation as a consequence of the domestic setting. The state establishes and mandates the migration/residency/work permit regime, then often relies for its administration on migration agents to perform a distributive function in favour of the employers and themselves. The migration/labour nexus ensures a steady supply of MDWs for the market, offering services which might otherwise be required of state institutions, and contributing significantly to consolidated revenue through worker levies. When the state uses regulation to play a market corrective function (such as an increase in levies to temper market demand), its consequences seldom favour the MDW, as against its own interests or those of more powerful domestic market stakeholders.

Stage 3: Decent Working Conditions and Terms

Employment contract-drafting for migrant domestic workers in Singapore is a function delegated to the MDW agent. As part of their accreditation process, the agent has to learn basic principles of contract law. Meanwhile, the Ministry of Manpower (the relevant state executive agency) encourages the use of a standard form MDW employment contract and

---

[39] About 9,000 households have taken advantage of the programme since it was installed in 2005. Compared to figures of an estimated 600,000 migrants being employed in German households in total, these figures appear marginal.

[40] Hess (2005).

provides a template for the agents' use.[41] That said, agents are not required to ensure that agreements between the MDWs and their employers are specified in written contracts.

In 2007, Malaysia and Singapore, along with other Member States of ASEAN, declared their concern for migrant workers in the region.[42] However, despite the non-binding nature of the declaration, to date, the ASEAN Instrument on the Protection and Promotion of the Rights of the Migrant Workers has not been generally adopted by member nations.

Within the receiving (host) states, such as Singapore and Malaysia, the governments promulgate broad guidelines on ensuring work conditions and access to justice, which may be seen as an informal response to threats by sending countries to ban the movement of MDWs to these receiving countries in the wake of cases of serious worker abuse.[43] It should be noted that in neither of these host countries do agents provide any inspectorate function to ensure that conditions of work are in compliance with their contracted arrangements.

Malaysia has no definition of 'domestic work' in the Employment Act 1995. Further, MDWs are defined as 'servants' and are excluded from otherwise prevailing legislated employment regulations relating to rest days, hours of work and termination benefits. There is no minimum wage policy in both Malaysia and Singapore.

The Ministry of Manpower (MOM) in Singapore issues guidelines to MDW employers concerning employer obligations, employment application processes and advice on other facets of MDW working conditions.[44] Matters highlighted in such pronouncements include the use of an employment contract, management of salary payment, safety in high-rise buildings, and other well-being concerns such as the employer's bearing of medical costs, provision of accommodation, rest and so on. However, there is no mention of the recommended wage rate, reasonable work load, or mandatory rest days. In addition, MOM provides passive enforcement channels,[45] where aggrieved parties could call for assistance. There is no active enforcement of the conditions contained in the guidelines. Fundamental health and safety issues such as the wearing of harnesses when window cleaning at heights, and the provision of rest

---

41 Ministry of Manpower, Singapore website, Service Agreement Between Foreign Domestic Worker Employer and Employment Agency.

42 Arifin (2012), p. 32.

43 Habibu and Kong (2009).

44 Ministry of Manpower, Singapore, *Your Guide to Employing a Foreign Domestic Worker*.

45 Ministry of Manpower, Singapore website. Report to us.

days have not progressed beyond administrative guidelines despite the tragic history of loss of life, and of worker depression and suicide. There is, therefore, no legislative pathway for judicial oversight of worker conditions in the Asian host jurisdictions such as Singapore.

As will be developed in more detail in the next chapter, the protective jurisdiction of the European Court of Human Rights (ECHR) is applicable to every worker within the EU whether they are contracted and registered, or unlawful migrants.[46] The provision of judicial oversight in this form is a profound difference to the manner of legal regulation in ASEAN states such as Malaysia and Singapore.

EU Member States are obliged to guarantee the right of workers to enjoy just and favourable conditions of work, that is, to ensure safe and healthy working conditions (Article 7(b)). Detailed labour law standards exist across EU states, many drawn from international convention compliance (although some International Labour Organization (ILO) instruments contain clauses that allow exceptions for migrant workers). EU Council Directive 89/391/EEC on the safety and health of workers excludes coverage of domestic servants. Member States such as Italy have enacted specific legal regimes regulating domestic work in their general labour laws, but this is not the norm throughout the EU.[47] In addition, because domestic and care work in the EU is so widely the province of unregistered migrant workers, their conditions of work and safety remain largely ungoverned.

Under Article 30 of the EU Charter of Fundamental Rights, every worker has the right to protection against unjustified dismissal, in accordance with Union law *and national laws and practices*. The Termination of Employment Convention, 1982 (No. 158) requires a valid reason for the termination of employment, however domestic workers are again excluded from this requirement.

---

[46] While access to the labour market in the EU can be restricted to nationals, once a person is working within the jurisdiction, a set of human rights and labour rights will apply, even if the work relationship does not adhere to legal standards. These rights include fair working conditions, unjustified dismissal or freedom of association and access to justice for violation of these rights.

[47] Purely cleaning jobs have a lower minimum salary. The more the work involves specialised and complex tasks (for example personal care and in particular assisting non-self-sufficient persons, or overall management of the household), the higher the salary. The typology of domestic work in Italy is thus based on a combination of the qualifications needed for the tasks at hand, previous experience of the worker, and the difficult or demanding nature of the job.

In Germany, there is no specific legislation for domestic work. General labour law instead applies.[48] At least 80 per cent of regular domestic work falls into a category called 'Minijobs', that is, a highly state-subsidised domestic work system where workers are employed through specific employment agencies with a maximum wage of EUR 400 per month and enjoy similar labour rights under general labour laws and collective agreements, if any such exist and are applicable. However, because Germany does not stipulate a national minimum wage, the hourly wages are low and Minijobs lack coverage by pension, health and unemployment insurances.[49] Further, by failing to recognise or regularise the legal employment status of a MDW in a comparable fashion to that of native workers, Germany avoids having to ensure that the MDWs within its jurisdiction have the coverage of just and favourable conditions of work, or the right to an effective legal remedy when rights are violated.

In Spain MDWs are also unlikely to enjoy protection by ECHR rulings and domestic worker legislation because the MDL market is largely informal. As a consequence of the financial crisis in 2008–2009 and resulting domestic employment pressures, Spain passed legislation imposing new limitations on migrants' rights (for example, repealing undocumented migrants' rights to public health care).[50]

In countries such as Germany and Singapore, where the MDW rights are poorly defined, there is also a specific direction by both the state and employer interests to *avoid the recognition* of such rights, either through a failure to provide MDWs with clear legislated legal employment status (beyond migration licensing) and/or differentiating MDWs from main-stream labour force where labour laws do apply. In this respect it is the nature of labour and devalued worker gender, status and marketability that are preyed upon and so well evidence how law through inaction is a powerful agent for discrimination.

Stage 4: End of Employment & Exit – Dispute Resolution Options and Repatriation

Under Article 8 of the Universal Declaration of Human Rights (UDHR), every citizen of the EU has the right to an effective remedy by the competent national tribunal for acts violating the fundamental rights granted to her by the constitution or law. Article 26 of the International Covenant for Civil and Political Rights (ICCPR) states that all persons

48 Carls (2012), p. 16.
49 Carls (2012), p. 16.
50 Gil Araujo and González Fernández (2014), p. 17.

are equal before the law and are entitled, without any discrimination, to the equal protection of the law. Articles 9(1) and 9(2) of the ILO Convention No. 143 on Migrant Workers stipulate that a migrant worker even in an irregular employment situation shall have the possibility of presenting her dispute to the responsible adjudicatory body, in person or through a representative.

In Germany, domestic workers are covered by general legal dismissal protections, restricting possible reasons for dismissal to specific negative employee behaviour and/or particular economic situation of the employer. However, collective agreements, which give benefit to these provisions on domestic work, apply only to cases where both employer and employees are members of the few trade unions and employers' associations which have signed the agreement.[51] As a large proportion of the MDWs in Germany are part of a shadow (unregistered) economy, they are unlikely to receive such protection.

In Spain[52] domestic workers can be fired without any particular reason, or simply at the employer's discretion, and severance pay is lower than for other workers. However, employers are obligated under any written employment contract to tender a written dismissal statement.

While the MDWs in Singapore and Malaysia generally have legal status through employment contracts and migration licensing, this does not ensure access to legal assistance and representation in situations of dispute, and there are anything but attendant fair extradition processes. In these two societies, the home is defined by the state as a private sphere, in which MDWs are confined. Employers commonly retain a MDW's legal documents such as their passport, and in this dependency context MDWs are discouraged from leaving the private sphere to access legal help when in need.

In Singapore, MDW employers can terminate the employment contract unilaterally. The Ministry of Manpower issues guidelines on how employers ought to deal with terminating the employment contract with the MDW[53] (for example, the employer ought to give notice of termination to the MDW). However, enforcement of such termination guidelines is not available without the worker seeking very limited and practically restricted disputation facilities. Compounding the abdication of its migration obligations, the Singapore state requires that MDW employers are responsible for the cost and activation of repatriating

---

51 Carls (2012), p. 16.

52 Carls (2012), p. 14.

53 Ministry of Manpower, Singapore, *Your Guide to Employing a Foreign Domestic Worker*.

migrant workers if the work permit is revoked or cancelled, or the contract is terminated.[54] To deal with this state-delegated responsibility, the employer engages the services of MDW agencies and their repatriation companies. These include booking plane tickets, transporting the MDW from the employer's home to the airport, cancelling the work permit on behalf of the employer and so on. The MDW could be told of the contract termination and be repatriated within 24 hours. Many of these repatriations in dispute situations involve the physical and forceful transport of migrants.

Following the amendments to the Employment Agency Act (EAA) in 2011, the Ministry of Manpower released the "Employment Agency Licence Conditions for Comprehensive Licence"[55] which requires the licensee (that is, the MDW agency) to ensure that the employment agreement 'clearly states a dispute resolution mechanism to deal with any dispute that may arise between the licensee and the employer'. There is no mention of the requirement for a dispute resolution clause to be included in the agreement to deal with disputes arising between the employer and MDW. Meanwhile, the MOM website highlights to the employer that, in case of a dispute, the worker should contact the agency or the Ministry which offers a free-of-charge conciliation service to resolve such employment disputes.[56] In general, workers are largely ignorant of even these oblique dispute resolution options. These apparent facilities in reality provide no real access to dispute resolution as the employer has total control over contract repudiation and worker repatriation. With the immediate termination of the work permit as a result of disputation, the MDW fears the punitive consequences of her lack of immigration status and generally has no choice but to comply with the repatriation. Overstaying in Singapore is an offence punishable by imprisonment and also caning for men.

AGENCY AND PRINCIPLE POLLINATION

Throughout this chapter we have been working with a disjunction, even a paradox. The principles of agency law and the relationships they forge, indistinct as these can be in the migrant labour context, not only require

[54] Ministry of Manpower, Singapore, *Your Guide to Employing a Foreign Domestic Worker*, p. 15.

[55] Ministry of Manpower, Singapore website, EA Licence Conditions for Comprehensive Licence.

[56] Ministry of Manpower, Singapore website, Work Passes and Permits.

loyalty but more general notions of fiduciary prudence. Yet the place of agency in the migration chain generates distinct exploitation and dependency situations and relationships which disempower workers as they progress through the influence of one agent to another. Law, its imbalance and its absence are clearly implicated in this alienation of labour force.

Somewhat like our position with a revision of legal regulation through contracting, we argue for a return to the fiduciary context of agency and not one limited to loyalty afforded to the principal. Perhaps, however, agency law has not quite so strong ideals of fairness and conscionability as those which underpin contract law theory. Certainly the webs of obligation developed through agency can be more complex and obscure than those created by contract bonds. That said, we have identified in the migrant labour chain critical decision sites where the agent-to-worker relationship is apparent and where bilateral worker/agent/employer connections unite the three prevailing market interests beyond the state. We have also revealed through the direct and the implicit divesting of its responsibility to agents, insufficiently governed, how the state is drawn into the agency web.

There are, in our view, crucial occasions where state-sponsored legal regulation, that ensures at the very least adequate knowledge transfer to enable workers to contract in a more empowered fashion, could be required and enforced through both public and private legal regulation. The onus on the state is through legitimating agent registration or at least allowing their participation in the market, that a higher order agency bond, state-to-agent, is forged. Along with this, and certainly when fundamental state powers in migration are transferred to agents, the state has a duty to ensure that these and other preferential powers affect vulnerable migrant workers in an egalitarian fashion. The state chooses to intervene in the market through migration registration and the exclusion of the unregistered, and chooses to divert or deny general employment rights to migrant workers, so any argument that these issues are for the market or not for the state is unconvincing and unwise.

Principle pollination is a role for the state in setting agency arrangements, including:

- minimum fiduciary standards
- clear pathways of obligation
- essential conditions of transparency when employment/migration obligations are on offer
- required information provision to workers, enabling some degree of informed consent in entering employment/migration arrangements

- specific and apparent agency relationships at different stages of the migration chain
- actionable dispute conditions, wherein migration and employment status can be severed so that workers can remain in the jurisdiction for deliberation and determination
- basic health and safety protections for workers to be the responsibility of agents on-going

In order that it has credibility in principle pollination, the state must reposition itself as a responsible market regulator. One area in which we see this as crucial is *state agency obligations* in migration, residency, employment and repatriation. These cannot, it is our view, be dispossessed to other market players, seeing that the state stands as their legislative sponsor. Many of the uncertainties of the migrant labour market are not for the state to cure. However, if migrant workers had confidence that their residency and employment status deserved basic protection beyond the whim of the employer and the commercial imperatives of the market, then some levels of vulnerability and dependency would be reduced.

If agent best practice is stipulated and malfeasance punished and deterred then the resulting more equitable agency consciousness will have spill-over effects on the behaviour of employer principals. Some argue that as with contracting, the overriding principle should not be some vague notion of fairness but rather clearer considerations of freedom to engage. Both objectives we suggest are premised on a freer, more complete and more shared flow of knowledge and information at crucial decision sites in the agency chain.

6. Regulatory preferencing: a comparative study

Input driven growth is an essentially limited process … once one allows for their rapid growth of inputs, the productivity performance of the 'tigers' falls from 'the heights of Olympus to the plains of Thessaly.'[1]

INTRODUCTION

The simple hypothesis that increasing regulation of the migrant labour market improves the quality of the market experience for its most vulnerable stakeholders, has been challenged in Chapter 2. To understand why this correlation does not naturally hold, the following argument focuses on preferential private property arrangements as forces which disembed migrant labour markets and undermine their sustainability. In particular, we examine how law, its shadow, or its selective absence promote and perpetuate private property relationships determined to disempower migrant labour force, so that its commodification enables agents, employers and the state to profit at the expense of realistic and fair labour pricing.[2]

The empirical core of this chapter is a brief and targeted account of the migrant labour market (MLM), in certain receiving countries, and the regional regimes (the European Union (EU) and the Association of Southeast Asian Nations (ASEAN))[3] which may exert some regulatory

---

1 Krugman (1994), pp. 69, 71–2.

2 It is just this cycle of market discrimination that makes the artificially devalued pricing of migrant labour both uncompetitive in any free market model, and attractive for those stakeholders who participate in the process of labour pricing deflation.

3 These two regional alliances have been consciously selected because of their very different constitutional bonds, their different approaches to the obligations and interests of members, and as a consequence their different approaches to regulation.

influence over identified nation state regulation.[4] The comparative endeavour engages state-to-state practice, nation state to regional regulatory approaches, and specifies the dynamics of migration/employment frameworks through a staged migrant labour process. Each of the four selected stages in the migrant labour flow are crucial decision sites where, in particular, the impact of contracting and agency (introduced more fully in chapters 4 and 5) would be anticipated as relevant regulatory domains:

1. identifying and engaging potential workers prior to migration
2. facilitating entry into the receiving country and receiving residency/ employment status[5]
3. determining work conditions after entry that relate to remuneration and industrial health and safety
4. controlling exit from the market.

Different private property relationships (influenced by the action or absence of public and private law) will form the focus for the staged comparison of decision sites. In stage 1 we pick up the discussion briefly introduced in Chapter 5 of the role of agency in migration/employment recruitment arrangements. In stage 2, the application of migration residency and labour permit regulation is explored as an intersection between state regulatory responsibility and the creation of dependency relationships within the market. Recognising the vast scope of worker welfare and employment rights considerations, stage 3 addresses the lifestyle and welfare conditions associated with the peculiar work/life context of migrant labour and its particular vulnerabilities. Stage 4 investigates the problematic connections between labour dispute resolution options and extradition/repatriation practices.

The overarching intention behind the decision-site/migration flow methodology is to target where law's activity or absence fosters private property arrangements which specifically and apparently endanger market sustainability, instead preferencing the economic interests and standing of agents, employers and the state. The analysis is concerned with legal regulation in action, and in retreat.

[4] The international regulatory dimension is not ignored through reference to its representation (or absence) in regional and national regulatory regimes and compliance.

[5] For the purposes of containing the analysis it has been determined to focus primarily on documented workers, and only to discuss black market labour where it has a direct connection with the documented market.

ANALYTICAL ASSUMPTIONS

In order to advance a comparative approach which is not merely a catalogue of synthesis and difference, it is necessary to work with a limited range of theoretical assumptions that will intentionally delimit drilling into the context of each referent, looking across comparative fields and then along process pathways. Having this purpose in mind, the assumptions below are advanced as consistent with our wider theoretical premises that:

- law currently instrumentalises private property arrangements which disembed migrant labour markets through frameworks of exploitation and dependency; and
- law in the future could offer a regulatory force which reimagines private property and its relationships in order to advance rather than endanger market sustainability, with migrant labour force and pricing as the case in point.

The assumptions are:

1. The regulation of a migrant labour market employs law for the implementation of social–economic policy objectives.[6] Legal regulatory instruments may arise out of public law in the forms of legislation, regulations, administrative guidelines and so on, or from private law as contracts, agency agreements, licences and so on.
2. From its commercial and regulatory nature, a migrant labour market reveals a mix of private and state actions, generating regulatory opportunities and possibilities projecting from the directions of private and public interests.
3. Migrant labour markets in different jurisdictions are under-regulated for diverse reasons. Characteristic of these regulatory lacunae is the selective absence of public and private law both in their expressive and facilitative functions.
4. Among under-regulated migrant labour markets, the reasons behind an absence of law can be unequivocal. For instance, as a primary sponsor and driver of legal regulation the state's divesting of regulatory responsibility (in migration and employment contexts) to agents and employers goes to legitimate preferencing the positions of the later stakeholders within market frames of benefit.

---

[6] den Hertog (2010), p. 3.

5. The current economic attraction of the migrant labour market rests on the exploitation of undervalued migrant labour, and its deflated pricing. To ensure this financial climate favouring some property arrangements over others, migration and employment regulations intersect to produce for workers lifestyle consequences of vulnerability and dependency. This discriminatory conditioning, in turn, disempowers workers when negotiating the commodification of their labour and practically dispossesses from actionable property rights in that labour.
6. The migrant labour markets chosen in the study, and their regional contexts, reveal common features of market disembedding across all migrant labour market regulatory frameworks.
7. The crucial decision sites and the exercise of various discretions in decision-making demonstrate a patterned process of worker commodification and disempowerment which are the product of preferential private property arrangements, constituted in part by law.
8. These decision sites will suggest and contextualise regulatory opportunities for repositioning legal regulation to fundamentally alter the essential conditions of market stakeholder engagement, which in turn will ensure market sustainability.

A DECENTRED REGULATORY LANDSCAPE

Behind the enquiry to follow is a desire to understand the ways in which regulation stimulates discriminatory market benefit (such as in Europe) or where a dearth of regulation allows the exploitative interests of market players with power over property to flourish (the ASEAN way). In either and both scenarios the nation state exercises a *light touch* regulatory approach in order to prefer labour market mobility and foster the market contexts that depress labour market value. This policy confluence reveals how regional and national market stimulus (even against perceived domestic labour market interests) exploit globalised labour flows, almost irrespective of regulatory activity.

A conclusion to be drawn from the variability of regulation, national and regional, is that either through protecting market flow, or by enabling space for the generation and maintenance of market conditions that stimulate labour migration, regulatory activity is not the essential variable in migrant labour market disembedding. Rather it will be argued that both active and dispossessed regulatory direction from the state as law's sponsor, and the discriminatory application of private law arrangements in a public law discretionary void enable private property arrangements which destructively commodify labour value and worker dignity.

Some say that despite employment climates of employment discrimination in migrant labour markets, everyone eventually benefits. As we have earlier noted, this view ignores the more permanent structural changes in labour valuing market-to-market which could bring value more generally without the unsustainable social consequences of massive labour disembedding. Ha-Joon Chang criticises Paul Krugman's controversial assertion that a poorly paid, under-regulated job opportunity is better for many migrant workers than no job or survival employment in their home country.

> Neoclassical economics is too accepting of the status quo. In analysing individual choices, it accepts as given the underlying social structure – the distribution of money and power, if you will. This makes it look at only choices that are possible without fundamental social changes. For example, many Neo-classical economists, even the 'liberal' Paul Krugman, argue that we should not criticise low-wage factory jobs in poor countries because the alternative may be no job at all. This is true, *if* we take the underlying socio-economic structure as given. However, once we are willing to change the structure itself, there are a lot of alternatives to those low-wage jobs. With new labour laws that strengthen worker rights, land reform that reduces the supply of cheap labour to factories (as more people stay in the countryside) or industrial policies that create high-skilled jobs, the choice for workers can be between low-wage jobs and higher-wage ones, rather than between low-wage jobs and no jobs.[7]

Migrant labour market exploitation depends on push/pull factors. In the process analysis that follows it will be revealed that many structural failings in the valuing of labour and the dignifying of work beyond commodity which characterise the economic environment of home states, are the essential preconditions for worker vulnerability and dependency all along the migration flow. As a consequence it is inadequate to evaluate the lot of migrant workers within the context of their eventual labour exploitation alone. The interactive influences of disembedding private property arrangements from home to host market contexts require dynamic consideration if the complicit role of legal regulation is to be understood, addressed and transformed. We fail in that endeavour if we trade sustainable market relations for remittance reimbursement, and the push of impoverishment for devalued labour pricing, only to ultimately benefit those few stakeholders who control property relations. The state

---

[7] Chang (2014), pp. 126–7.

as a recentred regulatory force has a role to play in this transformation of dignified labour transaction, state-to-state, and in regional alliances.

The chapter examines migrant labour market flows in a regional environment where the regulatory stimulus for free labour migration across state borders (within a contained migrant labour market) is complemented by domestic migration/employment regulation which devalues labour price by disembedding migrant labour life contexts. The EU prioritises free labour flow, enabling transitional employment growth less fettered by employment protections, and nation states directly exclude migrants from the ancillary social benefits which otherwise attach to paid work and link workers to their social context.

LABOUR MARKET IN EUROPE – MARKET PRIORITISATION

Insecure Tenure

The central tenet of the European Union (EU) internal labour market is free movement of workers across Member States through the gradual reduction of internal border barriers to workers and the fortification of external borders against any non-EU citizen workforce.[8] In order to facilitate free movement, workers are granted rights of entry to EU state markets for three months, and additional residency privileges in another Member State beyond the normal three-month period if a worker or a self-employed person has sufficient personal resources for subsistence, thereby not posing a drain on the social security system of the receiving state.[9] Article 7(1)(d) of the EU Treaty also offers a right to family reunification without any other conditions attached.[10] This concession is

---

[8] Consolidated version of the Treaty on European Union and the Treaty on the Functioning of the European Union, Article 45. 2012/C 326/01; Lesinska (2014), pp. 45–6.

[9] European Union: Council of the European Union, Council Directive 2004/38/EC of 29 April 2004 on the Right of Citizens of the Union and Their Family Members to Move and Reside Freely within the territory of the Member States, Art. 7.

[10] European Union: Council of the European Union, Council Directive 2004/38/EC of 29 April 2004 on the Right of Citizens of the Union and Their Family Members to Move and Reside Freely within the territory of the Member States; Davies (2012), p. 79; *Blaise Baheten Metock* v. *Minister for Justice, Equality and Law Reform*, European Court of Justice, Grand Chamber, C-127/08, [2008] ECR I-6241, [67]–[68].

to ameliorate the social dislocation associated with the translocation of citizen workers within the EU when it is read in conjunction with a generous definition of who is a 'worker'.[11]

In terms of migrant labour preferencing, temporary/part-time or successive fixed-term contracts are growing trends in the EU as opposed to permanent employment relationships.[12] Transitional labour arrangements are encouraged as part of the EU's 'flexicurity' agenda, designed to maximise labour's contribution to economic productivity, a policy envisaged to promote as many people into jobs as possible, even if these positions fluctuate in availability and tenure. Associated with its labour productivity purpose, 'flexicurity' is said to increase EU competitiveness against other international markets.[13]

In earlier policy arrangements temporary workers (especially those provided by an agency – as is typical of migrant workers) were not entitled to equivalent pay or leave benefits as those enjoyed by permanent workers.[14] A series of EU 'atypical work' directives provided that temporary workers should receive treatment equal to permanent employees.[15] Even so, these remain insecure and indeterminate working arrangements only buffered by the most basic employment protections. At the same time the temporary work policy normalises a form of employment that, although benefitting employers by providing a flexible workforce, destabilises working contexts and market positioning for the otherwise more disadvantaged employee groups (for example, women and migrants who are more inclined to take up such part-time work) who are less likely to be protected by trade unions or through balanced collective bargaining.[16]

Countered by some promise of judicial oversight, the directives also maintain what has come to be known as the *Luxembourg* approach (see below) whereby any further restrictions/conditions placed on temporary agency work are subject to review/dismissal by the European Court of

---

11 Atypical work directives: temporary agency (2008/104/EC), part-time (97/81/EC) and fixed-term contracts (1999/70/EC); Davies (2012), p. 80; *Levin* v. *Staatssecretaris van Justitie*, European Court of Justice, Case 53/81, [1982] ECR 1035, [11]–[16]; *Lawrie-Blum* v. *Land Baden-Wuttemberg*, European Court of Justice, Case 66/85, [1986] ECR 2121, [17].

12 Cremers (2010), pp. 193–4.

13 Davies (2012), pp. 178–83.

14 Crush (2011).

15 European Union, Council of the European Union, Council Directive 2008/104/EC of 19 November 2008 on Temporary Agency Work, Art. 5.

16 Countouris and Horton (2009), pp. 332–5; Fredman (2004).

Justice (ECJ) if deemed detrimental to the 'general interest' and freedom of the EU internal market.[17] In this respect, judicial interventions are for market benefit rather than originating with individual worker interests.

Posting or 'Social Dumping'

The European Commission (EC), as part of its free internal market and 'flexicurity' agenda, encourages the practice where workers are contracted in one EU Member State and then temporarily posted to undertake work in another (primarily occurring in the construction and agricultural sectors). Consistent with this policy, the ECJ held that states cannot ban or impose disproportionate restrictions on the posting of workers from another state.[18] However, the practice raises concerns about the potential *social dumping* of workers from Member States with lower wages and working conditions posted to Member States with more developed labour law protections and higher wages to undercut the local labour market. The Rome I Regulation deems it lawful for these workers to be operating on lower wages contracted under, and governed by, the law of the sending state.[19]

The EC passed the Posted Workers Directive in 1996 to ameliorate some of these concerns for inequity and market imbalance, requiring that minimum wages, conditions, health and safety guarantees and break periods must be governed by the law of the host state.[20] However, restrictive interpretations by the ECJ have determined that the list of protections provided by the Directive is exhaustive, and any further restrictions to posted workers can only be justified if they do not disproportionately challenge the right to freedom of movement.[21] Subsequent industrial action attempting to raise the wages/conditions of posted workers above the minimums dictated in the Directive must be for

---

[17] European Union, Council of the European Union, Council Directive 2008/104/EC of 19 November 2008 on Temporary Agency Work, Art. 4(1).

[18] Davies (2012), p. 93; *Rush Portuguesa Ld* v. *Office national d'immigration,* European Court of Justice, C-113/89, [1990] ECR I-1417, [15]–[20]; *Commission* v. *Luxembourg*, European Court of Justice, C-319/06, [2008] ECR 1-4323, [50]–[54]. Some restrictions may be imposed for 'public policy reasons' in accordance with Article 3(10) of the Directive but this must be interpreted strictly.

[19] Davies (2012), pp. 94–5.

[20] European Union: Council of the European Union, Directive 96/71/EC of the European Parliament and of the Council of 16 December 1996 Concerning the Posting of Workers in the Framework of the Provision of Services, Art. 3(1).

[21] *Commission* v. *Luxembourg*, [26].

legitimate public interest concerns and must not disproportionately interfere with freedom to provide services in the internal market.[22] Labour lawyers and the International Labour Organization (ILO) have criticised the Court's approach for prioritising business freedom over workers' rights and the power of trade unions[23] and having the potential to uniformly drive down wages and working conditions in the more developed states.[24]

The original draft of the Directive for Services in the Internal Market 2006/123/EC (Bolkenstein Directive) was particularly controversial because of fears about a race to the bottom for local workers, coupled with concerns that, in making migrant worker movement easier under depressed sending state employment conditions, firms would always prefer migrants to locals and even move commercial operations to where labour was cheaper.[25] While the later drafts adopted a more neutral tone, they still incorporated the *country of origin* principle, and designated that any national laws which put in place restrictions on freedom of movement and establishment must be justified and shown to be non-discriminatory.[26] Through these pronouncements, the Commission and the Court clearly favour free movement of business/workers at the expense of national protectionist measures or any associated attempts by trade unions/collective agreements to maintain the labour market status quo for native workers.[27]

The Blue Card Directive 2009/50/EC is one of the administrative *survivors* of proposed directives for uniform EU approaches to migration after the Amsterdam Treaty, later abandoned in favour of a 'Fortress Europe' discourse in the early 2000s and during the 2004 EU enlargement.[28] The Directive addresses the need for a free flow of a more highly skilled and mobile migrant labour force. However, the Directive takes a cautious approach with considerable discretion given to Member States in terms of imposing quotas, preferencing nationals and granting equal

---

22 *Laval* v. *Svenska Byggnadsarbetareforbundet*, European Court of Justice, C-341/05, [2007] ECR I-11767; *International Transport Workers' Federation and Finnish Seamen's Union* v. *Viking Line ABP and OÜ Viking Line Eesti*, European Court of Justice, C-438/05, [2007] ECR I-10779; Cremers (2010), pp. 302–5.

23 Davies (2008); also International Labour Organization (2013).

24 Davies (2012), pp. 9–12.

25 Barnard (2008), pp. 328–9.

26 Barnard (2008), p. 362.

27 Chang, Hanf and Pelkmans (2010).

28 Gsir (2013), pp. 100–105.

treatment rights.[29] Stimulating labour flow at the top end of the skills scale, however, presents the devastating potential for 'brain drain' from developing countries.[30]

The free movement of labour force across EU Member States, so the argument goes, benefits the union's economy, gets more people into work, and makes the labour market more productive. As will be shown below, the selective mobility of labour, at the costs of labour protection and employment stability, has destructive effects on worker dignity and labour market sustainability as a vital context for social bonding.

EMPLOYMENT CONTRACT AND WORKING CONDITIONS IN EUROPE

The Employee Information Directive 91/533EEC designates that all employers (apart from those contracting casual workers) must provide a written statement to employees outlining terms of contract and employment.[31] The ECJ held in *Kampelmann* that such a statement in no way affects the terms and actionability of the employment contract, being of probative value only, along with an evidential presumption that the statement correctly reflects the contractual terms.[32] Kenner and Barnard note that although this notification requirement represents a small departure from freedom of contract in favour of employees, it is in fact solely concerned with the provision of information and has little value in enforcing better conditions or employee rights.[33]

---

[29] Davies (2012), pp. 104–6; European Union: Council of the European Union, Council Directive 2009/50/EC of 25 May 2009 on the Conditions of Entry and Residence of Third-country Nationals for the Purposes of Highly Qualified Employment.

[30] Gumus (2010), pp. 448–9; Davies (2012), pp. 103–7.

[31] European Union: Council of the European Union, Council Directive 91/533/EEC of 14 October 1991 on An Employer's Obligation to Inform Employees of the Conditions Applicable to the Contract or Employment Relationship, Art. 2(2).

[32] *Helmut Kampelmann and others* v. *Landscaftverband Westfalen-Lippe*, European Court of Justice, C-253/96 to 258/96, [1998] IRLR 333, [25]–[35]; *Stadtwerke Witten GmbH* v. *Andreas Schade*, European Court of Justice, C-258/96, [1982] ICR 54 (Browne-Wilkinson J), p. 58; and *Klaus Haseley* v. *Stadtwerke Altena GmbH*, European Court of Justice, C-258/96, [1983] ICR 351 (Ackner LJ), p. 355.

[33] Kenner (1999), pp. 223–8; Barnard (2012), pp. 566–7.

Equality directives effecting worker entitlements in line with gender equality (75/117/EC) and other equal treatment (76/207EEC) as well as parental leave (2010/18/EC) were represented as protecting against overall labour market degradation through employer preferencing of cheaper female labour. Such directives have since become regarded as regulatory methods for EU labour market efficiency removing barriers to individuals being retained as part of the labour force at fullest capacity.[34]

In general, rights-based regulation and the 'constitutionalisation' of EU labour markets are dependent on such equality directives, which in turn are operated as a replacement for traditional protections by state-centred trade unions and collective bargaining market influences[35] in repositioning employee interests.[36] The anti-discrimination directives (workplace discrimination (2000/78/EC) and racial discrimination (2000/43/EC)) are intended to constitutionalise basic worker rights protections across the EU, yet at the same time have been employed by the ECJ for reinforcing free worker movement and eliminating nation state protectionist measures.[37] As already mentioned the court has read these directives as only having effect without prejudice to immigration restrictions (see Article 3(2)), again preferencing the economic imperative of free labour movement above any prevailing and universal worker claims against discrimination.[38]

---

34 Davies (2012), pp. 111–15.

35 Kilpatrick (2006), pp. 125–9.

36 Bell (2014); *Mangold* v. *Helm*, European Court of Justice, C-144/04, [2005] ECR 1-9981, [74]–[78]. See Bell (2014) for the increasing importance of the Treaty on the Functioning of the European Union, European Charter of Human Rights and European Social Charter as a source of 'general principles' of equal treatment in employment-related disputes, for example in *Mangold* v. *Helm*.

37 For instance the decisions of *Mary Carpenter* v. *Secretary of State for the Home Department*, European Court of Justice, C-60/00, [2002] ECR I-6279 and *Mangold* v. *Helm*.

38 In contrast note working time (2003/88/EC), participation in trade unions and collective bargaining (2009/38/EC and 2002/14/EC), redundancy and social security (79/7/EC, 86/388/EC, 98/99/EC) and their state opt-out provisions.

EU MIGRANT WORKER RECRUITMENT AND EMPLOYMENT AGENCIES

Growth of Private Employment Agencies

The European Union has seen a massive growth in number and scope of private employment agencies. In the UK alone the industry has increased four-fold since 1994 and is worth an estimated 25 billion dollars (US).[39] This market expansion is no doubt linked to the increasingly 'flexible' nature of migrant labour work (through temporary, seasonal, part-time and fixed-term contractual arrangements), especially after the most recent global financial crisis,[40] along with the relatively new regulatory acceptance of private employment agencies on the Continent.[41,42] Another stimulus to agency expansion is the complexity and tightening of immigration restrictions, whereby employers find it harder to register workers themselves and are more likely to rely on agencies and accept their fee frames. This shift has been accompanied by the decline in influence of public/state-controlled employment agencies (especially in Eastern Europe).[43]

The EU commitment to freedom of internal markets and the Bolkenstein Directive have also made it easier for agencies to operate across borders. Yet, agency services and their scrutiny vary widely as do the services provided by agents for workers in employment bargaining. Agency workers are often less well covered by health and safety standards as a result of the poorer negotiation of terms to work longer hours and for lower wages and their lack of knowledge about the nature of their employment. Agents seem to work from self-interest to ensure job placement at workers' cost.

---

[39] International Labour Office (2007), pp. 1–4; Scott (2007).

[40] Otto and Bolzonello (2012), pp. 1–3; Cangiano and Walsh (2014); Cremers (2010), pp. 193–4.

[41] For example, in Italy in the 1970s private employment agencies were effectively prohibited and public agencies held a monopoly over employment services. Now Italy as part of the European Union is dedicated to providing 'equal treatment' for millions of private agency sourced workers.

[42] See the *legislazione antifraudolenta* (particularly N1369/1960) which imposed a 'general prohibition of intermediation and interposition in the supply of work', also Art. 125 of *French Labour Code (Code du Travail)*; Countouris (2007), p. 38; cf. European Union: Council of the European Union, Council Directive 2008/104/EC of 19 November 2008 on Temporary Agency Work.

[43] Agunias (2013).

Similar to the Asian market experience discussed in Chapter 5, an initial and often enslaving financial burden for workers, at their entry into the migrant flow and when they are least able to bear it, are excessive recruitment fees and, in the worst cases, working in conditions that resemble forced labour.[44] Against this recipe for vulnerability and dependency, agency-recruited workers have little engagement with trade unions and their bargaining and protective capacities.[45]

EU Agency Regulation Confined to the Interests of the Internal Market

The only regulation of private employment agencies EU-wide is the provision of equal rights for temporary agency workers and posted workers, as established by Directives 2008/104/EC and 96/71/EC.[46] These are part of a series of legislative reforms (which also include the Part-time and Fixed-Term Directives) forwarding the European Commission's 'flexicurity' agenda. These Directives specifically anticipate that by requiring equal treatment for each class of worker (agency or otherwise), along with normalising atypical work, the employed labour force will increase together with the overall productivity of the market, and its competitiveness.[47] There also exists the overarching policy assumption that temporary work will act as a 'stepping stone' to a permanent position.[48]

No Uniform Licensing/Registration or Monitoring of Agencies Across the EU

No EU legislation exists to cover the common or uniform registration, operation or monitoring of employment and migration agencies.[49] The Temporary Workers Directive leaves discretion to Member States in

---

[44] Otto and Bolzonello (2012), p. 4; Sorrentino and Jokinen (2014), p. 7; see also International Labour Organization (2012), pp. 1–3.

[45] Otto and Bolzonello (2012), p. 4; Davies (2012), p. 180.

[46] European Union: Council of the European Union, Council Directive 2008/104/EC of 19 November 2008 on Temporary Agency Work; European Union: Council of the European Union, Directive 96/71/EC of the European Parliament and of the Council of 16 December 1996 Concerning the Posting of Workers in the Framework of the Provision of Services, Art. 3(1).

[47] Davies (2012), pp. 178–83; Countouris (2012), pp. 39–41.

[48] Davies (2012), p. 181.

[49] Association Francaise de Normalisation (2012), p. 14.

determining licensing requirements within their own borders.[50] The ILO Convention 181 provides guidelines for a uniform legislative approach but only 12 EU states have ratified this instrument.[51]

Throughout the Union there are different ways of conceptualising the employment/agency/worker relationship (as discussed in Chapter 5 more generally). The Continental approach is to regulate through contract, that is, as a 'triangular' relationship, with contracts concluded between the agency and worker, and then agency and employer, which are then subject to various controls and requirements. In such a market context agencies were previously not permitted to offer permanent and temporary employment, but had to be licensed for one or the other.

It would appear that the UK has more difficulty giving clear guidance regarding how agencies are regulated, so much so that workers are often unable to discern if there is an employment contract with either their agency or their employer.[52] This is a prevailing problem with uncertain triangulated agency obligations across ASEAN jurisdictions (see Chapter 5).

Increasingly Liberal 'Soft Touch' Approach on Agency Intervention

The turnaround in the EU from centralised state employment agencies, and discouraging private agency arrangements, to the withdrawal of state/agency sponsorship, in preference for private agency services is not a natural market correction. Private agencies and their promotion of transient working arrangements are now seen as more compatible with employment policy which values flexibility over security. These agencies have facilitated worker engagement in atypical/less regulated employment, which is part of the EU push for labour market flexibility, market growth and competitive advantage. The rush to increase EU labour market productivity has necessitated a new regulatory approach. It moves from restricting atypical work promoted through agency intermediaries, or the provision of incentives for atypical work to convert into standard

---

[50] Association Francaise de Normalisation (2012), pp. 16–17; European Union: Council of the European Union, Council Directive 2008/104/EC of 19 November 2008 on Temporary Agency Work, Art. 4(4).

[51] Belgium, Bulgaria, Czech Republic, Finland, Hungary, Italy, Lithuania, Netherlands, Poland, Portugal, Slovakia and Spain. Otto and Bolzonello (2012), p. 4.

[52] Countouris (2012), p. 95; see also Hepple (1999); Scott (2007), pp. 6–7.

employment, instead promoting normalisation of atypical work/agency arrangements in the context of equalising rights through employment security.

Because of the reservations in British nation state politics concerning the free flow of labour, the UK is the exception when it comes to regulatory stimulus for migrant labour markets. Although regulation has arguably increased with the introduction of the Gangmasters Licensing Authority and Employment Agencies Standards Inspectorate (following public opinion galvanising against migrant labour flows), the enforcement capacity of such inspectorate initiatives is still questionable, especially given the increasing number of agencies being established in the UK.[53]

On the other hand, in Germany and France the deregulation of agencies is viewed as an integral part of the flexible labour market agenda, through such local legislative instruments as the Hartz Laws and the Social Cohesion Law, respectively.[54] For Germany, Hartz saw the end of the Public Employment Service's monopoly over the provision of employment and the development of Personal Employment Services (being independent businesses attached to the Federal Public Employment Service (which secure temporary employment for unemployed persons)). Associated with institutional repositioning, the increased liberalisation of the rules surrounding temporary agency work (such as allowing temporary workers to be hired out to the same employer several times, and a reduction in the minimum time thresholds for temporary agency worker contracts), have grown the portfolios of the private sector agency industry.[55]

Although this deregulation of controls on atypical work has been matched in the EU by a declared recommitment to the idea of 'equal rights', in terms of migrant labour market conditions, the vulnerability and dependency consequences for workers have been exacerbated by job insecurity, increasing income inequality, and swelling ranks of the working poor. The negative impact of flexibility policies has been much greater for the already precarious employees (such as women, who make up 84 per cent of atypical workers).[56]

---

[53] See generally Scott (2007).

[54] Countouris (2012); Eurofound (2005).

[55] Countouris (2012), p. 138.

[56] See generally Jacobi and Kluve (2007); Leschke, Schmid and Griga (2006); Knight (2013); Heyes and Lewis (2014); Heyes (2011); Bonesmo Fredriksen (2012), p. 9.

CITIZENSHIP AND RESIDENCY

Discretions as to Long-term Residency

The EU Citizens Directive 2008/38/EC designates that upon gaining status of 'worker' in a new Member State an EU citizen has automatic right to residency, family reunification (even if family members are in third country nations – as in Article 7) and social assistance if job-seeking across the EU. The Long-term Residence Directive 2003/109/EC represents an original vision as encapsulated in the Tampere Council Agreement (1999) that foreign migrants who have been resident and working in EU Member States for long periods of time are important economic actors and sufficiently integrated to be permitted 'near-equality' of rights with EU citizens. The freedom of movement between states for work purposes offered to such a long-term migrant labour force is obviously designed to enhance internal EU labour market flexibility.[57] The Directive sets out that if a migrant has been granted residency in employment for five years continuously they should be granted long-term residency, and with it the right to family reunification, equal access to the labour market and intra-EU mobility.[58]

Despite what appears to be overarching residency stability in return for long-term labour, these arrangements still offer considerable discretion to Member States when imposing extra restrictions on this benefit. For example, by mandating integration conditions, such as insisting that reunification via marriage is tested to ensure that it is not a 'sham', along with wide interpretations of the requirement that applicants must have 'stable and sufficient resources',[59] the automatic connection between work service duration and permanent residency is not assured. Because of the uncertainty of 'near equality' approaches to workers providing labour value after the expiration of a designated number of years, many foreign/third country national migrants prefer to apply for citizenship rather than await the vagaries of long-term residency.[60]

---

[57] Halleskov Storgaard (2012), pp. 299–303; Maas (2008), p. 591.

[58] European Union: Council of the European Union, Council Directive 2003/109/EC of 25 November 2003 Concerning the Status of Third-Country Nationals Who Are Long-Term Residents (23 January 2004).

[59] See generally Halleskov Storgaard (2012), and Wray (2012); *Rhimou Chakroun* v. *Minister van Buitenlandse Zaken*, European Court of Justice, C-578/08, [2010] ECR I-01839, [47]–[51].

[60] Halleskov Storgaard (2012), pp. 323–37.

Gaining Citizenship in an EU Member State

Dependent on the developing legal regulations of the Member States, over the last decade the requirements governing applications for citizenship have become tighter and more onerous. The application process often requires high fees, demonstrated language proficiencies and substantial independent income thresholds before a migrant is permitted to naturalise.[61]

REPATRIATION – THE UNREGISTERED WORKER FOCUS AND DRIVERS FOR MARKET LEGITIMACY

The EU Directive providing for sanctions against employers of illegal migrants (2009/52/EC) is intended as a deterrent measure against the eagerness of employers to engage unregistered migrant workers. Employer preferences for unregistered workers demonstrate a market demand for the cheapest and most unprotected labour force, acting as a strong 'pull' factor for irregular migrant labour arrangements and fuelling an unregulated black market. The Directive mandates common action across EU states, attacking a differential market advantage in regulatory weaker states or those with more employer-friendly domestic policies which benefit from and rely on unregistered migrant labour.

The regional approach to deterring unregistered migrant labour is also an important part of the recent shift towards a security-driven harmonisation of EU border protection policy.[62] Criminal sanctions, and significant economic penalties applying to employers and workers enforced through regularised and intrusive raids, are intended as a strong message to errant employers, illegal workers, and beyond to a concerned European populace, that action for the protection of citizen preferencing is being taken.[63] In reality, these measures only exacerbate worker dependency, alienating them further from domestic worker communities, and in fact increasing the benefits along with the risks of disempowered unregistered labour force from an employer perspective (discussed in Chapter 2).

Command and control is now the EU regulatory position when enforcing border protection and delimiting migrant labour markets. This

---

61 See e.g., Lesinska (2014), p. 44 for thorough commentary on this.

62 Carrera and Guild (2007), p. 1; Bloch, Kumarappan and McKay (2015), pp. 134–5; Wunderlich (2013).

63 Cholewinski (2012), pp. 151–4; Bloch, Kumarappan and McKay (2015), p. 136.

hardline approach should, however, be balanced against labour fields and some state jurisdictions (such as with agricultural work in the poorer Member States) where a blind-eye is turned to large-scale unregistered work. The official position is that in order to monitor the divide between legal and illegal migrant labour force, employers are required to keep detailed employment records, risking the suite of penalties for employment violations that includes fines (as well as the cost of repatriating the employee), and exclusion from public benefits and also from tendering for public contracts. In particularly serious repeated infringements, with highly exploitative conditions, or where employers have knowledge that their employees are victims of human trafficking, employers face criminal sanction.[64] Even so, Member States retain discretion as to actual penalties to be imposed for what violations, by the Directive simply outlining that the response must be 'effective, proportionate and dissuasive'.[65]

The Directive's provisions do not cover those workers who may be *semi-legal*, such as sectoral or seasonal workers, not officially deemed 'illegal' in terms of administrative status, or all those workers who may be exposed to labour exploitation through being required to work in violation of their limited conditions of permit.[66] This penalty-based deterrent approach may have dulled some more legitimate employer impetus to engage undocumented workers, however it does not address the social and economic reasons for hiring workers without papers, such as devalued labour price, or ethnic and family loyalties. In certain employment settings the demand for unregistered workers remains stable with employers being prepared to risk the fine in order to keep fragile businesses functioning.[67]

As highlighted in Chapter 2, from the employees' perspective the penal/deterrent approach may paradoxically make their work situation and residency status more precarious. Employers sometimes use the threat of being discovered to decrease wages and conditions. Workers collectively develop tactics and systems to avoid discovery which exacerbate their feelings of vulnerability, preferring constant movement from one degraded and dangerous job opportunity to another rather than face

---

[64] Carrera and Guild (2007), pp. 2–3.

[65] European Union: Council of the European Union, Directive 2009/52/EC of the European Parliament and of the Council of 18 June 2009 Providing for Minimum Standards on Sanctions and Measures Against Employers of Illegally Staying Third-country Nationals.

[66] Carrera and Guild (2007), p. 3.

[67] Bloch, Kumarappan and McKay (2015), pp. 143–7.

the prospect of deportation.[68] Experience has shown that the deterrent/penalty regulatory approach may also be exercised in a discriminatory fashion through selective investigation and enforcement, focusing on small- to medium-sized 'ethnic-run' businesses as routinely the most likely subjects for raids.[69] Along with employer discrimination exists the additional negative reality that the deterrent/penalty approach criminalises undocumented workers as well as exploitative employers, further disadvantaging the former in their employment and residency aspirations.[70]

Carrera and Guild argue that regulatory policy should instead make it easier for employers to ascertain the status of employees and then take responsibility for worker legitimacy:

> … a common immigration policy should not focus its action and efforts on applying a stricter criminal framework … employers and employees must first be provided with a clear, efficient, swift and transparent labour and residence permit(s) system.[71]

Another responsibilising regulatory approach could be to rely more specifically on the employment contract as a more universal frame of engagement for workers, registered or otherwise. In addition, expanding access for all migrant workers (registered or not) into local trade unions[72] would enable through greater transparency less punitive pathways where the black market may be absorbed into the regulatory context. These self-regulatory approaches are better at addressing the 'push' factors at work on labour migration in specific market contexts and could lead away from the hubris of 'blind-eye' market benefits for employers and states.[73] However, the more control-focused Directive also provides some important safeguards for employees, where if irregular migrants are apprehended and removed from the place of work the employer must settle any outstanding wages.[74]

Directives for sanctions against carriers, smugglers and traffickers in persons (2001/51/EC, EC Treaty) and the Directive rewarding

---

68 Bloch, Kumarappan and McKay (2015), pp. 138–43; Bacon and Hing (2010), p. 81.

69 Bloch, Kumarappan and McKay (2015), p. 143.

70 Bacon and Hing (2010), p. 83; Carrera and Guild (2007), p. 7.

71 Carrera and Guild (2007).

72 Inghammar (2010).

73 Carrera and Guild (2007); Bloch, Kumarappan and McKay (2015), pp. 147–8.

74 Inghammar (2010); Cholewinski (2012), p. 153.

cooperation with authorities (2004/81/EC) identify people traffickers as the penalty/deterrence focus against serious criminal activity. The directives stress the need for regulatory harmonisation[75] by moving criminal sanctions 'outwards' towards private carriers, to 'point of origin' and creating obstacles for entry, backed up by the Schengen positive and negative country lists in relation to granting visas.[76]

Expulsion and Readmission

A unified expulsion and return policy has been a long-term EU priority, outlined in the Vienna Action Plan and Tampere Conclusions, and in the Hague Programme.[77] This policy approach has involved the creation of the Schengen Information System and Directives on mutual recognition of expulsion decisions (which are then kept in the Information System) as well as strategies for cooperation in the removal of illegal migrants by air.[78] The 'Returns Directive' attracted controversy because it normalises the use of detention for irregular migrants who do not leave within the period of voluntary return (up to four weeks), allowing detention for up to six months (with the possibility of another 12-month extension if such is deemed to be 'proportionate'). The directive also makes possible the detention of women and children.[79] Other problematic provisions relate to re-entry bans, enabling wide discretion for Member States whether or not to impose such bans and retarding their duration (although the guideline is five years). Even though the re-entry bans proved popular

---

75 Cholewinski (2012), pp. 153–7.

76 Servent (2010), pp. 7–8.

77 See e.g., European Council (2005), at 1.6.4, calls for 'the establishment of an effective removal and repatriation policy based on common standards for persons to be returned in a humane manner and with full respect for their human rights and dignity'; Cholewinski (2012); also Carrera and Pusterla (2006), p. 3.

78 European Union: Council of the European Union, Council Directive 2001/40/EC of 28 May 2001 on the Mutual Recognition of Decisions on the Expulsion of Third Country Nationals; European Council: Council of the European Union, Council Directive 2003/110/EC of 25 November 2003 on Assistance in Cases of Transit for the Purposes of Removal by Air; Arcarazo (2012), pp. 182–3.

79 European Union: Council of the European Union, Council Directive 2008/115/EC of the European Parliament and of the Council of 16 December 2008 on Common Standards and Procedures in Member States for Returning Illegally Staying Third-country Nationals; Cholewinski (2012), p. 149.

with Member State constituencies in practice they appear to be compelling immigrants to use more illegal, and sometimes more dangerous, means for re-entry.[80]

Judicial oversight in *Kadzoev* saw the ECJ recognising an individual right to liberty for immigrants when there is no reasonable prospect of removal.[81] The European Return Fund allocated EUR 676 million over the period 2008–13 for migrants (usually those who are voluntarily returning) to re-establish in their country of origin. Even so this compensation has been impugned as not allowing sufficient funds to cover true expenses. Pragmatically, as funds are allocated per expulsion, Member States may be tempted to increase their expulsions to gain further access to fund allocations.[82]

Bilateral Readmission Agreements and Repatriation

The EC currently has readmission agreements with Macau and Hong Kong, Pakistan, Georgia, Moldova and the Ukraine, Russia, the Western Balkans (that is, Albania, Macedonia, Montenegro and Bosnia Herzegovina) and Sri Lanka.[83] Despite the recent focus on bilateral readmission agreements,[84] by offering unequal benefits to non-European states, the policy has been criticised as 'Eurocentric.'[85] From the perspective of human safety this readmission policy has the down-side of promoting circular migration, where if the only paths out of the readmitting state are back to the EU through dangerous routes, ejected migrants may now have no alternatives, as they see them, but to take such risks.[86]

When it comes to concerns for repatriation, the European approach demonstrates little interest in protecting the position of irregular migrants, apart from Directive 2009/32/EC which sanctions employers utilising irregular labour. For instance the *Convention on Legal Status of Migrant Workers* (Council of Europe treaty which preceded the EU) only covers registered migrants, as do the ILO conventions 97 and 143 on

---

[80] Baldaccini (2010), pp. 129–34.

[81] *Said Shamilovich Kadzoev (Huchbarov)*, European Court of Justice, C-357/09, [2009] ECR I-11189.

[82] Barbe and Johansson-Nogues (2008), p. 91; Carrera and Pusterla (2006), pp. 6–7.

[83] Jonjic and Mavrodi (2012), p. 33.

[84] Roig and Huddleston (2007), pp. 363–4.

[85] Roig and Huddleston (2007), p. 374; Barbe and Johansson-Nogues (2008), pp. 89–91.

[86] Roig and Huddleston (2007), pp. 379–82.

private employment arrangements. The EU Charter, although supposedly applying universal workers' rights, expressly excludes migrants in irregular[87] situations. While the UN *International Convention on the Rights of Migrant Workers* expressly recognises irregular migrants, no European States have ratified this convention.[88]

Having explored the migrant labour decision sites crucial in determining European labour flow, there is value in a specific and more detailed examination of national regulation. Reflecting on the transnational policy of labour mobility when contrasted with domestic protectionism and political sensitivity around the competition presented by migrant labour in the domestic labour and welfare settings, one might assume that the state/region comparison would reveal a tension in regulatory purpose and a sharpening in legal regulatory intervention.

DEREGULATING THE GERMAN LABOUR MARKET – IMPACT ON MIGRANT WORKERS

The demographics of the German labour market prior to 2008 revealed segmentation between 'standard' long-term employees and those in temporary or marginal employment, coupled with relatively high rates of long-term unemployment.[89] It appeared at that time the labour market picture was of 'insiders' and 'outsiders'. The 'insiders' were employees in stable long-term employment with open-ended contracts who were well protected by unfair dismissal provisions and their trade unions. 'Outsiders' were those in all other forms of employment, unable to reach the regulatory safe ground of secure long-term employment, enjoying lesser employment protections because of the atypical nature of their work. Prior to the 'flexicurity' push most Continental European states had deliberately curtailed the rights available to workers in atypical employment as an attempt to discourage this insecure labour form.[90]

---

87 Cholewinski (2012).

88 Cholewinski (2008).

89 Heyes and Lewis (2014); De Stefano (2014), p. 259; Knight (2013).

90 This also involved prohibiting or heavily regulating the activities of private employment agencies, and providing incentives for part-time or temporary work to be converted into full-time employment at the expiry of a stated period. Countouris (2007), pp. 30–42; Heyes and Lewis (2014); De Stefano (2014).

After 2008 a more flexible labour market became regarded in Germany as well as in the EU as a necessity in order to stimulate economic growth.[91]

Labour Market *Reforms*?

What are known as the Hartz reforms (2004–2005) and later policy initiatives by the Merkel government have flattened out the employment protection disparities between standard and atypical workers, and fundamentally altered the unemployment benefit system to make it incentive-based.[92] These structural changes to the existing (worker-centred) labour markets included:

- ending the monopoly of the Public Employment Service and allowing for private employment agencies to obtain short-term positions for the unemployed;[93]
- creating mini-jobs or midi-jobs which consisted of low wage and short-term forms of employment that would take an unemployed person off welfare payment but exempt them from tax, and their employer from paying the full amount of social insurance;[94]
- determining that only short-term unemployed are entitled to full welfare payments, with long-term unemployed being required to take up offers of any work that are made to them;[95]
- loosening of unfair dismissal provisions;[96]
- requiring equal regulatory treatment for temporary, temporary agency, part-time and fixed-term contract workers;[97] and
- pushing for standard employment contracting.[98]

The normative argument behind this radical labour market transformation was that employment equality and basic rights provisions would ensure 'great hope for European social policy and (act) as a significant countervailing force to the economic imperatives (of the reforms)'.[99] Aligned

---

91 Davies (2012), pp. 3–27.
92 De Stefano (2014), p. 258.
93 Jacobi and Kluve (2007).
94 Blankenburg (2012).
95 Kemmerling and Bruttel (2006), p. 97.
96 De Stefano (2014), pp. 260–72.
97 Jacobi and Kluve (2007); Leschke, Schmid and Griga (2006).
98 Deakin (2013), pp. 140–45.
99 Barnard (2014), p. 208.

with this prospect of balancing human rights with economic growth was the belief that the progression from insecure to more permanent work frames (which was naturally presumed to be the consequence of getting back to work, in whatever form) would encourage the regularisation of much migrant and domestic work, and thus eventually allow those workers access to greater protection and social security benefits.[100]

Impact across Labour Markets

There is little doubt that these policy changes stabilised unemployment rates through opening up opportunities to transient employment and enforcing 'work for the dole'.[101] The monetary and social benefits for those most exposed in the labour force, with the contraction of the welfare net were problematic, if present at all. On the other hand the advantages of this flexible and under-regulated market for employers were considerable and expansive. The flow-on effects in destabilising conditions associated with permanent and secure labour positions were inevitable. Employers now have access to many alternative levels of labour force beyond long-term or permanent job arrangements, and the financial attractions of cheaper labour and less social insurance payments (for those who employed *mini-jobbers*).[102]

When translated to the EU market form,[103] following the global financial crisis, the economic benefits came at the clear social cost of greater employment precariousness and dependency, even in the domestic/native labour sectors.[104] What was created across the Union was a culture of short-term low-wage employment. At the time the German Chancellor quipped 'we have created the best low-wage sector in the world', where in truth the most vulnerable worker groups (women, migrant workers) became trapped in a cycle of uncertain and temporary employment, with the dependency disempowerment that this inevitably generates.[105] Wages were uniformly depressed and the already dismal regulation of many work contexts experienced a universal 'internal devaluation' of employment protections.[106] Working poverty was on the

---

[100] Carls (2012), p. 19; Lutz and Palenga-Mollenbeck (2010), p. 425.
[101] Knight (2013), p. 1.
[102] Leschke, Schmid and Griga (2006); see also Heyes (2011).
[103] Davies (2012), p. 3.
[104] Leschke, Schmid and Griga (2006).
[105] Fredman (2004).
[106] See e.g., Barnard (2014), p. 209.

rise.[107] Private employment agencies burgeoned as did their self-interest in employment relations.[108]

In practice, the workplace restructuring initiatives in Germany never assisted in the regularising of migrant work (particularly for unregistered labour), especially domestic workers. Regulation through incentives such as tax deductions for employers of domestic labour, were progressively balanced out by the increased social insurance that they had to pay for the worker. As such the incentives did not appear to make enough difference to favour the employment of registered domestic labour. Approximately 95 per cent of all domestic workers in Germany remained unregistered following the freeing up of market mobility.[109] Along with the unintended push towards unregistered domestic labour force, migrant workers (registered or not) became further marginalised as the reforms made it far more difficult to gain regular, steady or permanent work. Along with the intransigence of work opportunities migrants were confronted with more difficulties in seeking long-term residency. The inability to produce evidence of stable contracted work (and its financial benefits) left migrants without essential qualifying characteristics. Further was the negative impact on welfare inclusion. Mini-jobs and *one-Euro* jobs are not entitled to social security benefits, and also may not provide sufficient evidence of regular and stable income that migrants need to demonstrate to be granted residency.[110]

Having documented the jurisdictional and market imperatives for free labour movement rather than employment and migration security in regional and domestic case studies where regulation is relatively vigorous, we now turn to the ASEAN confederation where labour regulation is lax, even if the *free labour flow for economic growth* mantra remains consistent. As constitutional background to this next comparative phase, it should be remembered that ASEAN, unlike the EU, does not bind its members legislatively or through an overarching executive. There is no ASEAN law, and ASEAN institutions do not have the capacity to require the compliance of Member State regulatory policy beyond the level of guidelines and voluntary conventions.

107 Knight (2013); Bonesmo Fredriksen (2012), p. 9.
108 International Labour Office (2007), pp. 1–4.
109 Shire (2012).
110 Kontos and Shinozaki (2007).

ASEAN REGULATION OF MIGRANT LABOUR

Recruitment

Regarding the migrant labour recruitment process, obligations at the ASEAN level consist of *ASEAN Declaration on the Protection and Promotion of the Rights of Migrant Workers*, in which Article 14 requires sending States to establish and promote legal practices to regulate recruitment of migrant workers.[111] However, due to consensus-based decision-making featuring in ASEAN agreements, and a strong emphasis on Member State autonomy, the Declaration and its detail are regarded more as guidelines and an aspiration rather than a binding instrument.[112]

In all ASEAN states recruitment is dominated by private sector agencies, operated as a 'fly now, pay later' scheme with agents' fees deducted progressively from the worker's salary.[113] At the domestic level, almost all states have implemented some tightening of regulations surrounding agents.[114] These regulations usually involve registration and licensing, and some commitment to providing the worker with basic agency and job information. Some states like Singapore only renew licences of accredited agencies, but this quality control process is problematic as it does so through the loose responsibility of several self-regulatory associations.[115]

---

[111] By 'adopting mechanisms to eliminate recruitment malpractices through legal and valid contracts, regulation and accreditation of recruitment agencies and employers, and blacklisting of negligent/unlawful agencies'. See also International Organization for Migration (2010), p. 6.

[112] Chavez (2007), p. 364. However, ASEAN is reportedly close to drafting a legally binding charter of migrant rights, see Wah (2014). This was followed by the establishment of an ASEAN Committee on Migrant Workers in 2009, however, it has encountered slow progress because of a lack of cooperation, and the Committee has only produced a 'zero draft' in which participant aspirations are summarised. The involvement of civil society organisations has also been limited, partially upon the request of some of the Member States involved, see Rother and Piper (2014).

[113] Indeed, the International Labour Organization (ILO) estimates that 34 per cent of the world's private employment agencies (approximately 72,000) are based in the Asia-Pacific Region; International Labour Organization Regional Office for the Arab States (2012), p. 1; International Labour Office (2007), p. 27; Varia (2007), p. 6.

[114] Kaur (2010), pp. 9–15; Silvey (2007), pp. 270–71; von Setyawati (2013), p. 269.

[115] Kaur (2007), [37].

The agency sector across the region does not offer basic protections to workers such as a cap on recruitment fees (Indonesia) or a basic wage (Singapore) or a binding standard employment contract (all states).[116] Overall, agency regulation is a varied and disorderly picture.[117] Even in some states such as Malaysia and Singapore which purport tougher licensing regimes, fundamental protections for workers on arrival, and regular inspections of working conditions after engagement are not a feature. Rather, regulation in the form of licensing provides revenue for the state, after which agents are largely left to complement the desires of private sector employers.[118]

In the Philippines, where there has been a long history of labour migration and a previous domination by the public sector in recruitment, strong regulation has featured backed up with regular public information campaigns. Licensed and blacklisted agents are published online and in employment brochures. However in recent years the system has become increasingly liberal, providing workers with basic information but then adopting a 'hands off' policy.[119] This transition might be explained by the paradox that despite the state's obligations to an army of its citizen workers who migrate across the region, the repatriation income which they provide is of such economic benefit to the balance of payments that the government is increasingly sensitive to market need whether that be pressure from prospective workers or a voracious agency sector.

Like the Philippines, Indonesia is a large sending nation, particularly of migrant domestic workers into Muslim households. Despite the many actors involved in the migrant flow domestically, and constant horror stories about worker treatment abroad, Indonesia is criticised for its lack of industry oversight, rampant corruption through the maintenance of hundreds of illegal agents, and discord between central and regional governments regarding appropriate and necessary regulatory policy. If, for instance, an impoverished province is keen to stimulate migrant flow and income repatriation it will be more inclined to derogate from even the most basic regulatory requirements proposed by central government.

---

116 Morgan and Nolan (2011), p. 12; Kaur (2010); although some states do provide templates for these employment contracts, see, e.g., Ministry of Manpower, Singapore website, Service Agreement Between Foreign Domestic Worker Employer and Employment Agency.

117 Varia (2007), p. 6.

118 See, e.g., Malaysia, which adopts pro-business and demand driven policy, as does Singapore. Kaur (2007); Kaur (2014), p. 359.

119 International Labour Organization Regional Office for the Arab States (2012), p. 18; Ball and Piper (2002), p. 1022.

The decentralisation of Indonesian governance stimulates regulatory inconsistency and webs of corruption.[120]

In all ASEAN states agents and labour brokers still maintain control over contractual terms, which are often only presented to the worker close to departure, and in some cases differ considerably from what might have been promised at recruitment and what even transpire at the time of employment.[121] NGOs have also questioned the extent of governmental oversight of compliance with what meagre regulations even exist.[122] Along with a lack of state or regional will for the task, regulation for worker benefit is challenging due to the many actors involved in the recruitment process, both in sending countries (village scouts, recruitment agents, government/immigration authorities) and receiving jurisdictions (partner agencies and eventual employers).[123] As noted in chapters 2 and 5 it is generally very difficult for workers to lodge a complaint about an agency once they have arrived in their destination state.[124] Dissatisfied and exploited workers also face barriers to redress once they arrive home, including costs, unfamiliarity with the legal system, absence of legal assistance and problems with jurisdiction.[125]

Bilateral Arrangements

The ASEAN 2020 vision, and integral to the creation of an ASEAN Economic Community, is the transformation of South-East Asia into a *single market* with a free flow of labour, not dissimilar to the economic growth/free labour market nexus promoted in the EU. However, with current ASEAN decision-making characterised by consensual bilateral agreements,[126] achieving some regulatory commonality across the regions is unlikely. Currently the free movement of labour ASEAN-wide is mainly confined to migration of highly skilled workers stimulated by

---

[120] International Organization for Migration (2010), p. 23.

[121] Farbenblum, Taylor-Nicholson and Paoletti (2015), p. 63.

[122] Transient Workers Count Too and Humanitarian Organisation for Migration Economics (2010), p. 28; International Organization for Migration (2010), p. 33.

[123] Farbenblum, Taylor-Nicholson and Paoletti (2015), p. 20; Transient Workers Count Too and Humanitarian Organisation for Migration Economics (2010).

[124] Au (2014).

[125] Farbenblum, Taylor-Nicholson and Paoletti (2015), pp. 123–32.

[126] Chavez (2007).

the divergence between rapid economic growth and educational investment.[127] Such a labour flow is also employed by developing Member States as a method of fulfilling the short-term demands of the market and making sure that the workers provided are temporary.[128] Other more developed autocratic states prefer 'foreign talent' rather than to expose their younger generations to critical thinking.

Largely because of cases where employers abuse workers or work conditions are exposed in the host country as oppressive or dangerous, or where public opinion in the host country turns more against the migrant population, bilateral arrangements come under strain. Malaysia in particular has been criticised for its erratically honoured bilateral migration policies.[129] Sending states regularly impose worker migration moratoriums as a method through which to secure certain rights for their workers or to put pressure on host states to actively ensure better conditions.[130] The problem with this open-and-shut market policy is that sending state economies are very vulnerable to the loss of repatriation revenue and to pressure from their worker population that might even so be willing to accept the pre-existing sub-standard conditions offered in host states, and the receiving states are aware of this market advantage.

Complex bilateral arrangements can also provide a disincentive for worker registration, such as in Thailand, where multiple bilateral agreements demand that the migrant undergo 'nationality verification' in their country of origin before applying for a work permit. Human Rights Watch notes that such requirements actually reduced the number of migrants using official channels, and by December 2007 just 14,151 migrant workers had engaged the government-to-government schemes to find secure legal employment.[131] Some high-demand receiving states, such as Singapore, simply avoid bilateral agreements with labour-sending countries in order to ensure for their market maximum levels of flexibility, while requiring strenuous immigration controls.[132] Preferences for this approach only vary where the supply of some labour types (such as aged carers) comes under strain when in the case of Singapore it was forced to seek out and negotiate arrangements with Cambodia.

---

127 Through, for example, Mutual Recognition Agreements, see Sugiyarto and Agunias (2014), pp. 4–7.

128 Kaur (2007).

129 Kaur (2007), p. 353; Piper (2008), pp. 7–8.

130 Kaur (2007), pp. 358–9.

131 Human Rights Watch (2010), pp. 23–4.

132 Hickey, Narendra and Rainwater (2013), p. 15.

Pre-departure Information and Training

Almost all states provide some form of information to prospective migrants, which appears to be the only feature of the ASEAN Declaration which has achieved tangible regulatory improvements.[133] Who should bear responsibility for this information delivery and training varies across the region. For instance, in the Philippines the government takes responsibility, whereas in Indonesia it is the responsibility of the agent (and associated costs are often then passed onto the worker).[134] Overwhelmingly, government-sponsored information programmes are found to be more effective in familiarising workers with their rights, and about possible (if limited) avenues for redress once overseas.[135]

REGISTRATION

Work Permit Systems

Most receiving countries (Singapore, Malaysia, Thailand and Brunei) that depend on large amounts of unskilled labour (in some instances making up to 30 per cent of the population) have this reliance predominantly in the construction and domestic industries, health care, agriculture and manufacturing.[136] Despite this crucial interdependency, nationality policies, particularly as regards the conferring of rights for migrants consequent on residency/immigration/work registration, are narrow and restrictive:

> ... in all cases, the historical focus of receiving countries ... has been on controlling migration in order to maximise the economic contributions of migrants, while minimising and even actually preventing migrants' claims (and potential claims) for social services, legal protections, family reunification and permanent settlement.[137]

Generally the migrant employment registration process is part of a two-tiered system which differentiates between unskilled and skilled

---

[133] Larga, Tunon and Baruah (2013), pp. 38–40.

[134] von Setyawati (2013), pp. 275–6.

[135] Farbenblum, Taylor-Nicholson and Paoletti (2015), p. 51.

[136] Tan (1996), pp. 49–50; Kaur (2007); Piper (2008). For an extended discussion of public rhetoric surrounding unskilled migrant workers in Singapore, see Rubdy and McKay (2013); Human Rights Watch (2010), p. 20.

[137] Hickey, Narendra and Rainwater (2013), p. 9.

workers. Skilled workers are encouraged as part of boosting economic growth, whereas unskilled workers are on a 'use and discard basis', often diminishing the vital role played by unskilled and semi-skilled foreign workers in maintaining and developing crucial markets such as real estate, and ameliorating the state's responsibility to provide care and welfare to the native population.[138]

Commonly for migrant workers the duration of their stay is limited to two or three years or less, with a levy being placed on employers for their use, and that employment being restricted to certain sectors. The levy system is a significant earner for state-consolidated revenue. In addition, it is meant through quotas and 'dependency ceilings' to temper the market appetite for cheap foreign labour. In reality these quotas seem to have little impact on the major employers and agents but rather hurt the limited profit margins of small businesses.[139] As a device for preferring or better balancing local worker employment opportunities, quotas (or equal worker ratios) tend to drive down salaries for locals and increase the likelihood of employing the aged and unproductive in basic manual work so more fit and productive foreign workers can be employed as a quota counterweight.

These levies also provide a regulatory device through which the employer can restrict the freedom of the worker.[140] The use of levies has encouraged employers in some sectors (for example, construction, where a large amount of workers are required) to hire workers illegally.[141] Often an employer will illegally *on-sell* their worker's labour to defray or to subvert the levy restrictions and black markets for augmented labour of this type are common. The levy is the law and as legal regulation is designed to control labour supply and market viability. In fact levies provide a useful example of how legal regulation primarily for the interests of thc statc will be subverted by the interests of the agents/ employers and damage the legitimate market frame as well as further disempowering workers in vulnerable market positions.

Responsibility for the Worker

When it comes to the maintenance and governance of migrant workers in the region, responsibility is placed on employer, with the state consciously divesting its obligations beyond often vigorous inspectorate

138 Low, Liu and Soh (2008), p. 212.
139 Piper (2008); Kaur (2014), [45]–[60].
140 Devasahayam (2010), pp. 55–6; Au (2014).
141 Au (2014).

functions to ensure compliance with registration and licensing requirements.[142] In Singapore the state requires a 'security bond' of $5,000 (Sgd) which is paid by the employer and forfeited if any of the Work Permit conditions are breached.[143] In Thailand the employer is responsible for accommodation that can be easily inspected, and liable for any damage or nuisance that the worker might cause.[144] Encouraging the employer to police migrant workers has led, in the domestic environment in particular, to employers retaining travel documents, and prohibiting workers leaving the home in case they form relationships or engage in social activities deemed by the wider civil society as in some ways unacceptable.

Consistent with employer obligations over migrant workers, flows the power to terminate workers' employment, after which they must inform the authorities and have the worker repatriated (usually within seven days).[145] In Singapore the state has also shifted repatriation responsibilities to employers with often brutal consequences (discussed in Chapter 5). In Singapore and Malaysia, dismissal of a worker on its own if the procedures have been complied with cannot be the subject of legal or industrial relations dispute as an arbitrary dismissal.[146]

Conditions of Employment

Migrant workers, through their work permit and residency conditions, cannot change their employers without the permission of the current employer (in Thailand this must be written permission in the form of a 'transfer form' signed by both employers accompanied by permission from the authorities).[147] It is not difficult to imagine worker vulnerability if they are in dispute with the original employer over conditions.

All countries in the region prohibit migrant workers from forming a trade union or political organisation. However, in Singapore and Malaysia, such workers theoretically can join unions but levels of trade union

---

142 Devasahayam (2010), pp. 55–6; Transient Workers Count Too and Humanitarian Organisation for Migration Economics (2010).

143 Transient Workers Count Too and Humanitarian Organisation for Migration Economics (2010), pp. 30–31.

144 Human Rights Watch (2010), pp. 28–73.

145 See, e.g., Ministry of Manpower, Singapore website, Work Passes and Permits.

146 Employment of Foreign Manpower Act (Cap, 91A), section 9(4); Employment (Restriction) Act 1968 (Act 353) (Malaysia), section 10(3).

147 Employment of Foreign Manpower Act (Cap. 91A), Part IV; Immigration Department of Malaysia website, Recruitment Terms and Conditions of Foreign Workers; Human Rights Watch (2010), pp. 2–3.

engagement by migrant workers are low.[148] This may be due to the fact that union organisations in these countries are not independent of government and do not encourage association with the transient work force.

On a broader social front, migrant workers are not permitted to have personal relations with citizens of the destination country, marry, 'break up families or become involved in immoral behaviour', or get pregnant. The intrusiveness of these conditions is exemplified in Singapore where this regulation takes the form of biannual pregnancy testing for which the employer is responsible.[149]

In Thailand, provincial regulations dictate that migrant workers cannot own or register motor vehicles, own mobile phones, cannot move out of area of employment without written permission and are subject to curfews (generally after 10pm).[150]

Labour Law Protections?

In Malaysia, Singapore and Thailand to varying degrees migrant workers are covered by elements of labour law but excluded from others. Such limited coverage does not apply to foreign domestic workers.[151] It has been estimated by an ASEAN Task Force on Migrant Workers that 60 per cent of all workers in ASEAN are not covered by labour law, either because of the nature of their work, or being deemed to be irregular migrants.[152]

The selective nature of this legislative coverage has been discussed in chapters 2 and 5 and it is largely directed towards limiting state obligations and further divesting responsibility for worker welfare and rights protections. Singapore requires that employers take out a minimum of $15,000 per year medical insurance for each employee. However the nature and proliferation of workplace related injuries (particularly in construction work) often produce medical costs well above the insured

---

148 Ball and Piper (2002); Piper (2008).

149 See Employment of Foreign Manpower Act 1990 (Cap. 91A), Part IV; also Devasahayam (2010), p. 51.

150 According to Human Rights Watch, this is in the form governmental decrees in the provinces of Phang Nga, Phuket, Surat Thani, Ranong and Rayong. See Human Rights Watch (2010), pp. 28–33.

151 Employment of Foreign Manpower Act 1990 (Cap. 91A), Part IV; Immigration Department of Malaysia website, Recruitment Terms and Conditions of Foreign Workers; Human Rights Watch (2010). This is not, however, the case in Brunei, see Hickey, Narendra and Rainwater (2013), p. 28.

152 Bandial and Begawan (2013).

limit (bearing in mind as foreigners they are charged at the maximum rate for medical expenses). In addition, while waiting for their medical or other dispute claims to be heard migrant workers are placed on a 'Special Pass' which allows them to stay in Singapore but does not allow them to work or generate any means of supporting themselves.[153] In the situation of medical claims, workers are still required to pay their accommodation fees while not receiving a salary for the leave period. Such externalities encourage workers not to claim medical insurance and to work on injured rather than face impossible subsistence expenses. No arrangements as yet exist between Singapore and sending countries for the transfer of labour law or social security benefits between nations.[154]

TRANSITION INTO CITIZENSHIP

Ability to Acquire Citizenship

Citizenship or permanent residency is not available to unskilled migrant workers in any ASEAN receiving state.[155] Unskilled foreign workers or

---

[153] See Employment of Foreign Manpower Act 1990 (Cap. 91A), Employment of Foreign Manpower (Work Passes) Regulations 2012, Schedule 1, Conditions and Regulatory Conditions of In-principle Approval for a Work Permit, section 2; Transient Workers Count Too and Humanitarian Organisation for Migration Economics (2010).

[154] Piper (2006), p. 11.

[155] In Singapore, to qualify for citizenship a worker needs to first gain Permanent Residency, which is only offered to Employment Pass (professional earning above $3,300 per month and with necessary qualifications) or S Pass holders (highly skilled/technician, earning above $2,100 per month) with two to six years of working in Singapore. Even if an unskilled migrant worker was to attempt to gain long-term visitor status or residency through family reunification this would be dependent on having a family member who was a Singaporean Citizen or a Permanent Resident earning above $4,000 per month, see Ministry of Manpower, Singapore website, Work Passes and Permits. In Malaysia, residency is open to experts and professionals, or to individuals who qualify under a points-based system, which awards points for years of stay over five years, language proficiency and tertiary qualifications. As unskilled workers are limited to a stay of two years and do not usually have the educational or personal income requirements under the points-based system, they are effectively prevented from gaining the 65 points necessary for residency. See Immigration Act 1959 (Act 155) (Malaysia); Immigration Department of Malaysia website, Entry Permit; Bowring (2011). Thai citizenship is also dependent on permanent residency, which requires three consecutive years of residence as well as an

persons previously employed as unskilled foreign workers are prohibited from marrying Singaporean citizens or permanent residents, and to do so permission is required from the Controller of Work Passes. In Malaysia marriage, either between migrant workers or with Malaysian citizens/ residents, is prohibited.[156]

The ASEAN regulatory picture, despite massive labour migration flows, and several developed recipient countries with socio-demographics and economies which would crumble without their cheap migrant labour force, features:

- a regional convention with worker protection aspirations that has all but been ignored by Member States (with some home state exceptions);
- sending-state expressive concerns regarding citizen/worker conditions and the regulatory intransigence of receiving states;
- short-term moratorium reactions by sending states against this regulatory inaction, but an eventual return to exploitative conditions due to weak bilateral bargaining power and economic pressure from home;
- agency self-interest and exploitation of workers through excessive fees;
- crucial information deficits affecting worker bargaining power;
- tough migration and employment licensing regimes;
- regulatory divestment by the state to employers;
- excessive and potentially discriminatory controls to employers over work conditions, worker lifestyles and repatriation;
- ineffective dispute resolution opportunities for workers;
- dangerously inadequate health and safety provisions for workers; and
- attacks on worker dignity through constructive social exclusion.

---

income of over 80,000–100,000 Baht per month for two years; see Royal Thai Embassy in London website, Notification of Immigration Commission: Criterion and Conditions of Foreign Nationals' Residential Permit Considerations, para 3.2.3. As above, because of the low-paid and transitory nature of their employment, unskilled workers are unlikely to fulfil these requirements.

156 Employment of Foreign Manpower Act 1990 (Cap. 91A), Employment of Foreign Manpower (Work Passes) Regulations 2012, Schedule 4, Conditions and Regulatory Conditions of Work Permit, Part VI, section 6; The New Paper (2015); Immigration Department of Malaysia website, Application for Employment Pass; Immigration Department of Malaysia website, Application for Foreign Worker.

Overall it is a story of worker commodification and exploitation without even the basic materialist recognition of the vital role played by migrant workforce in the value-added growth 'miracles' of Asian tiger economies.

REGULATING MARKET SECTORS – LABOUR DIGNITY V WORKER MARGINALISATION

This chapter does not have a simple preference for more or less regulation, or in favour of domestic before regional regulation or vice versa. Instead it has revealed that irrespective of the degree of regulation and its source, if the principle behind the regulatory approach, the relationships it fosters and its outcomes prioritise the property arrangements of employers, agents and the state over worker dignity and fair labour pricing, this will inevitably lead to social disembedding.

> A more sophisticated regulatory framework for controlling unfair power relations in adhesion contracts needs to seek to regulate market sectors rather than individual contracts. This type of regulation requires the standard business terms in a particular sector to be tested for their fairness prior to being put into circulation in the market. One way to achieve this might be to require representatives of the two sides of the trade to negotiate the standard terms to be used and to invalidate departures from the agreed model. Another method is to employ a government agency to negotiate and fix standard terms of business in particular sectors … in order to achieve effective regulation of mass contracts for the purpose of the redistribution of power, the key lies in the development of regulatory schemes that are designed to analyse market sectors as collective actors.[157]

In his very apposite discussion of the role of private legal instruments in constructing markets,[158] Collins identifies certain crucial variables which are essential for the creation and growth of trust relationships. Whether it is the *regulation for growth* EU approach, or the *responsibility divestment* model in ASEAN, the reality of migrant worker commodification shows little or no regard for trust bonding as essential for market sustainability.

In the comparative discussion of regulatory absence and action we have set out a dysfunctional terrain where law is complicit in the creation of discriminatory and dependent labour relations that in turn reflect and are exacerbated by the power imbalances which Collins suggests are suitable for repositioning through the use of reconceived contracting.

157 Collins (1999), pp. 234–5.
158 Collins (1999), chapter 5.

> Markets are comprised of patterns of entry into transactions by individuals. They choose to do so where the perceived benefits of the transaction outweigh the perceived risks of disappointment or betrayal. When transactions take place, the risks of disappointment or betrayal have not been eliminated, but they have been displaced, so that they no longer present a formidable obstacle to trade. Displacement occurs when the parties have a relation of trust … much activities in relation to contract should be understood as creating the conditions under which this trust can be established.[159]

Obviously from the comparative analysis preceding, trust is not necessarily created or maximised through the volume or scope of regulation, but rather it is importantly dependent on the regulatory purpose, and the benefits it offers to market players. Law can have a significant influence, we argue, in redirecting the regulatory purpose from individualised profit towards social solidarity. However, placed against the contemporary irrelevance of law in market sustainability, preferring market discrimination and property preferencing, the critic might be forgiven for wondering whether legal regulation can ever have a reformative dimension.

> Aside from the construction of the normative system of property rights that is presupposed in all trading activity, the legal system [currently] makes a marginal contribution to the construction of markets. Legal sanctions rarely make a significant contribution to the construction of trust, and the invocation of the legal process can often damage perceptions of trust-worthiness. (Inclusions added)[160]

The story does not, either for Collins or for us, stop there. Techniques of legal regulation (particularly through private instruments like contracts, and processes such as agency) are already evolving new capacities. The sustainable pairing of private law with other more open-textured regulatory market standards depends on law orienting its regulatory interest and capacity towards market sectors rather than individualised market interests and partial or sectoral stimulants. To escape private law's weaknesses in recognising and reinforcing public goods and collective interests, there is a need for legal regulation to steer other regulatory schemes for the benefit of particular market sectors such as labour force, rather than individualised interests of powerful market players through externalities like the free flow of workers.

We share Collins' concluding optimism that:

---

159 Collins (1999), p. 125.
160 Collins (1999), p. 126.

> Despite this record of failure … the collision between private law and public law regulation … creates a fresh productive capacity for regulation. The insights of the reflexive capacity of private law combined with the collective policy orientation of public regulation can provide a springboard for more productive regulation [in a sustainable sense].[161]

[161] Collins (1999), p. 361.

Conclusion: designating dignity

> … the principle of equality often takes the form of a quasi-proportionality between replacement income and lifetime earnings … modern redistribution is built around a logic of rights and a principle of equal access to a certain number of goods deemed to be fundamental.[1]

INTRODUCTION

The US Declaration of Independence (1776) asserts for everyone an equal right to the pursuit of happiness. If we are to accept the earlier-vaunted notion that men are born free and that social distinction rests on *common utility*, then equality in virtue and inequality as market reality are extant. Why is this not so?

The central tension in any *rights-based* foundation for legal/regulatory repositioning when it comes to private property arrangements is the realistic limits to how far equal rights extend. In Chapter 4 we explored the virtue of equitable contracting within inequitable market frames, and yet the context of labour pricing exposed how only through the aggressive intervention of law might more than the semblance of less inequalities be achieved.

The rights-based frame advanced in this analysis is variegated. Law is employed to reverse or at least mediate and modify the current commercial onus. Law is not to protect the exploitation of the vulnerable and the dependent but rather to demand when market inequality appears mechanical, of those mechanisms the measure of *common utility* and its market value appropriate for and commensurate with sustainable societies.

This conviction may sound like a reaffirmation of Rawls' 'difference principle'[2] and Sen's 'capabilities' approach.[3] While giving credit to these views,[4] we recognise the need (in providing substantive reconciliation between social justice and market inequalities) for critical analysis to

1 Piketty (2014), p. 779.
2 Altham (1973).
3 Sen (2004).
4 Findlay and Lim (2014a), chapter 4.

return to the specific historical and economic contexts which have informed the empirical component of our text. If we are to advance repositioned legal regulation and its influence over private property arrangements as a pathway for market and social realignment, then it is essential to practically explore how the living conditions of those most disadvantaged can be improved in a better socially located market.

In determining this process of more equitable and realistic revaluation we advocate measures of happiness that do not only reallocate wealth, recognising the prevailing material wealth = happiness equation is partly to blame for the inequality leading to market imbalance.[5] If wealth and growth are created and maintained in markets where access to capital, pricing productivity, and sharing profit are skewed in favour of those who predominate in private property arrangements, then along with regulatory influence over these market frames there will be a need to augment the values which the market can provide to a wider stakeholder base. In the context of social sustainability these values may reflect and reaffirm *goods* representing the conditions of *human dignity in community*.

Employing law to assist in the necessary democratic deliberation and political confrontation attendant on market equalisation as a *social good* will neither prove axiomatic nor easy. Some argue that the origins of law are violence that essentially promotes as well as depends on the inequalities on which it feeds.[6] We understand this position but, as with the argument that law is inextricably wedded to private property discrimination, prefer to recall law's normative significance for communitarian ordering and its historical relevance before property was king.[7] Moving equality of rights beyond absolute principle to a political imperative that would almost routinely emerge from the wreckage of economic and social revolution, law will also shift its own current regulatory emphasis in championing private property protection, on to facilitating a radical reordering of rights valuation.

---

[5] A more detailed discussion of this is found in Findlay and Lim (2014a), chapter 4.

[6] Rousseau (1754).

[7] Berman (1987); Twining (2009).

LAW AS ECONOMISM

Evgeny Pashukanis simultaneously theorised the destruction and survival of law.[8] He saw law as more than the balance of state power or the record of class forces. Finding as we do much merit in exercising an alternative approach to the need for more extensive law theorising put by Pashukanis,[9] we do not accept the assertion that law can only be a reflection and a pre-condition of simple commodity exchange. Seeing law as little more than an appendage to commodity relations enables through the elimination or even just contracting of exchange market arrangements, law's withering away, along with its cognate principles of justice. Collateral damage would be the diminished enunciation of individual rights in favour of some collective obligation and benefit proposed through other political and economic means, and neither enunciated in law's normative frame, nor protected by its facilitative capacity as a market regulator. Giving up on all of this would really make all we have argued so far, hot air.

While this book works within paradigms of economism it envisages law as broken free from them. Law has the potential as we see it to return exchange commodities such as wage labour to their extrinsic values as much as it has to their distortion. Restricting the consideration of law as form (Pashukanis could be faulted for this) fails to understand law's different substantive fields. At the same time, like we argue against labour rights discourse later in this chapter, it is specious to laud law for its normative declaration of rights equality, while declining to reveal its substantive inequality. Arthur in a defence of Pashukanis takes the form/substance dilemma further:

> Pashukanis should have laid greater stress on the need to criticise law not only as the basis of what it shows (the fetishization of relationships of commodity exchangers) but on what it does not, and indeed what it ideologically cloaks; the inner world of capitalism's appropriation of labour power once the latter has commodity form.[10]

Within the Marxist theoretical frame, by limiting the analysis of law to its market dimension without addressing its grounding in class is to miss:

---

[8] Pashukanis quoted in Kelsen (1966), p. 106 where Kelsen concluded that 'it follows from Pashukanis' identification of law with capitalist economy … that there can be no law in the communist society of the future'.

[9] Mullin (1980).

[10] Arthur (1978), p. 30.

> The inner connection between bourgeois legality and the relations of production founded upon the expropriation of labour.[11]

Class in our analysis is determined by the conditions of use as much as the control of the means of production and law currently determines both. As Sayer reflects:

> There is no logically compelling reason for assuming exploitation must rest in control of the physical means of production … under appropriate conditions control of any condition of production can serve as a possible basis for exploitation.[12]

Migrant labour force is economically exploited because laws of migration and labour relations are regulatory tools that benefit those who have citizenship and market dominance. It becomes important here to understand the connection between the social relations of market production, and legal form. In so doing it would be wrong to argue for the immortality of any particular legal form by wrenching it from its particular historical traditions. Rather we would search for ways to more sustainably incorporate juridical concepts (such as contracting, agency and legal personality) into ideological processes that as yet suffer without clear and sustainable applied reformative outcomes.

CAN LAW BE AN UNQUALIFIED HUMAN GOOD?

> … rights and democratic practises are discounted as camouflage or discounted as relics of bourgeois liberalism … this very often goes along with a wholesale dismissal of *all* law and *all* police, and sometimes with a sloppy notion that *all* crime is some kind of displaced revolutionary activity.[13]

We take the position that if wide-ranging social revolution is not yet on the cards, then there needs to be a continued struggle for equity, dignity and the civil rights that support them. The legal side of state power is not the impediment to these aspirations but rather the class bound procedures which determine the operation of legal arrangements. Law can impose effective inhibitions on market power, disaggregated as these presently may be, but what are its limits, what kind of inhibitions and what form can they achieve? Currently, as is the case with law's sponsorship of

---

[11] Fine (1979), p. 43.
[12] Sayer (1975), pp. 799–800.
[13] Thompson (1979), p. 15.

private property arrangements, these depend on the organisation of the working (labouring) classes to be dominated by the power of capital and the bourgeois state. What needs to be resolved in the context of private property arrangements and their potential contribution to sustainability is the way that law can stimulate extra-legal political regulation so that rule of law is no longer code for class domination. There is little doubt, even as so often is currently perceived, that rule of law is rule of class. In its most egalitarian representation, rule of law complements the class domination of capital and other means of production.[14] But this does not have to be so. If the driver behind rule of law discourse is not premised on the immutability of exploitative private property relations, then rule of law can drift from legitimating the market to reintegrating the social.

We have argued for law that, under the right market conditions which it facilitates through repositioned private property arrangements, it can promote social good. As our analysis of migrant labour suggests, law is also now a tool in the market for qualifying access to *economic good*. So that law, in its regulatory mode in particular, may represent as well as promote social good in the terms advanced through our analysis, it is necessary that it make way for choice, but not as an amoral individualist accession. Autonomy is regularly promoted and required by law as a condition of legal engagement.[15] Essentially autonomy is the capacity to choose. Law acts as a selective arbiter of options for choice. If there was an essence to this text it is the redirection of choice pathways through law, diversifying access to the benefits of property that currently law via contemporary private property arrangements is designed to constrain.

THE VALUE OF LIFE AND CHOICE – DISPLACEMENT AND REPLACEMENT

> The sense of honour, and personal dignity – that feeling of persons exaltation and degradation which acts independently of other people's opinion, or even in defiance of it; the love of beauty; the passion of the artist; the love of order, of congruity, of consistency in all things, and conformity to their end; the love of power, not in the limited form of power over other human beings, but abstract power, the power of making our volitions effectual; the love of action, the thirst for movement and activity, a principle scarcely of less influence in human life than its opposite; the love of ease: – ... . Man, that most complex being, is a very simple one in our eyes.[16]

---

14 Fine (1979), pp. 30–31.
15 Cotterrell (2007), p. 107.
16 Mill (1987), p. 132.

In his memoir on life as a senior government regulator (interestingly focusing on the value of life) Cass Sunstein defines regulation principally as legal controls that limit or authorise public or private conduct in order to promote some social good.[17] While recognising the paradox between universal rights recognition of the equality of human dignity and the discriminatory calibration of the value of life, Sunstein demands principled regulation should endeavour to work against inequality and inequity.

When looking at labour market regulation against a measure of the value of life, Sunstein identifies welfare and autonomy as important regulatory considerations. Similar to Hayek and Sen, he agrees that institutions such as the market can be judged by the extent to which they promote human liberty and freedom. This is a distinctly different vision of the market as the promoter of economic prosperity. In the context of worker integrity, and whether autonomy or welfare are the appropriate regulatory pathways, where the market is ordered so as to recognise stakeholder dignity, then choice becomes a reality. In terms of risk in the exercise of labour power, the quantification of an employer's willingness to pay as against the worker's willingness to accept will only go to ensuring a healthier market frame when there is some balance in the exercise of crucial choices about the nature and extent of labour power and their pricing.

In an earlier work looking at globalisation and crime we spent some time deconstructing choice, not in terms of individual but cultural values of life.[18] As we have asserted in our discussion of contracting and agency relations (chapters 4 and 5) choice at crucial decision sites in the development of migrant labour arrangements provides a tangible platform for rebalancing power relations, economic benefit and rationalising labour value without destroying market viability (see Chapter 2).

In *The Globalisation of Crime*, we identified opportunities for choice as essential if the options available open up to beneficial outcomes rather than primarily to a set of adverse eventualities (that is, rights protection v access to work). Motivation for opening up or constraining opportunity benefitting some stakeholders at some essential decision sites merit interrogation if we are to appreciate the dynamics of choice-making and wish to regulate for their more equitable divestment.

> Opportunity needs to connect with motive if (real) choice is to eventuate. Motive is more complex than rational choice theory suggests. An understanding of the nature of motive is crucial if the deactivation of (adverse) choice,

---

[17] Sunstein (2014), p. 3.

[18] Findlay (1999), chapter 6.

through the reduction of (distorted) opportunity is to occur. Otherwise tampering with opportunity will only lead to a deflection of (adverse) choice if the original motive is strong. (inclusions added)[19]

In the context of crime and control choices these reflections went on to develop a displacement/replacement dynamic which retains relevance for our consideration of regulating migrant labour arrangements. As suggested in Chapter 3, a new role for law in private property engagement offers legal regulation an important role in displacing exploitation, dependency, vulnerability and devalued labour price, replacing these with sustainable market conditions.

Even utilising powerful and institutionally set employment, contracting and agency laws that balance stakeholder interests, the *displacement and replacement* cycle is dynamic. Markets morph as choice flexes under fluid market conditions.

> In anything but a state of total indulgence, making choices is a comparative exercise. The factors which influence any choice outcome will almost always be determined against other choice scenarios … the process through which such comparative evaluation concludes is what displacement and replacement represent … displacement occurs when conventional features of opportunity are removed, and replaced by illegitimate substitutes … replacement and displacement processes are dynamic, relative and negotiable, reflecting the analytical position accorded to choice … like the passage towards globalisation, the choice process should both expand and unify the experience of those making choices where the motivation for choice is shared. There must be some logic in making choices. As such the logic need not be constrained within paradigms of reason or utility. To make much of this logic beyond mindless individualism it is necessary to suggest, in terms of fundamental contexts, what choice must be working towards.[20]

For us this eventuality is incontrovertibly social sustainability, not individual wealth creation and economic growth at any cost.[21]

QUANTIFICATION AND MONETISATION

It is not uncommon for regulators to talk about regulatory principles and outcomes in terms of numbers and money. Such an approach is driven by desires for accountability, transparency, consistency and stringency all

---

[19] Findlay (1999), p. 167.
[20] Findlay (1999), pp. 181–2.
[21] See Findlay (2013); Findlay and Lim (2014a).

deemed better likely if regulation promotes informed and responsible choice. The choice should enable empowered selection between the various 'good' consequences flowing from different regulatory endeavours.

> When regulators quantify and monetize relevant goods, the goal is to promote sensible choices, not to erase differences among quantitatively distinct goods. Nor should this point be unfamiliar from daily life. People … make trade-offs amongst these and countless other diverse goods, they do not pretend that they are quantitatively identical.[22]

There are two assumptions which underpin the argument that regulation recognises diversity rather than preferring uniformity in the search for, and the determination of, *goods*. Initially there needs to be both access to and not displacement from choice options within regulatory populations. The market, for instance, cannot promote choice for some at the cost of excluding other critical stakeholders. The second assumption is that those faced with choice can afford to make it. As we have seen with the options (where they exist) for migrant workers to claim minimum working conditions, choice becomes elliptical when these legitimate claims in turn decrease the attractiveness of their labour-power in a discriminatory market. The cost of the choice is disembedded market viability.

And what of the contexts in which, because of the knock-on effect of risks associated with choice, it becomes difficult to quantify the attractiveness or even the consequences of constrained regulatory decision-making and choice participation. The underlying difficulties in quantifying risks and outcomes may rest with the relativity of measurement. Standard cost–benefit may be neither useful nor appropriate if access to choice alternatives bringing good outcomes is crucially skewed in a market framework. In such settings, and largely for the most disadvantaged stakeholders, the calculation of *judgement-costs* and the benefits that could outweigh these, along with an explanation of the *judgement conditions and processes*, while important for informed regulation, become impossible if information deficit and choice disempowerment are not also an object of the regulatory project.

When looking at the importance of choice as a market *dignifier*, uniformity in valuation might be as illusive, as it is unrealistic. That said, a fully individualised approach to market choice is not feasible even if it is a worthy aspiration. This book has argued law's task in better individuating the role of migrant labour within private property relations

---

[22] Sunstein (2014), p. 70.

comprising disembedded labour markets. For achieving this end it is necessary to plot how individuation varies across clear and measurable risks. Further, individuation becomes more understandable as the structural impediments to equality in market participation are exposed and addressed. Both these regulatory trajectories are legitimate roles for law in repositioning private property arrangements.

TYRANNY OF AUTONOMY

Autonomy is often advanced as a major *dignifier of the individual*. In recent neo-liberal attacks on welfarism,[23] the argument goes that governments should not force people to spend more than the very small amount they have and are willing to spend even if the welfare gain is not trivial, and that governments (through compelled expenditure from consumers and tax payers) should in turn be willing to spend more than poor people are willing to pay to reduce a risk, simply because the welfare gain would not be trivial.[24] This policy conviction almost reads as an assertion that despite poverty and consequent choice constraint, every citizen should be at liberty to make their choices on risk reduction. Taken to its most extreme, this would speak as an endorsement for wholesale deregulation in the name of liberty, and justified by the dignity of individualist autonomy.

We reject that regulatory intervention challenges the dignity of individualised choice, and that autonomy and dignity in all social circumstances, are equivalent. If we move from the autonomy of choice to the autonomy of life, it is compelling that people have a right not to be subjected to risk and that right should not be conditional on their intrinsic *value* in any market sense. We assert due to the malignance of law's current role in crafting and maintaining private property relations, labour markets are in the grip of behavioural failure. Therefore, resting the protection of the individual on their willingness to pay can only be argued if that preference for transaction does not violate prerogative rights that are declared as evidence of human dignity. With the exploitation and vulnerability on which the current profitability of migrant labour markets depend, it is the mechanics of the market that disempower migrant workers from gaining realistic labour pricing which might then project them into positions where a willingness to pay is a reality of choice. Instead these workers are regulated out of contributing to tax or

23 Hall (2011); Spies-Butcher (2014).

24 Sunstein (2014), p. 114.

welfare frames. Beyond the problematic contention that individuals should be considered citizens and not merely consumers constantly at the edge of choice, migrant workers as market variables are kept out of deliberative democracy, with their access to autonomy being equally dead-ended.

In a section to follow we advance our critical consideration of migrant labour commodification by recognising that the ownership of their labour has been leeched from them in markets of vulnerability and dependency. Migration displaces the migrant, making residency the fiat of employers and the state, while denying any genuine role to the worker in determining labour price. Even the withholding of labour to achieve better conditions falters on the realisation that employers turn off and on employment availability, and thereby can exile migrant labour from any monetary valuing at the stroke of a pen.

Living a life of perpetual risk, the migrant worker is denied the dignity of basic certainties. Law is currently complicit in the destabilisation and devaluing of migrant labour value which then fuels the outsider's view that these units of production are expendable as such, worth much less in risk measurement terms.

GLOBAL AND TRANSNATIONAL RISK VALUATION – ARE THE LIVES OF THE VULNERABLE WORTH LESS?

In its second report in 1995,[25] the Inter-governmental Panel on Climate Change calculated that a life in an industrialised country was worth 1.5 million USD whereas the life in a developing country was worth 150,000. The measurement of differential life valuing (removed from more integral and essential determinants) raises important problematics regarding dignity. Monetarisation such as this (and crude as it seems) is only regularly advanced in policy terms as a comparative. Providing a way of viewing differential dignity across the globe such comparatives require critical consideration, regarding why actuarial measures are even attempted and contrasted. Do these comparisons call for a balancing (through transnational and global regulation) of the factors on which valuations of statistical life (VSL) are advanced? If more equivalent VSL is utopian, or generates its own comparative challenges, should we not at

---

[25] Intergovernmental Panel on Climate Change (1995).

the very least qualify the meaning and application of these figures often as arbitrary as they are offensive?

We do not wish to sink into the mire of monetarisation where the value of dignity is at stake. However, what these comparative measures suggest is that, in a world of multi-national commerce and the mass migration of labour force, containing VSL to national jurisdictions is both distracting and very probably divisive. In so doing, the argument allows for the incapacity of poorer nations, through regulatory action, to lift the 'value' of their citizens, as an excuse for limiting regulatory vigour. Chapter 2 establishes, in the short-term, that migrant labour markets benefit a small portion of the rich in national economies, damage the viability of the native labour market at large, and exacerbate dangerous wealth gaps. For multi-national corporations benefitting from the globalised migration of cheap labour, the competitive advantages are much greater and the wealth generation minus social sustainability costs is indeed attractive. Recognising this, to limit the value of life and its correction to the capacity of disadvantaged and denuded nation states for rectifying an imbalance perpetuated by international commercial market advantage reads as irresponsible and pedestrian. The costs involved in addressing what are obscene comparisons in life valuation across the globe must be sheeted home to those market players who drive prices (and values) down for their own market advantage. Nation states may in part be responsible for this inversion (and benefit from it in terms of welfare cost displacement, and superficial economic growth through transitory injections of capital – see Chapter 6) but by comparison with multi-national commercial exploitation state responsibility so measured, is far less significant.

In this book, the argument in favour of repositioning regulatory responsibility for market imbalance and towards market sustainability will not be embraced by those players against who it should be directed, without incentivisation. Here is where the demand for law should gain new drivers. In order to sensitise other *low hanging fruit* in market economies (like semi and unskilled local workers) against distorted (often consciously inverted) probability risk perception (such as migrants steal our jobs and challenge our national image) and towards the benefits of this regulatory redirection, law's expressive role will need to advance the real dangers in exclusive private property relations. All workers with marginalised influence over labour pricing need to understand that presently endorsed, exclusive private property arrangements undermine general social good in the form of fair labour valuing at large, rather than holding out the plunder from further exploiting migrant labour force as the rich if restricted rewards of citizenship and individualised meritocracy.

Unfortunately in recent debates across the European Union (referred to in chapters 5 and 6) organised domestic labour (trade unions) has fought the advancement of basic rights for migrant workers on the genuinely delusional platform that the presently limited pool of social welfare is not enough to go around. This position basically ignores the shared dilemma of disempowered labour force migrant or otherwise, and plays into the hands of those interests that financially benefit from further destabilising the social presence of migrant labour.

INDIVIDUAL HUMAN RIGHTS AND DIGNITY – THE TROJAN HORSE?

Rights discourse is part of the problem when endeavouring to revalue and dignify labour. Too often it talks in model terms approaching the utopian, making its motivation behind legal regulation all to ephemeral and, from the perspective of those it is designed to protect, tragically peripheral. For instance where is this sentiment reflected in the plight of undocumented domestic workers in the Middle East?

> Migrants are not commodities nor are they just economic or political actors. They are producers and drivers of social change. Throughout the world migrants are best placed to contribute to society when their rights are respected … Human beings are now recognised as being at the core of migration, no longer seen as merely economic agents. It is only through the protection of the human rights of all migrants that migrant workers are able to contribute to the economic, social and human development of both their countries of origin and host countries.[26]

The stark disconnect between human rights discourse and the life experiences of migrant workers in the states of the Gulf Co-operation Council (Bahrain, Kuwait, Oman, Qatar, Saudi Arabia and the United Arab Emirates) (GCC) calls into question conventional international humanitarian law recourse to effective regulation.

After the mid 1970s oil boom these state economies became dependent on cheap temporary migrant labour, primarily in construction and domestic markets.[27] The most common countries of origin for these low-skilled

[26] Office of the High Commissioner for Human Rights (2013).
[27] Baldwin-Edwards (2011), pp. 14–24.

workers are India, Pakistan, Nepal, Sri Lanka, Indonesia, Ethiopia, Eritrea, China, Thailand, Korea and the Philippines.[28]

At the other end of the labour supply chain these economies remain reliant on highly skilled expatriates to staff the private sector.[29] GCC nationals are primarily employed in the public sector where there are higher wages and better protections (under 'localisation' policies public sector jobs are primarily available to GCC citizens).[30] Altogether migrants comprise 88.5 per cent of the population in the UAE, 85.7 per cent in Qatar and between 30–70 per cent in the other GCC states.[31]

For low-skilled workers recruitment agencies in sending countries sometimes require workers to pay between $2,000–3,000 (USD), including visa and transportation costs to recruiters.[32] Relationships of crippling financial dependency and impoverishment commonly feature at the outset of the work arrangements, where migrants are both economically and emotionally most at risk from fundamental rights violations.

Migration into the GCC is governed by the kafala system, which further institutionalises dependency relations on which residency is confirmed. In this arrangement a GCC citizen acts as sponsor of the migrant and assumes all legal and financial responsibility for them once they have entered into the receiving state.[33] In return the migrant is bound to that sponsor/employer and cannot change employers without written consent (and in some states without first working two years for that sponsor).[34] Further, by restricting mobility and binding the worker to the employer, good or bad, the migrant cannot change to a job of a different nature, cannot leave the receiving state without consent, cannot join a trade union, and enjoys no minimum wage, in an employment

---

[28] Human Rights Watch (2014), p. 11; Human Rights Watch (2006), p. 23; Auwal (2010), pp. 87, 105.

[29] Ruhs (2013), p. 99; Baldwin-Edwards (2011), p. 15.

[30] Ruhs (2013), p. 98; Harry (2007), pp. 135–42.

[31] Shah and Fargues (2013), p. 2.

[32] Human Rights Watch (2006), p. 8; Al Jazeera (2012).

[33] Murray (2012), p. 467.

[34] Human Rights Watch (2006), p. 36; see *Cabinet Resolution No. (25) of 2010 concerning Internal Work Permits Applicable in the Ministry of Labor (UAE)*. The employee may still apply to terminate their contract and work permit to leave the country, however unless they have the consent of their employer and have worked the requisite two years they are likely to be subject to a re-entry ban.

pricing regime where standard industry wages are based on ethnicity rather than skill.[35]

Migrant workers face fines, deportation and one year re-entry bans for absconding from sponsor/employers. Those who harbour domestic worker migrants who have absconded without a visa can also be liable to penalties (Articles 95 and 96(a) of the *Executive Regulations of the Entry and Residence of Foreigners*).[36]

Contracting conditions do little to ameliorate these contextual opportunities for exploitation. As an example the United Arab Emirates (UAE) utilises a standard form contract for domestic workers to nullify whatever contract terms or instruments the migrant may have agreed to with the recruitment agency in their sending state.[37] If this regulatory device were applied to correct the earlier exploitation through agency contracting it would have a positive influence on rights protection. In reality the standard form contract entrenches or exacerbates these exploitative terms.

Low-skilled workers receive meagre wages in comparison to what they could be paid in other jurisdictions. For instance, in the GCC it is estimated that construction workers receive 2 per cent of what they would earn in the United States. Regarding high-skilled migrants, their wages are on par with international salaries and in many cases much higher.[38] With lower-skilled migrant workers it is common practice for sponsor employers to withhold wages (for at least the first two months) and to encourage migrants to work illegally for other sponsors/multiple sponsors at the same time, thus making a side-line business through sponsorship and subjecting workers to even greater labour demands for no financial return but to the sponsor.[39]

There are no citizenship opportunities available for migrant workers no matter how long might be their years of service and residency.[40]

Winckler and Murray identify five characteristics that both accord with, and differentiate the GCC employment/migration system from, any other comparable migration system:

---

35 International Labour Organization Regional Office for Arab States (2014); Human Rights Watch (2006), pp. 2–15.

36 Human Rights Watch (2014), p. 19.

37 Human Rights Watch (2014), p. 22; Consulate-General of the United States website, Domestic Employee Visa.

38 Auwal (2010), p. 95.

39 Human Rights Watch (2006), p. 8; see also Saberi (2006); Shah (2009), p. 12; Baldwin-Edwards (2011), pp. 40–41.

40 Murray (2012), p. 468.

1. no citizenship or permanent residency available to migrant workers
2. lack of employment stability (two years is usual length of work permits, then requiring renewal at the sponsor's discretion)
3. permanent settlement is not sought by workers
4. migrant workers constitute the majority of the workforce
5. GCC citizens (and not just the economic elite) gain enormous benefits from cheap migrant labour.[41]

The human rights challenges particular to the plight of migrant construction workers in the GCC include:

- high death rates due to industrial accidents, heat-related injuries and suicides (in 2004 Indian, Pakistani and Bangladeshi embassies counted 880 construction worker deaths).[42] The International Trade Union Confederation (ITUC) is predicting a further 4,000 deaths in Qatar associated with the construction work for the 2022 FIFA World Cup facilities;[43]
- scant health and safety regulation. For instance, in Qatar there are approximately 140–50 inspectors for over 240,000 construction related businesses, exacerbating workplace accidents and heat-related injuries, and the relatively high rates of suicides (approximately 80 in 2004);[44]
- frequent complaints concerning the non-payment of wages, especially after the global financial crisis where many construction firms went bankrupt and then exited the GCC, often leaving the migrant workers that they had sponsored without consent to go home or any means of repatriation.[45]

In the context of migrant domestic workers the human rights challenges specifically present as:

- no legal protection, with workers being explicitly excluded from labour laws or any minimum wage requirements (for example, Federal Law No 8 on the *Regulations of Labor Relations*, UAE);

---

41 Murray (2012), pp. 467–8; Winckler (2009).
42 Construction Week (2005).
43 International Trade Union Confederation (2014), pp. 14–15.
44 International Trade Union Confederation (2014), p. 25; Human Rights Watch (2006), p. 44.
45 Al Jazeera (2012); International Labour Organization (2010).

- conflicts of interest where complaints from domestic workers are also handled by the Ministry of Immigration rather than the Ministry of Labor (UAE);
- imprisonment/reduced mobility of workers virtually confining them in the home by sponsors where employers pay relatively high fees to recruitment agencies for securing the worker without guarantee of a replacement if the worker absconds;
- widespread physical abuse, sometimes sexual abuse, and the retention of wages, food and communication, as estimated by Human Rights Watch (HRW). If a migrant domestic worker escapes such abuse, they may face possible charges of absconding and/or theft, as well as zina (sexual crimes) when apprehended.[46]

What of the influence of legal regulation, international or regional? No GCC state is a party to the International Convention on Rights of Migrant Workers, and many have not ratified the core ILO conventions.[47] There exists no minimum standard wage, with workplace complaints usually being handled by the Ministries of Labour. Access to complaints mechanisms is further limited by the requirement that workers' complaints must be written and submitted in Arabic or English. Several other state agencies are responsible for policing migrants' conditions (for example, the Human Rights Department of the Dubai Police and the Permanent Committee on Labor Affairs). Even so, there remains a focus on worker compliance.

It is a sad fact that international condemnation of rights violations is more likely to be effective if it is directed to national reputation and economic viability rather than the individual integrity of the migrant worker. For instance, in light of criticism regarding pre World Cup preparation and particularly migrant worker conditions, Qatar has implemented the Qatar Foundation Standards and Supreme Committee Standards. This initiative, however, has been criticised as no more than window dressing, in that there is still little enforcement of these regulations, no minimum wage designated for migrant workers, and the kafala system remains in place.[48]

For us this is not a unidimensional story of human rights violations, to be answered by greater compliance with international conventions, more significant transfer of convention principles into domestic law, and more inspection enforcement. These developments may assist in at least casting a sharper light on employment abuse and human exploitation.

---

[46] Human Rights Watch (2014), pp. 60–62.
[47] Murray (2012), p. 478.
[48] Dickinson (2014), pp. 16–20.

However, as the sponsorship system, the restrictions on labour mobility, the slave wages, the denial of potential citizenship and the calibration of labour price in terms of status and ethnicity reveal, the more fundamental fields for change are the manner in which migrant labour is commodified and the labour market is discriminated in this region. With each state either adopting profound regulatory conflicts of interest, or totally abrogating regulatory responsibility to stakeholder self-interest, change will not come from the regulatory state without some fundamental market realignment. Law is vital in this repositioning.

The regulatory recipe of many NGOs and human rights academics continues to sidestep the commodification and market realignment issues, preferring instead to advocate:

- ratification of key human rights and ILO conventions, and the removal/amendment of the kafala system;
- transparency within sending countries about the conditions that migrants should expect when travelling to work in these countries, public education campaigns, especially for domestic workers as the most vulnerable group;[49]
- greater regulation of recruitment agencies within sending states;[50]
- a *naming and shaming* approach in the international arena, engaging with NGOs for assistance, and encouraging non-sending countries (such as the US and EU) to attempt to bargain better conditions for workers when negotiating free trade agreements with GCC;[51]
- embargoes by sending countries on certain categories of workers until the regulatory framework is tightened. Indonesia, for example, banned migration to Saudi Arabia for domestic work in August 2011 until greater legislative protections were introduced (which occurred in February 2014 in the form of Resolution No. 310 or the Household Regulation on Service Workers and Similar Categories).[52]

We say good luck to these aspirations but with little confidence. Is it not reasonable to question the efficacy of an international humanitarian law approach relying on nation state compliance and facilitation, where

49 Human Rights Watch (2006), pp. 17–18.

50 Human Rights Watch (2014), p. 75; Dickinson (2014), p. 6; Human Rights Watch (2006), p. 16.

51 Auwal (2010), pp. 101–9.

52 Burke (2011); Varia (2014).

nation states such as these are deeply complicit in the regulatory market abuses and regulatory lacunae that critics would want them to redress?

TRANSITION

In this book we have not attempted to set out law's regulatory role for some new and inevitable global epoch, a venture far too grand for even the most expansive market contexts. Rather the analysis of law's role in private property arrangements past, present and future has been with the purpose of exploring regulatory transition.

Our work on North/South Worlds[53] challenges regulatory scholarship to break free of the regulatory state. Without reiterating the argument for that here, it is relevant to suggest, as with the limitations of a public international law approach to controlling global crime and justice,[54] that seeing the law/state synergy as ineffable tends to constrain our consideration of transformative potentials in legal regulation.

Some of the confidence we have in law's capacity to act as a positive force in market transition, towards social embeddedness rather than away from it, rests on two important observations:

1. It is the expressive more than the facilitative function of the law (when we turn to contract and agency relationships) which sees contracts and agency arrangements as compliance mechanisms rather than breach frameworks. As such the *unspoken* terms of contract and agency generate the preference to comply and that these may not only emanate out of self-interest. If access to contract and agency influence and benefit is broadened through the regulatory measures earlier suggested in this work (see chapters 4 and 5) then the compliance imperative need not be undermined. In fact it would be the compliance imperative that enables any transition to a wider franchise of benefit occurring without substantive restructuring of the contract or agency instruments and processes.
2. Law is a regulatory device with the capacity to free-up and tie-down market relations. This regulatory duality suggests that law is not a singular or unidirectional influence over market trajectory, and as much as it now may stimulate market disembedding, it similarly possesses the potential to redirect market relationships

---

[53] Findlay and Lim (2014a).
[54] Findlay (2013).

> back in a social direction, without necessarily destroying the market as an exchange mechanism. Obviously this may mean that the market entities for exchange may vary from commodities to other material or non-material forms, the value which will not be dominantly material wealth, nor will their exchange sacrifice market sustainability for shorter-term economic growth goals.

But transition is not only about markets devoid of considering their crucial characteristics. This book has focused on the market plight of migrant workers, to observe their subservience AND to positively encourage legal regulation as a market balance, one that can promise the sustainability of social bonding through new understandings of property relations. To achieve this law needs to participate in the emancipation of these workers as lives and not livelihoods, as people and not units of production.

> Most people would say they own themselves, or own their labour, and this gives them the right to do X or Y. In the law of course, a person cannot have a property relationship with their own body, and the circumstances under which you can dispose of your labour are both restricted by laws as well as market possibilities and so forth. But nonetheless the colloquial notion that you 'own what you are' is incredibly strong … lawyers can talk until they are blue in the face about how an individual does not own their person, but the very language of property and its close association with proprietorship, says the opposite … From all sides this forms a very general sense that your identity in the world and the activities associated with you are part *of* you, they are your *own self*, and the self can in that sense *own* the self: the self and all its expressions. That is a very strong folk concept.[55]

Unfortunately against the struggle for human dignity, Strathern observes that property turns things into objects and requires the exercise of subjective control over these objects.[56] Like the monetarisation and commodification of labour without thought of the worker as man and woman, the ease in effecting undignified and dehumanising experience becomes a market routine.

A depressing feature of how migrant labour is positioned in the productivity frames of modernised economies is what we refer to as *speculative* enslavement; that the labour pool is perceived as limitless, and because of the seeming inevitability of selective global impoverishment, unlimited in its compliance with exploitation. A positive spin is

---

55 Strathern (2013), p. 212.
56 Strathern (2013), p. 216.

often attached to the speculation surrounding labour enslavement; being the argument that such workers are better off even in discriminating markets than if they were not even offered the exploitative conditions that currently characterise these market arrangements. The disturbing foundations of this justification reveal how those interests currently benefitting from migrant labour displacement are comfortable to hitch onto future profit forecasts projections about a regulatory environment continuing which is not designed to transform, but rather to preserve or at least ignore these unsustainable market arrangements.

> Speculation in and of itself, once put into circulation, creates its own set of facts, resulting in an altered material reality. For a system to be operational, to gain a level of reality, it does not have to be true in any provable sense. Instead, as is well known, it has to function only as a communal fiction that is shared by a sufficient number of people.[57]

At present worker, agent, employers, governments and the public at large share a belief (for different reasons) in the inevitability of speculative enslavement. If legal regulation is to be truly transformational of private property arrangements in migrant labour markets, it needs to confront this perception, and in a quest to invest dignity into migrant labour, law needs to clearly define sites of responsibility for denying and then igniting that dignity.

RESPONSIBLE WHO?

In the epilogue to his book, Cass Sunstein proposes four ways to humanise the regulatory state. In this he epitomises the constriction of Western regulatory scholarship. The blinkers of this vision, worthy as it may be, are encapsulated in the invocation that:

> … to decide how to handle social problems, governments should focus on the human consequences of their decisions.[58]

He tells us that first the state should appreciate costs and benefits not as arithmetic abstractions, but as efforts to 'capture' (and the verb is revealing) qualitatively diverse goods and to promote sensible trade-offs. Second he suggests that the state should take account of values that are difficult to quantify. Implicit in this is the inherent utility of quantified

---

[57] Hirsch (2013), p. 228.
[58] Sunstein (2014), p. 173.

values in general and the state's role as the principal quantifier. Next he argues that cost/benefit choices for regulation should be behaviourally informed. Again the contrariness of this is apparent. It should be the social rather than the economic which drives our consideration of the essence of behaviour and the responsibility of regulation to maximise its *good*. The final admonition is just why the state is not enough as the author of sustainable futures, being compromised in its participation in dysfunctional private property arrangements. The need to benefit from the dispersed information of a wide variety of human beings is just why we must return the state and its economic addictions to more fundamental obligations of the broad social.

In the preceding analysis we do offer a role for the state in the regulatory transition to sustainable market economies, particularly as it is the modern sponsor institution for law making. This role is given moral weight by the sometimes irresponsible benefit gained by states through the maintenance of current private property arrangements, at the expense of migrant workers. Add to this the market reality that states facilitate the preferential positions of employers and agents, making the obligations of redress apparent and pressing. An important stimulating function for the state in environments of sociability is to prominently and candidly broadcast the risks to the market if regulatory balance is not better achieved. In addition to this, the state can act to broker essential communication between market players in a spirit of interest mutualisation.

The central objection to the regulatory state literature is the presentation of the state as an impartial regulatory force. Surely by now, in the migrant worker case study, we have dismantled that pretence. The serendipity situation of the state as mastering migration regulation for national interests, and at the same time posturing adherence to workers' rights commitments, obliges the state to reconcile its crucial influence over the vulnerability and dependency contexts of migrant worker livelihoods.

NEW WAYS OF THINKING

A prevailing criticism of our analysis could be the perceived failure to tackle what would motivate a change in law's influence over private property arrangements. Why would law, or more specifically its powerful sponsors such as preferred commercial and state interests, jeopardise their even unbalanced market share through acceding to corrective principles and practices in legal regulation? The answer resides in sustainability, and for those who find it difficult to embrace the notion in its wider communal manifestations, the sustainability of market economies.

Take for example the recent global push, hegemonic and commercial, to ameliorate global poverty, particularly in Africa.[59] In part this may be an inevitable humanitarian concession. However, more likely with the repositioning of the global economic model,[60] anti-poverty campaigning is as much about strengthening and growing new consumer markets as it is about the recognition and revaluing of human dignity.[61] Bill Gates came to Davos with cassava to encourage the rich to feed the poor. His friends took up the challenge to benefit the starving but also to recognise the inherent productivity of the world's impoverished when lifted out of their desperation.

Following the downturn in the American economy after the sub-prime mortgage crash and consequent strains on the global financial industry,[62] China was confronted with the immanent and stark reduction of its major consumer market, on which its economic growth was in no small part dependent.[63] In response the Chinese government concentrated economic effort on growing its domestic middle class and expanding the scope and depth of its local consumer market.[64]

This market refocusing in China should not be read as some recognition that the nation state can determine its economic fate in isolation. If China sees sustainability through the limited lens of profit and gain then lending to the US to stimulate consumer markets through economic rejuvenation is no different than investing in the African or Chinese poor.

If this market growth/poverty eradication nexus is smart developmental policy and good for human dignity (both distinctly contestable assumptions) then global economic development policy must also move more distinctly into sustainability mode. The UN Millennium Goals enunciate this inevitability.[65] Yet prioritised mechanisms of modern global socio-economic development remain out of step. Take for instance, Foreign Direct Investment. This *aid technology* has become popular with world aid organisations because it enables more targeted and responsible

---

59 Sachs et al (2004); United Nations (2013), p. 7.

60 Hughes and Haworth (2011).

61 Spangenberg (2014).

62 United Nations Industrial Development Organization (2009).

63 Roach (2014), Preface.

64 Elms and Low (2013), chapter 5.

65 United Nations Sustainable Development website, with the Sustainable Development Goals building upon the Millennium Development Goals.

investment pathways, and implicitly avoids the complicated and often problematic intrusions of fragmented state bureaucracies. The down side of this development model is that by skirting the state, good or bad and for valid investment reasons, it contributes little to state capacity-building and disaggregated states remain the problem rather than part of the solution. A public/private partnership mix with directly accountable FDI frames would present a more viable developmental design in the medium-term if social sustainability is also a developmental priority.

Another problem is the *share-holder profit* investment model for FDI. If investment returns against domestic risk are to be almost entirely repatriated out of the host developing economy, then sustainable economic and social development are casualties rather than inevitable consequences of FDI.[66] The profit returns for the aid/investment dollar must, through balanced private property arrangements encouraged by law, be measured in terms of human dignity and social bonding in the host economy, even more than financial benefits for investors against economic risk. Without this expanded notion of investment value, market sustainability is not maximised. Nor will the essence of human dignity reiterated throughout this book be grown through social bonding and property concepts which rest in trust as much as transaction.

SOCIABILITY AND MARKET SUSTAINABILITY INTO THE FUTURE

At this point we are as intrigued as should be the reader, whether the link between dignified labour, reconstituted private property arrangements and their relationship to the law going forward will essentially and seamlessly demand broader social equality. The key to satisfying this conjecture lies in how these transformed market components work discreetly and then interact *within* the framework of current market economies. The impact on markets as we know them will be the empirical frame to answer whether markets need to change for the law to change or vice versa? It is the (as yet untested) belief in this analysis that as private property arrangements are transformed through a rehabilitated legal regulatory initiative (producing for instance more dignified labour valuing) then the social embedding of crucial market components, and therefrom the sustainability of the markets they accommodate, is inevitable.

---

66 Culpeper and Bhushan (2008).

Even if the regulatory direction of law over private property arrangements could be repositioned as our analysis argues, there remain questions concerning the sustainability of this transformation and its outcomes. As with suggestions that through regulatory sociability communities of shared risks can achieve mutuality across different interests and move to shared fate,[67] the larger transition from what came before to what comes after (chaos → orderliness shifts through sociability) is not simple or easy to determine. The uncertainty as to what will ensure the sustainable security of change is a consequence of there being so little empirical evidence as yet, that this happens in a market frame. There are many examples in the communitarian literature which explore collective dispute resolution incorporating divergent interests in crisis-to-mutuality management.[68] Also, much of the restorative justice literature uses a similar method for conflict resolution directed from initially opposing standpoints.[69] Where our efforts to reform regulatory principle with social sustainability as the driver differ from these modes of regulation (and what is not contained in corporate social responsibility literature)[70] is the conscious positioning of sociability in a market setting.[71] There is much theorising on market disembedding that has been discussed in our earlier work,[72] being the process of sociability in reverse, but we have found nothing convincing exists which studies in detail the social and market factors ensuring more permanent sustainability from sociability through market-embedding in an empirical sense.

How do we deal with what happens after market orderliness has been achieved, in particular, how do we prevent old self-interested patterns of behaviour creeping back in? In some earlier work on corporate sociability[73] we asserted that new regulation frameworks will become normalised through the more common and natural practice of sociability. Because mutualised 'fate' results are measurably more beneficial in a social sense than the triumph of exclusionist property rights, it will be difficult to remove them from a growing regulatory prominence. But what do we do about parties that might then use this improved social ordering and more sustainable market condition as a springboard to forward their own interests, and what of those who seek to go along with collaboration in

67 Findlay (2013).
68 Reimers and Chung (2010).
69 Bloomfield, Barnes and Huyse (2003).
70 D'Amato, Henderson and Florence (2009).
71 Findlay (2014).
72 Findlay (2013); Findlay and Lim (2014).
73 Findlay (2013).

times of crisis but then revert back to old profit-motivated regulation/lack of regulation when the crisis is over?

We offer two possible scenarios with very important reservations, and two consequential answers, one less satisfactory in terms of sustainable market societies. In one scenario communitarian regulatory engagement is the product of necessity. Therein the principle of regulation is so profoundly and irrevocably changed along with prevailing economic realities at large, from wealth creation in an individualist sense to more sustainable social relations through the contraction of economic growth. In addition, the limits on state resources have stimulated the general repositioning of social direction from materialism in the modern age to more collectivist sustainability in the 'after-modern'. We are seeing this already in *failed* (in the Western economic model sense) states, such as Greece,[74] and in economies where wage labour and commodification are less and less realistic aspirations for the next generations. In the case of Greece recovering from largely unregulated borrowing excess, epidemic tax evasion, profligate bank lending on unmanageable sovereign debt, corrupt economic and commercial governance, recent strangling austerity in public policy, and histories of savage wealth gaps, the necessity for sociability rather than more socially destructive austerity regulatory approaches is becoming clear. Tearing away the social fabric to shore up an economic culture, which in no small part got Greece to where it is today, and sacrificing future generations to structural exclusion from wage labour without the provision of alternative means of subsistence, is a recipe for dis-embedding at all levels. Even from an external regulatory perspective, ungoverned economic profligacy to unrelenting austerity is an unsustainable attack on modern social bonds – from no regulation to toxic regulation. In Greece, alongside austerity and economic restructuring we are seeing a re-emergence of communitarian social engagement which is more than a pastoral reinvigoration of lost agrarian days. There is beginning a widespread breakdown of individualistic regulatory directions out of necessity, consequent with the emergence of new regulatory principles, relationships and objectives designed to tolerate, and be resilient to the flight of individualist wealth creation and anticipated economic growth out of the ashes.[75] The other side of this transition at a time of great social pain through the collapse of the welfare state communitarian model is the emergence of negative nationalism, the seeds

74 Polychroniou (2014); BBC News (2011).
75 Slavo (2011).

or irredentist communitarianism and what has become known as disidentification.[76]

The second less attractive option is that of regulatory cycles, from crisis to crisis as a consequence of the inevitability of human greed. Short-term corrections in the international financial industry following the 2009 collapse evidence this tragic myopia.[77] However, with the nation state and wage labour essentially in decline as environments for mechanical social exclusion and regulatory dysfunction, communitarian evolution is inextricable in societies with still enough time to seek sustainable market arrangements. Whether the triumph of the *social* over the *individual* is sustainable will be the question.

Pashukanis suggested that because of its indelible stamp of bourgeois property interests, law would wither away. At the other end of the political spectrum *Washington consensus* neo cons argue away law in favour of market freedom.[78] Somewhere in the middle, Proudhon confirms that if private property arrangements are profoundly altered then law finds its place. We extend his optimism by proposing law as a crucial medium in revisioning property and embedding its markets, because of law's *essentially sociable* normative foundations, and its capacity to outlive the economic and political superstructures which since the emergence of capitalist commodification imbued law with little more than elite commercial value.

---

76 Prinos (2014).
77 Giovanoli (2009).
78 Kanbur (2009).

Bibliography

JOURNAL ARTICLES

Akerlof G. and Yellen J. (1985) A Near–Rational Model of the Business Cycle, With Wage and Price Inertia. *The Quarterly Journal of Economics* 100, 828–38.

Alexander G. (2000) Cognitive Theory of Fiduciary Relationships. *Cornell Law Review* 85/3, 767–85.

Altham J. (1973) Rawls's Difference Principle. *Philosophy* 48/183, 75–8.

Amaldas M. (2009) The Management of Globalization in Singapore: Twentieth century lessons for the early decades of the new century. *Journal of Alternative Perspectives in the Social Sciences* 1/3, 982–1002.

Ames J. (1909) Undisclosed Principal: His rights and liabilities. *The Yale Law Journal* 18/7, 443–53.

Amin S. (2011) Exiting the Crisis of Capitalism or Capitalism in Crisis? *Globalizations* 7/1–2, 261–73.

Anderson B. (2007) A Very Private Business: Exploring the demand for migrant domestic workers. *European Journal of Women's Studies* 14/3, 247–64.

Auwal M. (2010) Ending the Exploitation of Migrant Workers in the Gulf. *The Fletcher Forum on World Affairs* 34/2, 87–108.

Backer L. (2007) From Moral Obligation to International Law: Disclosure systems, markets and the regulation of multinational corporations. *Georgetown Journal of International Law* 39, 591–653.

Bacon D. and Hing B. (2010) The Rise and Fall of Employer Sanctions. *Fordham Urban Law Journal* 38/1, 77–105.

Baldaccini A. (2010) The EU Directive on Return: Principles and protests. *Refugee Survey Quarterly* 28/4, 114–38.

Ball R. and Piper N. (2002) Globalisation and Regulation of Citizenship – Filipino Migrant Workers in Japan. *Political Geography* 21(8), 1013–34.

Barnard C. (2008) Unravelling the Services Directive. *Common Market Law Review* 45, 323–94.

Barnard C. (2014) EU Employment Law and the European Social Model: The past, the present and the future. *Current Legal Problems* 67/1, 199–237.

Barnett R. (1986) A Consent Theory of Contract. *Columbia Law Review* 86, 269–321.

Barnett R. (1987) Squaring Undisclosed Agency Law with Contract Theory. *California Law Review* 75/6, 1969–2003.

Barbe E. and Johansson-Nogues E. (2008) The EU as a Modest 'Force for Good': The European neighbourhood policy. *International Affairs* 84/1, 81–96.

Barber P. (2000) Agency in Philippine Women's Labour Migration and Provisional Diaspora. *Women's Studies International Forum* 23/4, 399–411.

Benson P. (1989) Abstract Right and the Possibility of a Nondistributive Conception of Contract: Hegel and contemporary contract theory. *Cardozo Law Rev* 10, 1077–198.

Berman H. (1987) Individualistic and Communitarian Theories of Justice. *University of California, Davis Law Review* 21, 549–75.

Birmingham R. (1970) Breach of Contract, Damage Measures, and Economic Efficiency. *Rutgers Law Review* 24, 273.

Bloch A., Kumarappan L. and McKay S. (2015) Employer Sanctions: The Impact of Workplace Raids and Fines on Undocumented Migrants and Ethnic Enclave Employers. *Critical Social Policy* 35/1, 132–51.

Boettke P. (1994) The Reform Trap in Economics and Politics in the Former Communist Economies. *Journal des Economistes et des Etudes Humaines* 5/2/3, 267–93.

Boldrin M. and Horvath M. (1995) Labor Contracts and Business Cycles. *Journal of Political Economy* 103/5, 972–1004.

Bosniak L. (1991) Human Rights, State Sovereignty and the Protection of Undocumented Migrants Under the International Migrant Workers Convention. *International Migration Review* 25/4, 737–70.

Bratland J. (2004) Contestable Market Theory as a Regulatory Framework: An Austrian postmordem. *The Quarterly Journal of Austrian Economics* 7/3, 3–28.

Bridge M. and Braithwaite J. (2013) Private Law and Financial Crises. *Journal of Corporate Law Studies* 13/2, 361–99.

Brosius J. (1999) Green Dots, Pink Hearts: Displacing politics from the Malaysian rain forest. *American Anthropologist* 101, 36–57.

Cangiano A. and Walsh K. (2014) Recruitment Processes and Immigration Regulations: The disjointed pathways to employing migrant carers in ageing societies. *Work, Employment & Society* 28/3, 372–89.

Castles S. (2006) Migration and Community Formation under Conditions of Globalization. *International Migration Review* 36/4, 1143–68.

Castles S. (2007) Twenty-first Century Migration as a Challenge to Sociology. *Journal of Ethnic and Migration Studies* 33/3, 351–71.

Cawthorne P. and Kitching G. (2001) Moral Dilemmas and Factual Claims: Some comments on Paul Krugman's defense of cheap labour. *Review of Social Economy* 59/4, 455–66.

Chang M., Hanf D. and Pelkmans J. (2010) The Services Directive: Trojan horse or white knight? *Journal of European Integration* 32/1, 97–114.

Chavez J. (2007) Social Policy in ASEAN: The prospects for integrating migrant labour rights and protection. *Global Social Policy* 7/3, 358–78.

Cholewinski R. (2008) The Human and Labor Rights of Migrants: Visions of equality. *Georgetown Immigration Law Journal* 22/2, 177–219.

Construction Week (2005) Site worker death toll exceeds 800. *Construction Week* 83 (6 August 2005).

Coote B. (1988) The Essence of Contract (Part II). *Journal of Contract Law* 1, 183–204.

Cotterrell R. (2010) Justice, Dignity, Torture, Headscarves: Can Durkheim's sociology clarify legal values? *Socio & Legal Studies* 20/1, 3–20.

Countouris N. (2012) The Legal Determinants of Precariousness in Personal Work Relations: A European perspective. *Comparative Labour Law and Policy Journal* 34/1, 21–46.

Countouris N. and Horton R. (2009) The Temporary Agency Work Directive: Another broken promise? *Industrial Law Journal* 38/3, 329–38.

Cremers J. (2010) Rules on Working Conditions in Europe: Subordinated to freedom of services? *European Journal of Industrial Relations* 16/3, 293–306.

Dalton C. (1985) An Essay in the Deconstruction of Contract Doctrine. *Yale Law Journal* 94, 997–1114.

Davies A. (2008) One Step Forward, Two Steps Back? The *Viking* and *Laval* case in the ECJ. *Industrial Law Journal* 37/2, 126–48.

Deakin S. (2013) What Exactly is Happening to the Contract of Employment? *Jerusalem Review of Legal Studies* 7/1, 135–44.

Devasahayam T. (2010) Placement and/or Protection? Singapore's labour policies and practices for temporary women migrant workers. *Journal of the Asia Pacific Economy* 15/1, 45–58.

De Stefano V. (2014) A Tale of Oversimplification and Deregulation: The mainstream approach to labour market segmentation and recent responses to the crisis in European countries. *Industrial Law Journal* 43/4, 253–85.

Drahos P. and Parker S. (1990) Critical Contract Law in Australia. *Journal of Contract Law* 3, 30–49.

Duff A. (1982) Intention, Responsibility and Double Effect. *The Philosophical Quarterly* 32/126, 1–16.

Eisenberg M. (1982) The Bargain Principle and its Limits. *Harvard Law Review* 95, 741–801.

Elias O. (2004) The International Status of Taiwan in the Courts of Canada and Singapore. *Singapore Year Book of International Law* 8, 93–103.

Elrick T. and Lewandowska E. (2008) Matching and Making Labour Demand and Supply: Agents in Polish migrants' networks of domestic elderly care. *Journal of Ethnic and Migration Studies* 34/5, 717–34.

Findlay M. (2014) Corporate Sociability: Analyzing motivations for collaborative regulation. *Administration & Society* 46/3, 339–70.

Findlay M. and Lim S. (2014b) Relevance of the Regulatory State in North/South Intersections. *International Journal of Social Economics* 41/7, 542–55.

Finn P. (1989) Commerce, the Common Law and Morality. *Melbourne University Law Review* 17, 87–99.

Fotopoulos T. (2000) Beyond Marx and Proudhon. *The International Journal of Inclusive Democracy* 6/1, 1–17.

Fredman S. (2004) Women at Work: The broken promise of flexicurity. *Industrial Law Journal* 33/4, 299–319.

Geddes A. (2005) Chronicle of a Crisis Foretold: The politics of irregular migration, human trafficking and people smuggling in the UK. *The British Journal of Politics & International Relations* 7/3, 324–39.

Gibson K. and Graham J. (1986) Situating Migrants in Theory: The case of Filipino migrant contract construction workers. *Capital & Class* 10/2, 130–49.

Gil Araujo S. and González-Fernández T. (2014) International Migration, Public Policies and Domestic Work: Latin American migrant women in the Spanish domestic work sector. *Women's Studies International Forum* 46, 13–23.

Giovanoli M. (2009) The Reform of the International Financial Architecture After the Global Crisis. *International Law and Politics* 42, 81–123.

Goetz C. and Scott R. (1977) Liquidated Damages, Penalties, and the Just Compensation Principle: A theory of efficient breach. *Columbia Law Review* 77, 554.

Graveson R. (1941) The Movement from Status to Contract. *The Modern Law Review* 4/4, 261–272.

Gsir S. (2013) EU Labour Immigration Policy: Discourses and mobility. *Refugee Survey Quarterly* 32/4, 90–111.

Gumus Y. (2010) EU Blue Card Scheme: The Right Step in the Right Direction? *European Journal of Migration and Law* 12/4, 435–53, pp. 448–9.

Harry W. (2007) Employment Creation and Localization: The crucial human resource issues for the GCC. *The International Journal of Human Resource Management* 18/1, 132–46.

Hepple B. (1999) United Kingdom. In Private Employment Agencies. *Bulletin of Comparative Labour Relations* 36, 380.

Heyes J. (2011) Flexicurity, Employment Protection and the Jobs Crisis. *Work, Employment and Society* 25/4, 642–57.

Heyes J. and Lewis P. (2014) Employment Protection Under Fire: Labour market deregulation and employment in the European Union. *Economic and Industrial Democracy* 35/4, 587–607.

Humphries J. and Rubery J. (1984) The Reconstitution of the Supply Side of the Labour Market. *Cambridge Journal of Economics* 8/4, 331–46.

Inghammar A. (2010) The Employment Contract Revisited: Undocumented migrant workers and the intersection between international standards, immigration policy and employment law. *European Journal of Migration and Law* 12/2, 193–214.

Kanbur R. (2009) The Co-Evolution of the Washington Consensus and the Economic Development Discourse. *Macalester International* 24, 33–57.

Kaur A. (2007) International Labour Migration in Southeast Asia: Governance of Migration and Women Domestic Workers. *Intersections: Gender, History and Culture in the Asian Context*, Issue 15 (May 2007).

Kaur K. (2010) Labour Migration in Southeast Asia: Migration policies, labour exploitation and regulation. *Journal of the Asia Pacific Economy* 15/1, 6–19.

Kaur A. (2014) Managing Labour Migration in Malaysia: Guest worker programs and the regularisation of irregular labour migrants as a policy instrument. *Asian Studies Review* 38/3, 345–66.

Kemmerling A. and Bruttel O. (2006) New Politics in German Labour Market Policy? The implications of the recent Hartz reforms for the German welfare state. *West European Politics* 29/1, 90–112.

Kenner J. (1999) Statement or Contract? Some reflections on the EC Employee Information (Contract or Employment Relationship) Directive after *Kampelmann. Industrial Law Journal* 28/3, 205–31.

Krippner G. *et al.* (2004) Polanyi Symposium: A Conversation on Embeddedness. *Socio–Economic Review* 2, 109–35.

Laffont J. (1994) The New Economics of Regulation Ten Years After. *Econometrica* 62/3, 507–37.

Lesinska M. (2014) The European Backlash Against Immigration and Multiculturalism. *Journal of Sociology* 50/1, 37–50.

Maas W. (2008) Migrants, States, and EU Citizenship's Unfulfilled Promise. *Citizenship Studies* 12/6, 583–96.

Marin K. (1991) Employment Division v. Smith: The Supreme Court alters the state of free exercise doctrine. *The American University Law Review* 40, 1431–76.

Mason A. (1988) Australian Contract Law. *Journal of Contract Law* 1, 1–7.

Michaels R. and Jansen N. (2006) Private Law Beyond the State? Europeanization, globalization, privatization. *American Journal of Comparative Law* 54, 843–90.

Mullin N. (1980) Pashukanis and the Demise of Law: An essay review. *Contemporary Crises* 4/4, 433–8.

Mullins P. (1992) Judicial Activism Constructs Lenders' Nightmare. *Campbell Law Review* 15/1, 77–95.

Murray H. (2012) Hope for Reform Springs Eternal: How the sponsorship system, domestic laws and traditional customs fail to protect migrant domestic workers in GCC countries. *Cornell International Law Journal* 45/2, 461–85.

Pang E.F. (1991) Labour Migration in Singapore: Policies, trends and implications. *Regional Development Dialogue* 12/3, 22–36.

Pang E.F. (1992) Absorbing Temporary Foreign Workers: The experience of Singapore. *Asia and Pacific Migration Journal* 1/3–4, 495–510.

Portes A. (2007) Migration, Development and Segmented Assimilation: A conceptual review of the evidence. *The ANNALS of the American Academy of Political and Social Science* 610/1, 73–97.

Prinos I. (2014) Golden Dawn, Media Representation and the Neoliberal Restructuring of Social Welfare: On the Greek crisis and the mobilisation of disidentifications. *Sociological Research Online* 19/3, 5.

Reimers F. and Chung C. (2010) Education for Human Rights in Times of Peace and Conflict. *Development* 53/4, 504–10.

Roberts K. (1997) China's "Tidal Wave" of Migrant Labor: What we can learn from Mexican undocumented migration to the United States? *International Migration Review* 31/2, 249–93.

Rother S. and Piper N. (2014) Alternative Regionalism from Below: Democratizing ASEAN's migration governance. *International Migration* 52(6).

Rounds C. (2009) The Common Law is Not Just about Contracts: How legal education has been short-changing feminism. *University of Richmond Law Review* 43/4, 1185–217.

Rubdy R. and McKay S. (2013) Foreign Workers in Singapore: Conflicting discourses, language politics and the negotiation of immigration identities. *International Journal of the Sociology of Language* 222, 157–85.

Ruhs M. and Anderson B. (2010) Semi-compliance and Illegality in Migrant Labour Markets: An analysis of migrants, employers and the state in the UK. *Population, Space and Place* 16/3, 195–211.

Sassen S. (1994) The Informal Economy: Between new developments and old regulations. *The Yale Law Journal* 103/8, 2289–304.

Sayer D. (1975) Method and Dogma in Historical Materialism. *Sociological Review* 23/4, 799–805.

Schwartz A. (2000) Contract Theory and Theories of Contract Regulation. *Revue d'Economie Industrielle* 92/2, 101–10.

Schwartz A. and Scott R. (2003) Contract Theory and the Limits of Contract Law. *Yale Law Journal* 113, 521–620.

Sen A. (2004) Capabilities, Lists, and Public Reason: Continuing the conversation. *Feminist Economics* 10/3, 77–80.

Shire V. (2012) Who Cares? Gender, migration and care work in Austria and Germany. *Unikate* 41, 48–57.

Silver H. (1994) Social Exclusion and Social Solidarity: Three paradigms. *International Labour Review* 133/5–6, 531–78.

Silvey R. (2007) Unequal Borders: Indonesia transnational migrants at immigration control. *Geopolitics* 12/2, 265–79.

Singh B. (2008) Singapore: Success at home, challenges from abroad. *Southeast Asian Affairs*. Institute of Southeast Asian Studies, Singapore.

Sirianni C. (1984) Justice and the Division of Labour: A Reconsideration of Durkheim's *Division of Labour in Society*. *The Sociological Review* 32/3, 449–70.

Smyth L. (2011) Anthropological Critiques of Sustainable Development. *Cross-sections* Volume VII, accessed on 16 February 2015 at https://eview.anu.edu.au/crosssections/vol7/pdf/ch07.pdf.

Spangenberg J. (2014) Institutional Change for Strong Sustainable Consumption: Sustainable consumption and the degrowth economy. *Sustainability: Science, Practice & Policy* 10/1, 62–77.

Spies-Butcher B. (2014) Marketisation and the Dual Welfare State: Neoliberalism and inequality in Australia. *The Economic and Labour Relations Review* 25/2, 185–201.

Stark D. (1986) Rethinking Internal Labor Markets: New insights from a comparative perspective. *American Sociological Review* 51/4, 492–504.

Sterk S. (2005) Trust Protectors, Agency Costs, and Fiduciary Duty. *Cardozo Law Review* 27, 2761–806.

Sugiyarto G. and Agunias D. (2014) A 'Freer' Flow of Skilled Labour within ASEAN: Aspirations, opportunities and challenges for 2015 and beyond. *Migration Policy Institute* 11, 1–12, accessed on 25 February 2015 at http://publications.iom.int/bookstore/free/MPI_Issue11_2Dec2014.pdf.

Tan C. (1996) Employee Relations in Singapore – Current Issues and Problems. *Employee Relations* 18/3, 48–61.

Terranova T. (2000) Free Labor: Producing culture for the digital economy. *Social Text* 18/2, 33–58.

Unger R. (1983) The Critical Legal Studies Movement. *Harvard Law Review* 96, 561–675.

Van Ginneken W. (2013) Social Protection for Migrant Workers: National and International Policy Challenges. *European Journal of Social Security* 15/2, 209–21.

von Setyawati D. (2013) Assets or Commodities? Comparing regulations of placement and protection of migrant workers in Indonesia and the Philippines. *Austrian Journal of Southeast Asian Studies* 6/2, 264–80.

Waldron J. (1985) What is Private Property? *Oxford Journal of Legal Studies* 5/3, 313–49.

Wishnie M. (2007) Prohibiting the Employment of Unauthorized Immigrants: The Experiment Fails. *The University of Chicago Legal Forum*, 193–217.

Wong D. (1997) Transience and Settlement: Singapore's foreign labor policy. *Asian and Pacific Migration Journal* 6/2, 135–67.

Wray H. (2012) An Ideal Husband? Marriages of convenience, moral gatekeeping and immigration to the United Kingdom. *European Journal of Migration and Law* 8, 303–20.

Wunderlich D. (2013) Implementing EU External Migration Policy: Security-driven by default? *Comparative European Politics* 11/4, 406–27.

Yeoh B. (2006) Bifurcated Labour: The unequal incorporation of transmigrants in Singapore. *Tijdschrift voor Economische en Sociale Geografie* 97/1, 26–37.

REPORTS OF INTERNATIONAL ORGANISATIONS

Berg A. and Ostry J. (2011) Inequality and Unsustainable Growth: Two Sides of the Same Coin? *International Monetary Fund Staff Discussion Note*, SDN/11/08 (8 April 2011), accessed on 11 February 2015 at http://www.imf.org/external/pubs/ft/sdn/2011/sdn1108.pdf.

Carls K. (2012) *Decent Work for Domestic Workers: The state of labour rights, social protection and trade union initiatives in Europe.* International Training Centre, International Labour Organization.

Cazes S., Verick S. and Heuer C. (2009) Labour Market Policies in Times of Crisis. *Employment Working Paper No. 35*, accessed on 16 February 2015 at http://www.ilo.org/wcmsp5/groups/public/ – ed_emp/ – emp_policy/documents/publication/wcms_114973.pdf.

Elms D. and Low P. (2013) Global Value Chains in Changing World. *World Trade Organization, Fung Global Institute, Temasek Foundation Centre for Trade and Negotiations*, accessed on 19 February 2015 at http://www.wto.org/english/res_e/booksp_e/aid4tradeglobalvalue13_e.pdf.

Gagnon J. and Khoudour-Casteras D. (2011) *Tackling the Policy Challenges of Migration: Regulation, Integration, Development.* OECD Development Centre, Paris.

Intergovernmental Panel on Climate Change (1995) *Second Assessment Report: Climate Change 1995*, accessed on 18 February 2015 at https://www.ipcc.ch/pdf/climate-changes-1995/ipcc-2nd-assessment/2nd-assessment-en.pdf.

International Centre for Migration Policy Development (2009) *Regularisations in Europe: Study on practices in the area of regularisation of illegally staying third-country nationals in the Member States of the EU.* International Centre for Migration Policy Development, Vienna, Austria.

International Labour Conference (2007) *Report VI: The Promotion of Sustainable Enterprises.* International Labour Office, Geneva.

International Labour Office (2007) Guide to Private Employment Agencies: Regulation, monitoring and enforcement. International Labour Organization, Geneva.

International Labour Office (2014) Fair Migration: Setting an ILO agenda. *Report of the Director-General, Report I(B)*, accessed on 18 February 2015 at http://ilo.org/wcmsp5/groups/public/ – ed_norm/ – relconf/documents/meetingdocument/wcms_242879.pdf.

International Labour Organization (2007) International Labour Standards: Rights of non-nationals. *IOM-UNITAR Briefing for Delegations on International Law Applying to Migration* (19 June 2007). International Labour Organization, New York.

International Labour Organization (2010a) Labour Inspection in Europe: Undeclared work, migration, trafficking. *Labour Administration and Inspection Programme LAB/ADMIN Working Document No. 7*, International Labour Organization, Geneva.

International Labour Organization (2010b) Deserted in the Sands: Migrant Workers in the UAE. *ILO Multimedia uploaded on to YouTube*

(30 July 2010), accessed on 18 February 2015 at https://www.youtube.com/watch?v=5Sum1taw2sM.

International Labour Organization (2012) Global Estimate of Forced Labour: Regional Factsheet European Union. Accessed on 25 February 2015 at http://www.ilo.org/wcmsp5/groups/public/@europe/@ro-geneva/@ilo-brussels/documents/genericdocument/wcms_184975.pdf.

International Labour Organization (2013) Report of the Committee of Experts on the Application of Conventions and Recommendations (Articles 19, 22 and 35 of the Constitution), *International Labour Conference, 102nd Session*, accessed on 24 February 2015 at http://www.ilo.org/wcmsp5/groups/public/ – ed_norm/ – relconf/documents/meetingdocument/wcms_205472.pdf.

International Labour Organization Regional Office for the Arab States (2012) Regulating Private Employment Agencies, *Regional Tripartite Conference on ILO Convention No. 189, Background Note* (22–24 October 2012), accessed on 25 February 2015 at http://www.ilo.org/wcmsp5/groups/public/ – arabstates/ – ro-beirut/documents/genericdocument/wcms_210535.pdf.

International Labour Organization Regional Office for Arab States (2014) Cooperating Out of Isolation: The case of migrant domestic workers in Kuwait, Lebanon and Jordan. *Discussion Paper, International Labour Organization Regional Office for Arab States* (14 December 2014).

International Organization for Migration (2010) Labour Migration from Indonesia, *International Organization for Migration Report* (27 October 2010), accessed on 25 February 2015 at http://www.iom.int/jahia/webdav/shared/shared/mainsite/published_docs/Final-LM-Report-English.pdf.

Jean S., Causa O., Jimenez M. and Wanner I. (2007) Migration in OECD Countries: Labour Market Impact and Integration Issues. *OECD Economics Department Working Papers No. 562*, accessed on 15 February 2015 at http://www.oecd.org/migration/46607889.pdf.

Markova E. (2006) Economic and Social Effects of Migration on Sending Countries: The cases of Albania and Bulgaria. OECD Development Center, Issy-Les-Moulineaux, Paris, accessed on 16 February 2015 at http://www.oecd.org/dev/38528396.pdf.

Office of the High Commissioner for Human Rights (2013) Statement by Committee on Migrant Workers and Migrant Workers' Rights: Ten years of progress but huge challenges remain, accessed on 18 February 2015 at http://www.ohchr.org/EN/NewsEvents/Pages/DisplayNews.aspx?NewsID=13502&LangID=E.

Shah N. (2009) The Management of Irregular Migration and its Consequences for Development: Gulf Cooperation Council. *International Labour Organization Asian Regional Programme on Governance of*

Labour Migration Working Paper No. 19, accessed on 18 February 2015 at http://www.ilo.org/wcmsp5/groups/public/ – asia/ – ro-bangkok/documents/publication/wcms_105105.pdf.

Sorrentino L. and Jokinen A. (2014) Guidelines to Prevent Abusive Recruitment, Exploitative Employment and Trafficking of Migrant Workers in the Baltic Sea Region. *European Institute for Crime Prevention and Control, Publication Series No. 78*, accessed on 25 February 2015 at http://www.heuni.fi/material/attachments/heuni/reports/Eviel1wVV/Heuni_reports_78_Guidelines.pdf.

Stark O., Taylor J. and Yitzhaki S. (2013) Labour Migration, Income Inequality and Remittances: A case study of Mexico, *World Bank DRD Discussion Paper – Report No. DRD283*, accessed on 15 February 2015 at http://www-wds.worldbank.org/external/default/WDSContentServer/WDSP/IB/2013/06/10/000356161_20130610153907/Rendered/PDF/DRD2830Box37730case0study0of0Mexico.pdf.

United Nations General Assembly (March 20, 1987) Report of the World Commission on Environment and Development: Our Common Future. Transmitted to the General Assembly as an Annex to document A/42/427 – Development and International Co-operation: Environment; Our Common Future, Chapter 2: Towards Sustainable Development, accessed on 16 February 2015 at http://www.un-documents.net/ocf-02.htm.

United Nations Industrial Development Organization (2009) The Global Financial Crisis and the Developing World: Transmission channels and fall-outs for industrial development. *Research and Statistics Branch Working Paper 06/2009*, accessed on 19 February 2015 at http://www.unido.org/fileadmin/user_media/Publications/RSF_DPR/WP062009_Ebook.pdf.

United Nations Sustainable Development website, accessed on 19 February 2015 at https://sustainabledevelopment.un.org/topics/sustainabledevelopmentgoals.

United Nations (2013) The Millennium Development Goals Report 2013, accessed on 19 February 2015 at http://www.un.org/millenniumgoals/pdf/report-2013/mdg-report-2013-english.pdf.

PUBLISHED PAPERS

Agunias D. (2013) What We Know About Regulating the Recruitment of Migrant Workers. *Migration Policy Institute, Policy Brief No. 6*, accessed on 24 February 2015 at http://www.migrationpolicy.org/sites/default/files/publications/LaborMigration-Recruitment_0.pdf.

Arifin B. (2012) *Critical Analysis of Domestic Worker Condition in Malaysia and Singapore: Ameliorated economic condition vs. gateway to modern slavery or servitude*. Master Thesis at Malmo University, accessed on 18 February 2015 at https://dspace.mah.se/bitstream/handle/2043/13842/Critical%20Analysis%20of%20Domestic%20Worker%20Condition%20in%20Malaysia%20and%20Singapore.pdf?sequence=2.

Arrow K. (1971) The Theory of Discrimination. *Conference on Discrimination in Labour Markets*, Woodrow Wilson School and Conference Office of Princeton University, accessed on 11 February 2015 at http://www2.econ.iastate.edu/classes/econ321/rosburg/Arrow%20-%20The%20Theory%20of%20Discrimination.pdf.

Association Francaise de Normalisation (2012) Feasibility and Opportunity to Develop a European Standardization Work Programme Concerning "Business to Business" Recruitment Services, accessed on 25 February 2015 at http://www.kdl.din.de/sixcms_upload/media/3145/Project_7_-_Recruitment_Services.pdf.

Baldwin-Edwards M. (2011) Labour Immigration and Labour Markets in the GCC Countries: National patterns and trends. *Kuwait Programme on Development, Governance and Globalisation in the Gulf States* (March 2011), accessed on 18 February 2015 at http://www.lse.ac.uk/middleEastCentre/kuwait/documents/Baldwin-Edwards,%20Martin.pdf.

Barajas A., Chami R., Fullenkamp C., Gapen M. and Montiel P. (2009) Do Workers' Remittances Promote Economic Growth? *IMF Working Paper WP/09/153*, accessed on 15 February 2015 at https://www.imf.org/external/pubs/ft/wp/2009/wp09153.pdf.

Bix B. (2011) Theories of Contract Law and Enforcing Promissory Morality: Comments on Charles Fried. *Minnesota Legal Studies Research Paper 11-47*, accessed on 17 February 2015 at http://papers.ssrn.com/sol3/papers.cfm?abstract_id=1965557.

Bonesmo Fredriksen K. (2012) Income Inequality in the European Union, *OECD Economics Department Working Paper No. 952* (16 April 2012), accessed on 25 February 2015 at http://www.oecd.org/officialdocuments/publicdisplaydocumentpdf/?cote=ECO/WKP%282012%2929&docLanguage=En.

Carls K. (2012) Decent Work for Domestic Workers: The state of labour rights, social protection and trade union initiatives in Europe, ACTRAV/ITC-ILO Report.

Carrera S. and Guild E. (2007) An EU Framework on Sanctions against Employers of Irregular Immigrants: Some reflections on the scope, features and added value, *CEPS Policy Brief No. 140, Centre for European Policy Studies*.

Carrera S. and Pusterla N. (2006) The European Return Fund: Added value and vulnerabilities, European Parliament Policy Unit C: Citizens Rights and Constitutional Affairs, Briefing Paper II (31 January 2006).

Cotula L. (2010) *Investment Contracts and Sustainable Development: How to make contracts for fairer and more sustainable natural resource investment.* IIED, Edinburgh, accessed on 11 February 2015 at http://pubs.iied.org/pdfs/17507IIED.pdf.

Culpeper R. and Bhushan A. (2008) Domestic Resource Mobilization: A neglected factor in development strategy. *The North-South Institute, Ottawa* (April 2008), accessed on 19 February 2015 at http://r4d.dfid.gov.uk/PDF/Outputs/ProPoor_RPC/60667_Background_Paper.pdf.

den Hertog J. (2010) Review of Economic Theories of Regulation, *Tjalling C. Koopmans Research Institute, Discussion Paper Series No. 10-18.*

Dustmann C. (2000) Temporary Migration and Economic Assimilation. *IZA Discussion Paper Series 186*, accessed on 16 February 2015 at https://www.econstor.eu/dspace/bitstream/10419/21029/1/dp186.pdf.

Eurofound (2005) Legislation on Employment Placement Services Amended. *Eurofound Observatory of Working Life, EuroWORK News Update* (28 June 2005), accessed on 25 February 2015 at http://eurofound.europa.eu/it/observatories/eurwork/articles/legislation-on-employment-placement-services-amended.

European Council (2005) The Hague Programme: Strengthening freedom, security and justice in the European Union, 2005/C53/01, OJ C53/1 (3 March 2005).

Gennaioli N. (2006) Contracting in the Shadow of Law. *Innocenzo Gasparini Institute for Economic Research*, accessed on 17 February 2015 at http://papers.ssrn.com/sol3/papers.cfm?abstract_id=813664.

Gibson J., Le T. and Stillman S. (2007) What Explains the Wealth Gap between Immigrants and the New Zealand born? *Department of Economics Working Paper Series No. 2/07*, accessed on 15 February 2015 at http://researchcommons.waikato.ac.nz/handle/10289/1623.

Hanson G. (2008) The Economic Consequences of the International Migration of Labour. *NBER Working Paper No. 14490*, accessed on 15 February 2015 at http://www.nber.org/papers/w14490.pdf.

Hickey M., Narendra P. and Rainwater K. (2013) A Review of International and Regional Migration Policy in Southeast Asia. *Migrating Out of Poverty RPC Working Paper No. 8* (September 2013), accessed on 25 February 2015 at http://r4d.dfid.gov.uk/pdf/outputs/MigratingOutOfPov/WP8.pdf.

Human Rights Watch (2006) Building Towers, Cheating Workers: Exploitation of migrant construction workers in the United Arab

Emirates. Human Rights Watch, USA, accessed on 18 February 2015 at http://www.hrw.org/sites/default/files/reports/uae1106webwcover.pdf.

Human Rights Watch (2010) From the Tiger to the Crocodile: Abuse of migrant workers in Thailand. Human Rights Watch, USA, accessed on 25 February 2015 at http://www.hrw.org/sites/default/files/reports/thailand0210webwcover_0.pdf.

Human Rights Watch (2014) I Already Bought You: Abuse and exploitation of female migrant domestic workers in the United Arab Emirates. Human Rights Watch, USA, accessed on 18 February 2015 at http://www.hrw.org/sites/default/files/reports/uae1014_forUpload.pdf.

Inghammar A. (2010) The Employment Contract Revisited: Undocumented migrant workers and the intersection between international standards, immigration policy and employment law. *European Journal of Migration and Law* 12/2, 193–214.

International Trade Union Confederation (2014) *The Case Against Qatar.* ITUC Special Report, International Trade Union Confederation (March 2014), pp. 14–15.

Jacobi L. and Kluve J. (2007) Before and After the Hartz Reforms: The performance of active labour market policy in Germany. *Journal for Labour Market Research* 40/1, 45–64.

Jonjic T. and Mavrodi G. (2012) Immigration in the EU: Policies and politics in times of crisis 2007–2012, *European University Institute, EUDO Observatory on Public Opinion, Political Elites and the Media (Public Opinion)* (November 2012), accessed on 25 February 2015 at http://www.eui.eu/Projects/EUDO/Documents/2012/Publications/EUDOReport5.pdf.

Kontos M. and Shinozaki K. (2007) Integration of New Female Migrants in the German Labor Market and Society and German State Policies on Integration: A state of the art, *Institute fur Sozialforschung an der J. W. Goethe Universitat Frankfurt, Frankfurt am Mainz.*

Larga R., Tunon M. and Baruah N. (2013) Background Paper: Progress on the implementation of the recommendations adopted at the 3rd and 4th ASEAN Forum on Migrant Labour, *International Labour Organization Regional Office for Asia and the Pacific*, accessed on 25 February 2015 at http://www.ilo.org/wcmsp5/groups/public/–asia/–ro-bangkok/documents/publication/wcms_219040.pdf.

Leschke J., Schmid G. and Griga D. (2006) On the Marriage of Flexibility and Security: Lesson from the Hartz-reforms in Germany, *Social Science Research Center Berlin, Research Unit: Labour Market Policy and Employment* (April 2006), accessed on 25 February 2015 at http://www.metiseurope.eu/content/pdf/allemagne/4_bilan_hartz_wzb.pdf.

Low S., Liu J. and Soh S. (2008) Chinese Foreign Workers in Singapore's Construction Industry. *Journal of Technology Management in China* 3/2, 211–23.

Lutz H. and Palenga-Mollenbeck E. (2010) Care Work Migration in Germany: Semi-compliance and complicity. *Social Policy and Society* 9/3, 419–30.

Mathä T., Porpiglia A. and Sierminska E. (2011) The Immigrant/Native Wealth Gap in Germany, Italy and Luxemburg. *European Central Bank Working Paper Series No. 1032*, accessed on 16 February 2015 at http://www.ecb.europa.eu/pub/pdf/scpwps/ecbwp1302.pdf.

Morgan G. and Nolan C. (2011) Step Up: Improving recruitment of migrant workers in Indonesia, *Business for Social Responsibility, Research Report* (3–7 May 2011), accessed on 25 February 2015 at http://www.bsr.org/reports/Improving_Migrant_Worker_Recruitment_in_Indonesia.pdf.

Northcutt S. (2007) Creative Commons and Intellectual Property, *Leadership Lab: Intellectual Property Series* (1 May 2007), accessed on 16 February 2015 at http://www.sans.edu/research/leadership-laboratory/article/ip-creative-commons.

Otto A. and Bolzonello F. (2012) The Quest for Decent Work for Migrant Workers, *SOLIDAR, Briefing Paper No. 51* (May 2012), accessed on 23 February 2015 at http://www.solidar.org/IMG/pdf/51_dwir_ii__migrants-2.pdf.

Pereira S. (2014) Migrant Workers and Labour Agency. *International Migration Institute Working Paper No. 99* (September 2014). International Migration Institute of the University of Oxford, Oxford, UK, accessed on 18 February 2015 at http://www.imi.ox.ac.uk/pdfs/wp/wp-99-2014.pdf.

Piper N. (2006) Country Study: Singapore, *Friedrich Ebert Stiftung Project on Migrant Labor I Southeast Asia Series*, accessed on 25 February 2015 at http://www.fes.de/aktuell/focus_interkulturelles/focus_1/documents/8_000.pdf.

Piper N. (2008) Country Study: Malaysia, *Friedrich Ebert Stiftung Project on Migrant Labor in Southeast Asia Series*, accessed on 25 February 2015 at http://www.fes.de/aktuell/focus_interkulturelles/focus_1/documents/6_000.pdf.

Roig A. and Huddleston T. (2007) EC Readmission Agreements: A re-evaluation of the political impasse. *European Journal of Migration and Law* 9, 363–87.

Sachs J. *et al.* (2004) Ending Africa's Poverty Trap. *Brookings Papers on Economic Activity,* accessed on 19 February 2015 at http://www.unmillenniumproject.org/documents/BPEAEndingAfricasPovertyTrapFINAL.pdf.

Scott S. (2007) Temporary Migrant Workers and the UK's Flexible Labour Market: Shifting policy narratives and regulatory rebalancing. *Migration Control and Narratives of Societal Steering, The University of Edinburgh*, accessed on 23 February 2015 at http://www.stis.ed.ac.uk/__data/assets/pdf_file/0018/9126/Scott.pdf.

Servent A. (2010) The European Parliament and the 'Returns' Directive: The end of radical contestation; the start of consensual constraints?, *Sussex European Institute, University of Sussex, Working Paper No. 117* (July 2010), accessed on 25 February 2015 at https://www.sussex.ac.uk/webteam/gateway/file.php?name=sei-working-paper-no-117.pdf&site=266.

Shah N. and Fargues P. (2013) Determinants of Future Migration in the Gulf. *Gulf Research Center Foundation, Workshop of Fifth Gulf Research Meeting* (3 November 2013).

Stuber P. (2006) Creating an Intellectual Commons through Open Access, accessed on 17 February 2015 at http://dash.harvard.edu/handle/1/4552055.

Thompson E. (1979) The Secret State. *State Research Pamphlet No. 1*. Independent Research Publications, London, UK.

Transient Workers Count Too and Humanitarian Organisation for Migration Economics (2010) Justice Delayed, Justice Denied: The Experiences of Migrant Workers in Singapore, accessed on 25 February 2015 at http://twc2.org.sg/wp-content/uploads/2013/09/Justice-Delayed-Justice-Denied-ver2.pdf.

Twining W. (2009) Normative and Legal Pluralism: A global perspective. *The Seventh Annual Herbert L. Bernstein Memorial Lecture in International and Comparative Law*, accessed on 18 February 2015 at http://scholarship.law.duke.edu/cgi/viewcontent.cgi?article=1049&context=djcil.

Varia N. (2007) Globalization Comes Home: Protecting migrant domestic workers' rights, accessed on 25 February 2015 at http://www.hrw.org/legacy/wr2k7/essays/globalization/globalizationcomeshome.pdf.

Yeh J. and Chang W. (2009) The Emergence of East Asia Constitutionalism: Features in comparison. *Asian Law Institute Working Paper Series No. 006*, accessed on 16 February 2015 at http://www.law.nus.sg/asli/pdf/WPS006.pdf.

Zegers de Beijl R. (2000) *Documenting Discrimination Against Migrant Workers in the Labour Market*. International Labour Office, Geneva.

NEWS ARTICLES AND MEDIA PUBLICATIONS

Ahmad R., Zolkepli F. and Yuen M. (2013) The Maids May Be Here Soon. *The Star Online* (27 December 2013), accessed on 18 February 2015 at http://www.thestar.com.my/News/Nation/2013/12/27/The-maids-may-be-here-soon-Indonesian-firms-ready-to-talk-on-sending-workers/.

Al Jazeera (2012) The Plight of Qatar's Migrant Workers. *Al Jazeera, Inside Story* (14 June 2012), accessed on 18 February 2015 at http://www.aljazeera.com/programmes/insidestory/2012/06/201261472812737158.html.

Aruna P. (2013) End to Stalemate on Indonesian Maids in the Offing in Malaysia. *AsiaOne News* (20 December 2013), accessed on 18 February 2015 at http://news.asiaone.com/news/malaysia/end-stalemate-indonesian-maids-offing-malaysia#sthash.iwwmHwe7.dpuf.

Bandial Q. and Begawan B. (2013) 60% ASEAN Workers Uncovered by Labour Laws, *The Brunei Times* (6 November 2013), accessed on 25 February 2015 at http://www.bt.com.bn/2013/11/06/60-asean-workers-uncovered-labour-laws.

BBC News (2011) Has Western Capitalism Failed? *BBC News* (22 September 2011), accessed on 19 February 2015 at http://www.bbc.com/news/business-14972015.

Blankenburg S. (2012) 'Mini-jobs' Don't Work in Germany, and They Won't Work in Britain. *The Guardian* (21 August 2012), accessed on 25 February 2015 at http://www.theguardian.com/commentisfree/2012/aug/21/mini-jobs-germany-britain.

Burke J. (2011) Maid 'Held Hostage' for 14 Years in Saudi Arabia. *The Guardian* (22 June 2011), accessed on 18 February 2015 at http://www.theguardian.com/world/2011/jun/22/maid-held-hostage-saudi-arabia.

CCTV.com (2007) Migrant Workers and Trafficking (IV): Illegal Immigration to Singapore. *CCTV.com* (21 January 2007), accessed on 16 February 2015 at http://www.cctv.com/program/asiatoday/20070123/105677.shtml.

Crush P. (2011) Agency Workers Directive Could Price Temps Out of the Market. *The Guardian* (16 September 2011), accessed on 24 February 2015 at http://www.theguardian.com/money/2011/sep/16/agency-workers-directive-temps.

Dancel R. (2014) The Dark Side of Maid Recruitment. *The Straits Times* (19 August 2014), accessed on 18 February 2015 at http://www.straitstimes.com/st/print/2742126.

De Soto H. (September 1993) The Missing Ingredient: What poor countries will need to make their markets work. *The Economist*.

Dickinson E. (2014) The Case Against Qatar. *Foreign Policy* (30 September 2014), accessed on 18 February 2015 at http://foreignpolicy.com/2014/09/30/the-case-against-qatar/.

Farbenblum B., Taylor-Nicholson E. and Paoletti S. (2015) Migrant Workers' Access to Justice at Home: Indonesia, *Open Society Foundations, Migrant Workers' Access to Justice Series.*

Habibu S. and Kong L. (2009) Najib: Act fast to check maid abuse. *The Star Online* (27 June 2009), accessed on 18 February 2015 at http://www.thestar.com.my/story/?sec=nation&file=%2f2009%2f6%2f27%2fnation%2f20090627155143.

Hall S. (2011) The March of the Neoliberals. *The Guardian* (12 September 2011), accessed on 18 February 2015 at http://www.theguardian.com/politics/2011/sep/12/march-of-the-neoliberals.

Knight B. (2013) 'Hartz Reforms': How a benefits shake up changed Germany. *The Guardian* (1 January 2013), accessed on 25 February 2015 at http://www.theguardian.com/commentisfree/2013/jan/01/germany-hartz-reforms-inequality.

Krugman P. (1994) The Myth of Asia's Miracle. *Foreign Affairs* 73/6, 62–78.

Leith W. (2008) Still Looking for a Free Lunch. *The Guardian* (27 December 2008), accessed on 16 February 2015 at http://www.theguardian.com/books/2008/dec/27/return-of-depression-economics-paul-krugman.

Lewandowska M. and Ptak L. (2013) *Undoing Property?* Sternberg Press, Berlin.

Lim P. (2011) Missing migrant workers hunted down in Singapore. *Yahoo! News* (3 August 2011), accessed on 16 February 2015 at https://sg.news.yahoo.com/missing-migrant-workers-hunted-down-singapore-032501556.html.

Manjoo F. (2015) Uber's Model May Upend the very Idea of a Job. *International New York Times* (30 January 2015), p. 15.

Michnik A. (1990) The Two Faces of Eastern Europe. (trans. A. Husarska) *The New Republic* (12 November 1990), p. 24.

Rhee C. (2012) Inequality Threatens Asia Growth Miracle. *Financial Times* (7 May 2012), accessed on 21 May 2014 at http://www.ft.com/intl/cms/s/0/fba71e2c9607-11e1-9d9d-00144feab49a.html#axzz2htIfpfmW.

Saberi M. (2006) Hundreds Protest Over Non-payment of Wages. *Gulf News* (29 August 2006), accessed on 18 February 2015 at http://gulfnews.com/news/gulf/uae/employment/hundreds-protest-over-non-payment-of-wages-1.251737.

Tan J. (2013a) Former SMRT bus driver: Why we went on strike (Part 1). *Yahoo! News* (5 April 2013), accessed on 18 February 2015 at https://sg.news.yahoo.com/former-smrt-bus-driver–why-we-went-on-strike–part-1–135100687.html.

Tan W. (2013b) Concerns Raised at Forum on Racial Relations. *Today Online* (12 September 2013), accessed on 16 February 2015 at http://www.todayonline.com/singapore/concerns-raised-forum-racial-relations.

The New Paper (2015) Tough for Transient Workers to Marry Singaporeans, *Asia One* (20 January 2015), accessed on 25 February 2015 at http://women.asiaone.com/women/relationships/tough-transient-workers-marry-singaporeans.

Wintour P. and Traynor I. (2014) Angela Merkel Forces David Cameron to Retreat from EU Migrant Cap. *The Guardian* (28 November 2014), accessed on 18 February 2015 at http://www.theguardian.com/uk-news/2014/nov/28/angela-merkel-david-cameron-migrant-cap.

CHAPTERS IN BOOKS

Arcarazo D. (2012) The Good, the Bad and the Ugly in EU Migration Law. In E. Guild and P. Minderhoud (eds.) *The First Decade of EU Migration and Asylum Law*, pp. 179–206.

Athukorala P., Fukao K. and Yuan T. (2009) Economic transition and labour market integration in China. In R. Ganaut, L. Song and W.T. Woo (eds.) *China's New Place in World Crisis.* ANU Press, Canberra.

Bauer T., Dietz B., Zimmermann K. and Zwintz E. (2005) European migration: What do we know? In K. Zimmermann (ed.) *Migration and Development*. Oxford University Press, Oxford, UK.

Beck T. and Levine R. (2004) Legal Institutions and Financial Development. In C. Menard and M. Shirley (eds.) *Handbook of New Institutional Economics*. Kluwer Dordrecht, the Netherlands.

Bell M. (2014) Constitutionalization and EU Employment Law. In H. Micklitz (ed.) *The Constitutionalization of European Private Law.* Oxford University Press, Oxford, UK, pp. 137–69.

Bergene A., Endresen S. and Knutsen H. (2010) Re-engaging with Agency in Labour Geography. In A. Bergene *et al.* (eds.) *Missing Links in Labour Geography.* Ashgate, Farnham, UK, pp. 3–14.

Cholewinski R. (2012) The EU Acquis on Irregular Migration Ten Years On: Still reinforcing security at the expense of rights? In E. Guild and P. Minderhoud (eds.) *The First Decade of EU Migration and Asylum Law*, pp. 127–78.

Collins H. (1986) Contract and Legal Theory. In W. Twining (ed.) *Legal Theory and Common Law.* Blackwell Publishing, Oxford, UK, pp. 81–98.

Eisenberg M. (2000) The Theory of Contracts. In P. Benson (ed.) *The Theory of Contract Law: New essays.* Cambridge University Press, Cambridge, MA, pp. 206–64.

Fine B. (1979) Law and Class. In B. Fine *et al.* (eds.) *Capitalism and the Rule of Law: From deviancy theory to Marxism.* Hutchinson, London, UK, pp. 29–45.

Ford M. and Piper N. (2007) Southern Sites of Female Agency: Informal regimes and female migrant labour resistance in East and Southeast Asia. In J. Hobson and L. Seabrooke (eds.) *Everyday Politics of the World Economy.* Cambridge University Press, Cambridge, UK.

Halleskov Storgaard L. (2012) The Long-Term Residents Directive: A fufilment of the tampere objective of near-equality? In E. Guild and P. Minderhoud (eds.) *The First Decade of EU Migration and Asylum Law.* Martinus Nijhoff, The Hague, pp. 299–328.

Helma L. (2008) When Home becomes a Workplace: Domestic work as an ordinary job in Germany? In L. Helma (ed.) *Migration and Domestic Work: A European perspective on a global theme.* Ashgate Publishing, Aldershot, UK, pp. 43–60.

Hirsch A. (2013) Exchange and Circulation. In M. Lewandowska and L. Ptak (eds.) *Undoing Property?* Sternberg Press, Berlin, pp. 223–31.

Kilpatrick C. (2006) New EU Employment Governance and Constitutionalism. In G. de Burca and J. Scott (eds.) *Law and New Governance in the EU and US.* Hart Publishing, Oxford and Portland, OR, pp. 121–51.

Kreide R. (2011) Re-embedding the Market through Law? The ambivalence of juridification in the international context. In C. Joerges and J. Falke (eds.) *Karl Polanyi, Globalisation and the Potential of Law in Transitional Markets.* Hart Publishing, Oxford, UK, pp. 41–64.

Lacher H. (2007) The Slight Transformation: Contesting the Legacy of Karl Polanyi. In A. Bugra and K. Agartan (eds.) *Reading Karl Polanyi for the Twenty-First Century: Market Economy as a Political Project.* Palgrave Macmillan, Basingstoke, UK, pp. 49–64.

McBarnet D. (2010) Financial Engineering or Legal Engineering: Legal work, legal integrity and the banking crisis. In I. MacNeil & J. Obrien (eds.) *The Future of Financial Regulation.* Hart Publishing, Oxford, UK, pp. 67–82.

Mill J.S. (1987) Bentham. In A. Ryan (ed.) *John Stuart Mill and Jeremy Bentham: Utilitarianism and other essays.* Penguin, Harmondsworth, pp. 131–75.

Pasquinelli M. (2013) The Sabotage of Debt. In M. Lewandowska and L. Ptak (eds.) *Undoing Property?* Sternberg Press, Berlin, pp. 29–35.

Pentecost C. (2013) Fields of Zombies: Biotech agriculture and the privatization of knowledge. In M. Lewandowska and L. Ptak (eds.) *Undoing Property?* Sternberg Press, Berlin, pp. 83–91.

Rao B. (1996) Income Inequality in Singapore: Facts and Policies. In C.Y. Lim (ed.) *Economic Policy.* Addison-Wesley Publishing Company, Singapore.

Schneider F. (2013) Imaginary Property. In M. Lewandowska and L. Ptak (eds.) *Undoing Property?* Sternberg Press, Berlin, pp. 197–205.

Stadler M. (2013) From Ownership to Belonging. In M. Lewandowska and L. Ptak (eds.) *Undoing Property?* Sternberg Press, Berlin, pp. 173–81.

Stapleton J. (2004) Regulating Torts. In C. Parker, C. Scott, N. Lacey and J. Braithwaite (eds.) *Regulating Law.* Oxford University Press, Oxford, UK, pp. 122–43.

Strathern M. with Lewandowska M. (2013) Reproducing the Future. In M. Lewandowska and L. Ptak (eds.) *Undoing Property?* Sternberg Press, Berlin, pp. 209–20.

Szreder K. (2013) The Cruel Economy of Ownership. In M. Lewandowska and L. Ptak (eds.) *Undoing Property?* Sternberg Press, Berlin, pp. 39–51.

Topel R. (1999) Labor Markets and Economic Growth. In O. Ashenfelter and D. Card (eds.) *Handbook of Labor Economics, Volume 3, Part C.* Elsevier, Amsterdam, pp. 2943–84.

Vishmidt M. in conversation with Ptak L. (2013) Abstraction and the Currency of the Social. In M. Lewandowska and L. Ptak (eds.) *Undoing Property?* Sternberg Press, Berlin, pp. 161–9.

Winckler O. (2009) Labor and Liberalization: The Decline of the GCC Rentier System. In J. Teitelbaum (ed.) *Political Liberalization in the Persian Gulf.* Columbia University Press, New York, US, pp. 59–86.

Yamanaka K. (1999) Illegal Immigration in Asia: Regional patterns and a case study of Nepalese workers in Japan. In D. Haines and K. Rosenblum (eds.) *Illegal Immigration in America: A reference handbook.* Greenwood Press, Westport, Conn., pp. 471–99.

BOOKS

Arthur C. (1978) Editor's Introduction. In E. Pashukanis, *Law and Maxism: A general theory.* Ink Links, London, UK.

Atkinson B. (1992) *The Selected Writings of Ralph Waldo Emerson.* The Modern Library of New York, New York, NY.

Barnard C. (2012) *EU Employment Law* (4th edn). Oxford University Press, Oxford, UK.

Bloomfield D., Barnes T. and Huyse L. (2003) *Reconciliation After Violent Conflict: A handbook.* Institute for Democracy and Electoral Assistance, Stockholm, Sweden.

Bookchin M. (1991) *The Ecology of Freedom.* Black Rose Books, Montreal.

Buckley R. and Arner D. (2011) *From Crisis to Crisis. The Global Financial System and Regulatory Failure.* Wolters Kluwer, The Hague.

Chang H. (2014) *Economics: The User's Guide.* Penguin Books, London, UK.

Cohen R. (2006) *Migration and Its Enemies: Global capital migrant labour and the nation-state.* Ashgate Publishing, Aldershot, UK.

Collins H. (1999) *Regulating Contracts.* Oxford University Press, Oxford, UK.

Cotterrell R. (1996) *Law's Community: Legal Theory in Sociological Perspectives.* Clarendon Press, Oxford, UK.

Cotterrell R. (2007) *Law, Culture and Society: Legal ideas in the mirror of social theory.* Ashgate Publishing, Aldershot, Hampshire.

Countouris N. (2007) *The Changing Law of the Employment Relationship: Comparative analyses in the European context.* Ashgate Publishing, Aldershot, Hampshire.

Dale G. (2010) *Karl Polanyi: The Limits of the Market.* Polity Press, Cambridge, UK.

Davies A. (2012) *EU Labour Law.* Edward Elgar Publishing, Cheltenham, UK.

D'Amato A., Henderson S. and Florence S. (2009) *Corporate Social Responsibility and Sustainable Business.* Center for Creative Leadership, Greensboro, NC.

Dennis I. (2013) *The Law of Evidence* (5th edn). Sweet and Maxwell, London, UK.

Dixon R. and Ginsburg T. (2014) *Comparative Constitutional Law in Asia.* Edward Elgar Publishing, Cheltenham, UK.

Edelman M. and Haugerad A. (2004) *The Anthropology of Development and Globalization: From classical political economy to contemporary neoliberalism.* Blackwell Publishing, Oxford, UK.

Escobar A. (1995) *Encountering Development: The making and unmaking of the third world.* Princeton University Press, Princeton, NJ.

Findlay M. (1999) *The Globalisation of Crime: Understanding transitional relationships in context.* Cambridge University Press, Cambridge, UK.

Findlay M. (2013) *Contemporary Challenges in Regulating Global Crises.* Palgrave Macmillan, Basingstoke, UK.

Findlay M. and Lim S. (2014a) *Regulatory Worlds: Cultural and social perspectives when North meets South.* Edward Elgar, Cheltenham, UK.

Fried C. (1981) *Contract As Promise: A theory of contractual obligation.* Harvard University Press, Cambridge, MA.

Groenendijk K. and Hampsink R. (1995) *Temporary Employment of Migrants in Europe*. Reeks Recht & Samenleving, Nijmegen.

Grugel J. and Piper N. (2007) *Critical Perspectives on Global Governance: Rights and regulation in governing regimes.* Routledge, London, UK.

Hall A. (2011) *Migrant Workers' Rights to Social Protection in ASEAN: Case Studies of Indonesia, Philippines, Singapore and Thailand.* Freidrich Ebert Stiftung, Singapore.

Hess S. (2005) *Globalized Housework: Au pair as a migration strategy of women from Eastern Europe.* VS Verlag, Wiesbaden.

Hyams E. (1979) *Pierre-Joseph Proudhon: His revolutionary life, mind and works*. John Murray, London.

Joerges C. and Falke J. (2011) *Karl Polanyi, Globalisation and the Potential of Law in Transitional Markets.* Hart Publishing, Oxford, UK.

Kelsen H. (1966) *The Communist Theory of Law.* Stevens & Sons, London, UK.

Kenny A. (1975) *Will, Freedom and Power*. Blackwell Publishing, Oxford, UK.

Knowles R. (2004) *Political Economy from Below: Economic thought in communitarian anarchism, 1840–1914.* Routledge, New York, NY.

Kuhner T. (2014) *Capitalism v. Democracy: Money in politics and the free market constitution*. Stanford University Press, Stanford, CA.

Lanier J. (2014) *Who Owns the Future?* Simon & Schuster, New York, NY.

Lipton M. (1977) *Why Poor People Stay Poor: A study of urban bias in world development.* Maurice Temple Smith, London, UK.

Massey D. *et al.* (1987) *Return to Aztlan: The social process of international migration from Western Mexico.* University of California Press, Berkeley, CA.

Maurer B. and Schwab G. (2006) *Accelerating Possession: Global futures of property and personhood.* Columbia University Press, New York, NY.

Mill J. (2010) *On Liberty.* Penguin Classics, New York, NY.

Morgan B. and Yeung K. (2007) *An Introduction to Law and Regulation.* Cambridge University Press, Cambridge, MA.

Norrie A. (2001) *Crime, Reason and History: A critical introduction to criminal law.* Butterworths, London, UK.

Offer J. (2000) *Herbert Spencer: Critical Assessments, Volume VI: Political aspects of social evolution.* Taylor and Francis, London, UK.

Ostrom E., Gardner R. and Walker J. (1994) *Rules, Games and Common-Pool Resources.* University of Michigan Press, Ann Arbor, MI.

Parreñas R. (2001) *Servants of Globalisation: Women, Migration and Domestic Work*. Stanford University Press, Stanford, CA.
Piketty T. (2014) *Capital in the Twenty First Century*. Harvard University Press, Cambridge, MA.
Polanyi K. (1944) *The Great Transformation: Economic and Political Origins of Our Time*. Rinehart, New York, NY.
Proudhon P. (1846) *System of Economical Contradictions: or the Philosophy of Misery*, translated from the French by B. Tucker, 1888. John Wilson & Son, Cambridge, MA.
Rawls J. (2008) *Lectures on the History of Political Philosophy*. Harvard University Press, Cambridge, MA.
Roach S. (2014) *Unbalanced: The co-dependency of America and China*. Yale University Press, New Haven, CT.
Ruhs M. (2013) *The Price of Rights: Regulating international labor migration*. Princeton University Press, Princeton, NJ.
Selznick P. (2002) *The Communitarian Persuasion*. Woodrow Wilson Centre Press, Washington, US.
Schutz E. (2011) *Inequality and Power: The economics of class*. Routledge, Abingdon, UK.
Scott J. (1998) *Seeing Like a State: How certain schemes to improve the human condition have failed*. Yale University Press, New Haven, CT.
Sunstein C. (2014) *Valuing Life: Humanising the regulatory state*. University of Chicago Press, Chicago, IL.
Thoreau H. (2005) *Civil Disobedience and Other Essays*. Digireads.com Publishing, Stilwell, KS.
Touchie J. (2005) *Hayek and Human Rights: Foundations for a minimalist approach to law*. Edward Elgar, Cheltenham, UK.
Trebilcock M. (1993) *The Limits of Freedom of Contract*. Harvard University Press, Cambridge, MA.
Weale A. (2013) *Democratic Justice and the Social Contract*. Oxford University Press, Oxford, UK.
Wellman C. (2002) *Rights and Duties: Property rights and duties of redistribution, Volume 6*. Taylor & Francis, London, UK.

INTERNET SOURCES

Au A. (2014) How the Migrant Labour System is Regulated Counts for a Lot, *Transient Workers Count Too* (25 October 2014), accessed on 25 February 2015 at https://twc2.org.sg/2014/10/25/how-the-migrant-worker-system-is-regulated-counts-for-a-lot/.
Bowring P. (2011) Foreign Workers Welcome, But No Permanent Residents, Please. *YaleGlobal* (11 November 2011), accessed on 25

February 2015 at http://yaleglobal.yale.edu/content/foreign-workers-welcome-no-permanent-residents.

Budapest Open Access Initiative website, accessed on 17 February 2015 at http://www.budapestopenaccessinitiative.org/read.

Cave du Marmandais website, Ephemeral Was Yesterday, Sustainability Is Tomorrow, accessed on 16 February 2015 at http://www.cave-du-marmandais.fr/en/the-spirit/sustainable.html.

Communication from the Commission of 7 April 1998 on Undeclared Work (1998), accessed on 16 February 2015 at http://aei.pitt.edu/5111/1/5111.pdf.

Consulate-General of the United States website, Domestic Employee Visa, accessed on 18 February 2015 at http://dubai.usconsulate.gov/domestic_employee_visas.html.

Department of Labour, Malaysia website, Issue of Private Employment Agency Licence, accessed on 18 February 2015 at http://jtkswk.mohr.gov.my/index.php/en/our-services/private-employment-agency/issue-of-private-employment-agency-licence.

European Commission's Employment Guideline No. 9 on Undeclared Work, as adopted on 22 July 2003, accessed on 16 February 2015 at http://eur-lex.europa.eu/LexUriServe/LexUriServ.do?uri=OJ:C:2003:260:0001:0003:EN:PDF.

Immigration Department of Malaysia website, Application for Employment Pass, accessed on 25 February 2015 at http://www.imi.gov.my/index.php/en/main-services/expatriate/2nd-stage-application-for-employ ment-pass.

Immigration Department of Malaysia website, Application for Foreign Worker, accessed on 25 February 2015 at http://www.imi.gov.my/index.php/en/main-services/foreign-worker/7-perkhidmatan-utama/292-application-for-foreign-worker.

Immigration Department of Malaysia website, Entry Permit, accessed on 25 February 2015 at http://www.imi.gov.my/index.php/en/main-services/entry-permit.

Immigration Department of Malaysia website, Recruitment Terms and Conditions of Foreign Workers, accessed on 25 February 2015 at http://www.imi.gov.my/index.php/en/main-services/foreign-worker.

Ministry of Manpower, Singapore website, Service Agreement Between Foreign Domestic Worker Employer and Employment Agency, accessed on 18 February 2015 at http://www.mom.gov.sg/Documents/foreign-manpower/Employment%20Agencies/Recommended%20Service%20Agreement.pdf.

Ministry of Manpower, Singapore website, EA Licence Conditions for Comprehensive Licence, accessed on 18 February 2015 at http://www.

mom.gov.sg/Documents/foreign-manpower/Employment%20Agencies/EA%20Licence%20Conditions.pdf.

Ministry of Manpower, Singapore website, Employment Agency Search, accessed on 18 February 2015 at http://www.mom.gov.sg/eadirectory.

Ministry of Manpower, Singapore website. Report to us, accessed on 18 February 2015 at http://www.mom.gov.sg/contact-us/Pages/report-to-us.aspx.

Ministry of Manpower, Singapore website, Work Passes and Permits, accessed on 18 February 2015 at http://www.mom.gov.sg/foreign-manpower/passes-visas/work-permit-fdw/before-you-apply/Pages/default.aspx#disputes.

Ministry of Manpower, Singapore, *Your Guide to Employing a Foreign Domestic Worker*, accessed on 18 February 2015 at http://www.mom.gov.sg/Documents/others/FDW/FDW%20EG(Eng)%20Std.pdf.

NBS (2014) Maintaining Sustainability through Contracts, accessed on 11 February 2015 at http://www.thenbs.com/topics/Environment/articles/maintainingSustainability.asp.

Polychroniou C. (2014) Crushing Economy and A Failed State. *Truth Out* (19 January 2014), accessed on 19 February 2015 at http://truth-out.org/news/item/21265-the-greek-success-story-of-a-crushing-economy-and-a-failed-state.

Royal Thai Embassy in London website, Notification of Immigration Commission: Criterion and Conditions of Foreign Nationals' Residential Permit Considerations, accessed on 25 February 2015 at http://thaiembassyuk.org.uk/?q=node/58.

Rousseau J. (1754) Discourse on the Origin and Basis of Inequality Among Men, accessed on 18 February 2015 at http://www.constitution.org/jjr/ineq.htm.

Slavo M. (2011) Barter Society Emerges as Greek Crisis Deepens. *SHTFPlan.com* (29 October 2011), accessed on 19 February 2015 at http://www.shtfplan.com/emergency-preparedness/barter-society-emerges-in-greece-as-crisis-deepens-video_10292011.

Singapore Institute of Directors (2008) Managing the Five Capitals for Sustainable Wealth Creation!, accessed on 11 February 2015 at http://www.sid.org.sg/uploads/bulletin_sub/documents/196_feature6.pdf.

Tan Chuan-Jin, Acting Minister for Manpower & Senior Minister of State, National Development, Reply to Parliamentary Question on Foreign Worker Levies Collection, Notice Paper No. 369 Of 2012 For The Sitting On 12 Nov 2012, accessed on 22 May 2014 at http://www.mom.gov.sg/newsroom/Pages/PQRepliesDetails.aspx?listid=64.

Varia N. (2014) New Protections for Saudi Arabia's Domestic Workers. *Human Rights Watch Dispatches* (19 February 2014), accessed on 18

February 2015 at http://www.hrw.org/news/2014/02/19/dispatches-new-protection-saudi-arabia-s-domestic-workers.

Wah J. (2014) Is ASEAN Closer to Legal Protection of the Rights of Migrant Workers?, *News Update, ASEAN Civil Society Conference and ASEAN People's Forum* (22 March 2014), accessed on 25 February 2015 at http://aseanpeople.org/is-asean-closer-to-legal-protection-of-the-rights-of-migrant-workers/.

LEGISLATION

Act 246 (Malaysia), accessed on 18 February 2015 at http://www.agc.gov.my/Akta/Vol.%205/Act%20246.pdf. Employment Act (Cap. 91) (Rev. Ed. 2009) (Singapore).

Alien Employment Act of 2008 (Kingdom of Thailand).

Cabinet Resolution No. (25) of 2010 concerning Internal Work Permits Applicable in the Ministry of Labor (UAE).

Cambodia's 2011 Sub-decree 190; Law No. 39/2004 concerning the Placement and Protection of Indonesian Migrant Workers (Indonesia).

Employment of Foreign Manpower Act (Cap. 91A) (Rev. Ed. 2009) (Singapore).

Employment of Foreign Manpower (Work Passes) Regulations 2012, Schedule 1, Conditions and Regulatory Conditions of In-principle Approval for a Work Permit.

Employment of Foreign Manpower (Work Passes) Regulations 2012, Schedule 4, Conditions and Regulatory Conditions of Work Permit.

Employment (Restriction) Act 1968 (Act 353) (Malaysia).

Employment Agencies Act (Cap. 92) (Rev. Ed. 2012) (Singapore).

French Labour Code (*Code du Travail*), accessed on 24 February 2015 at http://www.legifrance.gouv.fr/affichCode.do;jsessionid=1F75337AA49AFEEF20C0AB85DB94D303.tpdjo05v_2?cidTexte=LEGITEXT000006072050&dateTexte=20090311.

Immigration Act 1959 (Act 155) (Malaysia).

Migrant Workers and Overseas Filipinos Act of 1995 (The Philippines).

EU DIRECTIVES

Commission of the European Communities, Commission Directive 86/388/EEC of 23 July 1986 amending Council Directive 83/229/EEC on the Approximation of the Laws of the Member States Relating to Materials and Articles Made of Regenerated Cellulose Film Intended to Come into Contact with Foodstuffs.

European Union: Council of the European Union, Council Directive 79/7/EEC of 19 December 1978 on the Progressive Implementation of the Principle of Equal Treatment for Men and Women in Matters of Social Security.

European Union: Council of the European Union, Council Directive 98/99/EC of 14 December 1998 Amending Directive 97/12/EC Amending and Updating Directive 64/432/EEC on Health Problems Affecting Intra-Community Trade in Bovine Animals and Swine.

European Union: Council of the European Union, Council Directive 1999/70/EC of 28 June 1999 Concerning the Framework Agreement on Fixed-term Work Concluded by ETUC, UNICE and CEEP.

European Union: Council of the European Union, Council Directive 2001/40/EC of 28 May 2001 on the Mutual Recognition of Decisions on the Expulsion of Third Country Nationals.

European Union: Council of the European Union, Council Directive 2002/14/EC of the European Parliament and of the Council of 11 March 2002 Establishing A General Framework for Informing and Consulting Employees in the European Community – Joint Declaration of the European Parliament, the Council and the Commission on Employee Representation.

European Union: Council of the European Union, Council Directive 2003/109/EC of 25 November 2003 Concerning the Status of Third-Country Nationals Who Are Long-Term Residents (23 January 2004).

European Council: Council of the European Union, Council Directive 2003/110/EC of 25 November 2003 on Assistance in Cases of Transit for the Purposes of Removal by Air.

European Union: Council of the European Union, Council Directive 2003/88/EC of the European Parliament and of the Council of 4 November 2003 Concerning Certain Aspects of the Organisation of Working Time.

European Union: Council of the European Union, Council Directive 2004/38/EC of 29 April 2004 on the Right of Citizens of the Union and Their Family Members to Move and Reside Freely within the territory of the Member States.

European Union, Council of the European Union, Council Directive 2008/104/EC of 19 November 2008 on Temporary Agency Work.

European Union: Council of the European Union, Council Directive 2008/115/EC of the European Parliament and of the Council of 16 December 2008 on Common Standards and Procedures in Member States for Returning Illegally Staying Third-country Nationals.

European Union: Council of the European Union, Council Directive 2009/38/EC of the European Parliament and of the Council of 6 May

2009 on the Establishment of a European Works Council or a Procedure in Community-scale Undertakings and Community-scale Groups of Undertakings for the Purposes of Informing and Consulting Employees.

European Union: Council of the European Union, Council Directive 2009/50/EC of 25 May 2009 on the Conditions of Entry and Residence of Third-country Nationals for the Purposes of Highly Qualified Employment.

European Union: Council of the European Union, Directive 2009/52/EC of the European Parliament and of the Council of 18 June 2009 Providing for Minimum Standards on Sanctions and Measures Against Employers of Illegally Staying Third-country Nationals.

European Union: Council of the European Union, Council Directive 91/533/EEC of 14 October 1991 on An Employer's Obligation to Inform Employees of the Conditions Applicable to the Contract or Employment Relationship.

European Union: Council of the European Union, Directive 96/71/EC of the European Parliament and of the Council of 16 December 1996 Concerning the Posting of Workers in the Framework of the Provision of Services.

European Union, Council of the European Union, Council Directive 97/81/EC of 15 December 1997 concerning the Framework Agreement on Part-time Working Concluded by UNICE, CEEP and the ETUC.

INTERNATIONAL TREATIES

Consolidated version of the Treaty on European Union and the Treaty on the Functioning of the European Union, Official Journal, 2012/C 326/01.

CASES

Balfour v. *Balfour* [1919] 2 KB 571.

Blaise Baheten Metock and Ors v. *Minister for Justice, Equality and Law Reform*, European Court of Justice, Grand Chamber, C-127/08, [2008] ECR I-6241.

Commission v. *Luxembourg*, European Court of Justice, C-319/06, [2008] ECR 1-4323.

International Transport Workers' Federation and Finnish Seamen's Union v. *Viking Line ABP and OÜ Viking Line Eesti*, European Court of Justice, C-438/05, [2007] ECR I-10779.

Helmut Kampelmann and others v. *Landscaftverband Westfalen–Lippe*, European Court of Justice, C-253/96 to 258/96, [1998] IRLR 333.
Klaus Haseley v. *Stadtwerke Altena GmbH*, European Court of Justice, C-258/96, [1983] ICR 351 (Ackner LJ).
Laval v. *Svenska Byggnadsarbetareforbundet*, European Court of Justice, C-341/05, [2007] ECR I-11767.
Lawrie-Blum v. *Land Baden-Wuttemberg*, European Court of Justice, Case 66/85, [1986] ECR 2121.
Levin v. *Staatssecretaris van Justitie*, European Court of Justice, Case 53/81, [1982] ECR 1035.
Mangold v. *Helm*, European Court of Justice, C-144/04, [2005] ECR 1-9981.
Mary Carpenter v. *Secretary of State for the Home Department*, European Court of Justice, C-60/00, [2002] ECR I-6279.
Raymond Kohll v. *Union des caisses de maladie*. European Court of Justice, C-158/96, Judgment (28 April 1998).
Rhimou Chakroun v. *Minister van Buitenlandse Zaken*, European Court of Justice, C-578/08, [2010] ECR I-01839.
Rush Portuguesa Ld v. *Office national d'immigration,* European Court of Justice, C-113/89, [1990] ECR I-1417.
Said Shamilovich Kadzoev (Huchbarov), European Court of Justice, C-357/09, [2009] ECR I-11189.
Stadtwerke Witten GmbH v. *Andreas Schade*, European Court of Justice, C-258/96, [1982] ICR 54 (Browne-Wilkinson J).
Waltons Stores (Interstate) Ltd v. *Maher* (1988) 164 CLR 387.

Index